P9-BJE-113

Out of the Locker Room
of the Male Soul

OUT OF THE
LOCKER ROOM
OF THE
MALE SOUL

STEVE MASTERSON
WITH GEORGE MCPEEK

HORIZON BOOKS
CAMP HILL, PENNSYLVANIA

Horizon Books
3825 Hartzdale Drive, Camp Hill, PA 17011

Faithful, biblical publishing since 1883

ISBN: 0-88965-136-1

© 1997 by Steve Masterson

All rights reserved
Printed in the United States of America

97 98 99 00 01   5 4 3 2 1

Unless otherwise indicated,
Scripture taken from the
HOLY BIBLE:
NEW INTERNATIONAL VERSION ®.
© 1973, 1978, 1984 by the
International Bible Society.
Used by permission of
Zondervan Bible Publishers.

TABLE OF CONTENTS

Foreword

In years to come, the late 1990's will be remembered as a time when the Almighty God moved powerfully in the hearts of men, calling each one to a life of integrity, holiness and wholeness. Answering that call, men have risen to the challenge and embarked on a pilgrimage back to the heart of God, re-focused their attention on those things that are eternally significant and launched our into uncharted seas of vulnerability and accountability to vitally link into relationships. In short, men have started to be real in how they perceive themselves, real in their relationship with God and real in their relationships with their families.

In this pilgrimage toward honesty and integrity, we inevitably wrestle with issues that haunt us, entangle us and make us stumble. Who really am I? What makes me act and react in ways that hurt people? Why is there an incessant tug on my heart by passions that need more light? In our past, we may have hid the vulnerable real self from ourselves and others by tightly wrapping a coat of identity bases on what we do rather than who we are. It is time to take off our coats, bring understanding and shed light. In this trek of increasing our self-awareness, we need a trail-guide, one who has gone before to survey the terrain. I firmly believe that Steve Masterson is an able guide, qualified by decades of pastoring, teaching, counseling and living out a life of integrity.

Reading this book has brought new insights into my own life, unearthing the basis of my own personal struggles. Steve Masterson has challenged me to peel off the coats of identity that I so closely guard and to take a honest look at the inner core of who I really am. In my pilgrimage toward holiness and wholeness, I desire to be real to God, to my wife, to my children, to my friends and to myself but I still struggle with the facades of pride that hide the fact that I am needy.

I believe that this is a significant book for times like these. We are in the midst of an epidemic of decaying marriages, broken families, eroding moral and spiritual values and financial and political insecurity. Like the swarms of locusts in the book of Joel, sin, compromise and relative moralism have devoured the stalks of integrity in the land. But the voice of God continues to go out, calling us, one by one, to rise up, stand in the gap, turn the tide and return to Him. Men experiencing God in a fresh way, meeting in small groups, worshiping Him with thousands of others in packed hockey arenas and football stadiums, are becoming real in their walk. We shall witness these new "Joshuas and Calebs" taking back territory held captive by Satan for far too long.

Like the bathroom mirror that reveals what we really look like before the razor, toothbrush and comb have done their work, this book will reflect who we really are as men before we cover ourselves with the masks of occupation, position and prestige. It takes courage to take a long, hard look at ourselves but, I believe, God is looking for courageous men, honest men—men of integrity.

Therefore also now, says the Lord, turn and keep on coming to Me with all your heart, with fasting, with weeping, and with mourning (until every hindrance is removed and the broken fellowship is restored). Rend your hearts and not your garments and return to the Lord your God, for He is gracious and merciful, slow to anger, and abounding in loving-kindnesss, and He revokes His sentence of evil (when His condition are met). (Joel 2:12, 13).[1]

Tom Iwanna, M.D.
Chairman, Board of Directors
Promise Keepers Canada

Endnote
[1] The Amplified Bible (Grand Rapids, MI: Zondervan, 1965), 1027-1028.

Acknowledgments

I would like to express my deepest heartfelt appreciation to the following people:

- To my wife *Jackie* for her hours, days and months of labor of love in entering the original and corrected drafts of the book into the computer, and for her input and feedback from a wife's and woman's perspective. Also for the way God has used her to be a godly challenge in helping me to grow as a man, husband and father.

- To *Trudy Sands* for her time and help in going over the computer entries of each chapter for formatting, and for overseeing the printout of each draft of the book.

- To *Mike Walrod* and his son, *Marty*, for the hours of editing, correcting and worthwhile feedback on the grammar, flow and content of the book.

- To *Martin Lewadny* for his input and feedback on the biblical content of the book.

- To *George McPeek* for his faithful friendship, hours of working with the script to make it readable to men, and for his belief in me and the message of this book.

- To *Dr. Larry Crabb* and *Dr. Dan Allender* for mentoring, modeling and teaching me about how to love God and others. Who I am as a man and what I have written has been influenced and shaped by them.

Becoming a Man

Christmas Eve, 1952—it's still as clear in my mind as though it was yesterday. I was seven and we were gathered as a family to open our presents. Waiting my turn with four brothers and one sister seemed to take forever. Finally, Dad held out the gift he and Mom had chosen for me.

As I tore off the wrapping, my sense of excitement skyrocketed. I just knew it was that pair of hockey skates I had been eyeing for months in the Eaton's catalog. The plain box beneath the paper puzzled me for a moment, but I was too anxious to pay much attention.

At last the box gave way to my eager fingers, and there to my horror was a used pair of white high-top girl's skates. After the initial shock, I tried to hide my shame and disappointment from my parents, and especially from my four younger brothers. I knew Mom and Dad had done the best they could. Being in the ministry, with six children and very little money, they could not find and afford more than this.

I spent the next four months of the hockey season trying to hide the white of those skates with black shoe polish. But no polish could cover the inner shame I experienced as a seven-year-old boy. All my friends had the latest and newest hockey equipment. Wearing girl's skates to play hockey with them not only caused me embarrassment, but also stirred something deep inside my boyish sense of maleness.

Many years later, something else in my sense of maleness was stirred, and the Holy Spirit used my wife, Jackie, to do it. After a particular incident, she called me to account and got very specific. In essence she said, "Steve, this is what I see in you and this is how it makes me feel!"

In that moment of confrontation, the hidden sin of my heart was exposed. Even talking about it now, I feel again that deep dread in the bowels of my masculine soul. But at the moment of confrontation, my immediate awareness was not of the Holy Spirit's presence nor any degree of guilt, just a sense of vulnerability over having my sin exposed. I was found out, plain and simple. There I stood naked of soul before her without any place to hide. In that moment, I was deeply aware that as a man and a husband I was not what she or others had thought I was.

There you have it: two painful episodes, decades apart, but both impacting my journey as a man. I used that word "journey" on purpose; becoming a man is a pilgrimage, not a short hike in the woods. God created me male; I had no choice. I will always be thankful for the passion of His heart by which He sought to mold me over a period of more than fifty years. The journey He brought me through has been filled with events like that with the girl's skates and with people like my wife. And of course, there is the impact of culture, of choices I made, good and bad, and of God Himself.

Nowhere in this process have I learned more from God about what it means to grow into manhood than in the context of my entire family. For that is where my maleness has been shaped, stretched, honed, sinned against, wounded, challenged, built up and fashioned.

I also thank God for the male friends that constantly speak into my life.

To God, my entire family and my male friends, I say, "Thank you for your investment. For without you I would never have become the man that I am, nor would I be growing into the man I hope to be, by God's grace."

It's not that I constantly live in doubt of my manhood. I don't. I have been a husband for twenty-five years, a parent for twenty-three, and I have fathered four children. I have provided for my family. Over the years, I have been a decent athlete and still play some football, hockey and golf. I get along well with other men including my own family members and some good male friends.

All of this should be enough to convince me that my manhood is intact, that it can't be disrupted. So why do I, at my age, still vividly remember the white girl's skates? And when I think of my wife's confrontation, why do I still feel that deep dread lurking down in my male soul? Because, like every man who reads this, there is nothing that moves and disrupts me more deeply than calling the nature and authenticity of my maleness into question. Though I am secure in what I do as a man, deep down I am shaky about who I am, about whether or not I really measure up.

Men, we need a theology of pilgrimage, a theology that gives us permission to grow up over time, that

sees life as a maturation process. Most of us have
been through the passages—some farther along than
others—from one stage to the next, infancy into boyhood, teenager into manhood, young man into mature man. I've been through over fifty years of it and
I am discovering there is no end in sight. Becoming a
man is a lifelong journey. And nowhere is the ideal
for this journey better depicted than in Luke's description of Jesus' boyhood in Luke 2:40, 52: "And
the child grew and became strong; he was filled with
wisdom, and the grace of God was upon him. . . .
And Jesus grew in wisdom and stature, and in favor
with God and men."

How does a boy become a man? He is called into
manhood. The confusion comes from not knowing
which voice to heed: the voice of culture or the voice of
peers; the voice of his coach or the voice of his mentor;
the voice of his church; the voice of his father, uncle,
grandfather, mother; or the voice of his God.

Today many men are questioning their male identities. There is a spirit of gender confusion found in
boys, young men and even middle-aged males. What
does it mean to be a man in the '90s? Men are losing
their way as they set their hearts on a continued pilgrimage of manhood.

Feminism has redefined femininity and womanhood, leaving men to wonder where and how we as
males fit into our culture and world. The media has
played havoc with our sense of identity. In response,
the secular men's movement has defined who men are
and what they do. But is this really what manhood is
all about?

So many voices are pronouncing on manhood, so
many conflicting messages are being sent, but who is

right? Who has the authority to make a definitive state-
ment that impacts roughly half the world's population?
For many there is no answer, only uncertainty. To be
macho and dominating is no longer politically correct
or legally sanctioned. To be passive and "wimpy" is
what infuriates women and children. Out of the midst
of today's social confusion, men question, "Who am I?
What does it mean to be a man?"

In the cultural ethos of our day where reconstruc-
tionism (flux) is in vogue, including the remaking of
our gender identities, God is raising His voice to call
out men. In the midst of cultural confusion, He is ral-
lying godly males who in turn are beginning to call out
their sons' manhood and to prize their daughters' femininity. God's call is not being drowned by the many
conflicting voices of our day. The worse the confusion,
the louder God speaks His clear directives.

As I speak across the country, I find that many men
are already in tune with the reality of the times and
that God has prepared them to listen to His voice.
These brothers are like the men of Issachar "who understood the times and knew what Israel should do" (1
Chronicles 12:32). Today's Christian males are wanting to be taught by men who model authentic, godly
manliness. They want sound teaching rooted in the Bible and spoken by men of God.

There is a new, fresh movement of God in the lives
of men. The hearts of fathers are being turned back to
their children. The hearts of sons are moving toward
their fathers. Husbands are wanting to love their wives
like Christ loves the Church. Men who are single are
choosing to remain sexually pure and alive toward
God. Men in their vocations are counting the cost to be
morally pure and ethically sound.

Hosea the prophet said, "Sow for yourselves righteousness, reap the fruit of unfailing love, and break up your unplowed ground; for it is time to seek the LORD, until he comes and showers righteousness on you" (Hosea 10:12).

Men, this book is your invitation to let God plow the back forty acres of your soul. If you look closely, you will see that it needs it. Far too many of us are pictured in the words of Hosea 10:13-14: "But you have planted wickedness, you have reaped evil, you have eaten the fruit of deception. Because you have depended on your own strength . . . the roar of battle will rise against your people, so that all your fortresses will be devastated."

To those of us who fit that description—and that includes most of us—God has charted the course in the words of Hosea:

> "Come, let us return to the LORD.
> He has torn us to pieces
>   but he will heal us;
> he has injured us
>   but he will bind up our wounds. . . .
> Let us acknowledge the LORD;
>   let us press on to acknowledge him. . . .
> For I desire mercy, not sacrifice,
>   and acknowledgment of God rather than
>   burnt offerings. . . ." (Hosea 6:1, 3, 6)

Men, what is your pilgrimage like? God is calling us to Himself. Our choice is to respond, and when we do, the Lord will expose our multitude of sins. The Lord said through Hosea, "Whenever I would heal Israel, the sins of Ephraim are exposed and the crimes of Samaria revealed" (Hosea 7:1).

In order for us to experience His healing, we need to humble ourselves and face the sin of our hearts. We have not met the true God until we are offended by Him. He will plow deep. He will tear us to pieces if necessary; He will injure us in order to heal and bind up our wounds. This may repel us, but it is our holy, loving heavenly Father at work.

Out of the Locker Room of the Male Soul is about two realities with which I unapologetically face you. The first reality is the sin of our hearts. Adam's fall has left a legacy that each of us has inherited. God's curse of the ground as judgment upon Adam and all men fit both his crime and ours. As we navigate through these pages together, I will be calling you to face the impact of the curse on your maleness, to own the pervasive influence of the sin of your heart, your justified self-centeredness, which is fueled by the pain of your heart.

The second reality is an invitation for you as a man to rise up to the glory and honor of your redeemed manhood. The psalmist wrote, "What is man that you are mindful of him, the son of man that you care for him? You made him a little lower than the heavenly beings and crowned him with glory and honor" (Psalm 8:4-5).

This book is about pilgrimage. Come join me, men, as we journey into the essence and reality of manhood, because "Blessed are those whose strength is in you, who have set their hearts on pilgrimage" (Psalm 84:5).

—Steve Masterson
January 1997

PART I

SHATTERED GLORY

CHAPTER 1

Temptation and Retreat

Bob was frustrated and exhausted as he drove out of the church parking lot and headed home. He was ready to call it quits. The elders' meeting had been four hours long, four hours of conflict over Sunday morning worship styles. "Why do I bother?" he griped. "Nobody listens to my point of view anyway. Not even the pastor." Sometimes church politics was a royal pain. It would serve them right if he resigned and washed his hands of the whole mess.

Bob had been twenty-one when he made a personal commitment to Christ. It had not been easy following after the heart of God, but right from the first he had meant business. He hung in there. And though he was quick to admit he wasn't perfect, he was respected enough to be elected to the elders' board for a second term. But after a night like this, he wondered if it was worth it.

It was almost midnight when he flopped onto the couch in his living room. Everyone else was asleep and he was exhausted, but he was so wired from the meeting he needed a few minutes to unwind. Kicking off his shoes and leaning back, he pointed the remote and began channel-surfing. He wanted something exciting, maybe something with a little skin in it. Anything to ease his frustration over the evening's impasse.

He found what he wanted on the movie channel, and for two hours he felt himself coming alive inside, two hours of pounding pulse and adrenaline rush without once thinking of the meeting. Yet, as he turned off the television at 1:30 a.m., he felt unclean and empty.

The violence and the sex in the movie had momentarily stimulated him, but now as he climbed into bed beside his wife, a quiet guilt settled down around him. He loved this woman God had given him. He was faithful to her, but why did he get so turned on by the explicit sex in movies? If he had the opportunity himself, would he take the plunge? What would the other elders think, what would the church think, if they knew about the urges that surged inside him in these times of solitude? A Christian for twenty-five years, an elder for six, and still that civil war raged in his soul. Would freedom never come? Would he never be on the inside what he professed so boldly in public?

Bob was not the first man to flounder in his spiritual walk, and he certainly will not be the last. The conflict between godly desires and fleshly temptations is as old as Scripture itself. The biblical narrative is replete with explicit examples of stunning victory laced with bitter sorrow and dismal failure. Take Noah, for example. He walked with God, but also shamed himself in drunkenness. And then there was Abraham, God's friend, who jeopardized his wife's purity out of cowardice. And there were a host of others. Jacob, whom God loved, connived for the very gifts that God had freely promised. Moses, who spoke face to face with

God, forfeited the promised land through a fit of anger and direct disobedience. Job, the man who feared God and turned from evil like no one else on earth, needed to repent of his self-justifying pride. Even David, the man after God's own heart, messed up by committing adultery and murder.

Man Falls Short of God's Standards

Like these men of faith and like Adam, you and I have also deeply offended the Lord! Despite our best intentions, we continue to fall far short of His righteousness, and the result is a stench in His nostrils. A quick sampling of the Word makes this painfully clear.

God's testimony: "The LORD saw how great man's wickedness on the earth had become, and that every inclination of the thoughts of his heart was only evil all the time. The LORD was grieved that he had made man on the earth, and his heart was filled with pain." (Genesis 6:5-6)

David's testimony: "Surely I was sinful at birth, sinful from the time my mother conceived me" (Psalm 51:5); "The fool says in his heart, 'There is no God.' They are corrupt, and their ways are vile; there is no one who does good. . . . Everyone has turned away, they have together become corrupt; there is no one who does good, not even one" (53:1, 3); "If you, O LORD, kept a record of sins, O Lord, who could stand?" (130:3).

Jeremiah's testimony: "The heart is deceitful above all things and beyond cure. Who can understand it?" (Jeremiah 17:9); "Why should any living man

complain when punished for his sins? Let us
examine our ways and test them, and let us return
to the LORD. Let us lift up our hearts and our hands
to God in heaven, and say: 'We have sinned and
rebelled   and   you   have   not   forgiven.' "
(Lamentations 3:39-42; see also 4:1-2)

Jesus' testimony: "But the things that come out of
the mouth come from the heart, and these make
a man 'unclean.' For out of the heart come evil
thoughts, murder, adultery, sexual immorality,
theft, false testimony, slander. These are what
make a man 'unclean.' " (Matthew 15:18-20)

John's testimony: "If we claim to be without sin,
we deceive ourselves and the truth is not in us"
(1 John 1:8); "But the cowardly, the unbelieving,
the vile, the murderers, the sexually immoral,
those who practice magic arts, the idolaters and
all liars—their place will be in the fiery lake of
burning sulfur. This is the second death." (Revelation 21:8)

By sharp contrast with these lofty standards set by a
holy God—and to his detriment—man tends to take
sin a lot less seriously. To many, building their sense
of well-being is the bottom line of their agenda, regardless of right or wrong. Over the years, this self-centered, if-it-feels-good-do-it attitude has generated some
very disturbing male stereotypes—macho, domineer-
ing, power-mongers; unfeeling, insensitive, hard, un-
caring, success objects; violent, war-mongers; workaholics; mental, physical and sexual abusers; evil, dysfunctional, diseased, sex-crazy, subjugators of women

and children; paternalistic, economic saboteurs and ecological destroyers.

But one thing the media and the men's and women's movements have not called us is *sinners*—unworthy sinners and enemies of God! This is the root of our problem, men, the very core of what makes us what we are. The difficulty with our negative-but-true labels is that they are too focused on the symptoms of self-centeredness. They offer us no hope, no real solutions and they utterly fail to identify the underlying cause. Name-calling may serve as a form of venting for men-bashers, but it does absolutely nothing to foster change.

The Scriptures are guilty of no such negligence, as the verses cited above clearly prove. God the Father, David, Jeremiah, Jesus and John have all zeroed in on the core of our problem as men—sin. Their diagnosis is disruptive and offensive. We cringe with shame when we hear it. But hear it and admit it we must. This is our only hope if we are ever to achieve and celebrate true manhood; we've got to face the sin of our hearts and deal with it ruthlessly.

Sin Undermines, Weakens, Distorts

Sin is destructive. It seeks to undermine, weaken and distort all that is godly and good. That which God designed for purity, sin subverts for depravity. As a result of sin, our glory, like a beautiful but damaged plate glass mirror, has been impacted and shattered. Though our image is still reflected, the web of cracks has turned it into a grotesque caricature of what the Lord intended it to be. Like the sons of Zion, once worth their weight in gold, we are now considered as pots of clay (Lamentations 4:1-2). Because of the subtleties of sin, our maleness no longer fully reflects the image, likeness and glory of the Father. What a tragedy for us both! Our sinfulness is not only robbing us of what is rightfully ours, but it has also greatly hurt and offended our loving God!

Men, this is serious business. Our sinfulness can no longer be ignored or swept under the rug. If we are ever going to celebrate our manhood, we need to begin by embracing what God says is true about us. Becoming the men He designed us to be begins with facing our sinfulness, becoming totally disrupted by our offensiveness to Him. How can we ever be enticed to celebrate until we have dealt with that which keeps us from being celebrants—our own tragedy and offensiveness?

Our Only Hope

Our only hope is to cooperate fully with God's agenda. First, He must disrupt us by exposing our sinfulness. Only then can He entice us with something profoundly better—to find and know Him more passionately than anyone or anything else on earth. Under this divine agenda, a delightful new passion will begin to consume us. As men of God, our focus will be forever altered: from our own well-being to His glory; from our justified selfishness and self-fulfillment to loving others even at the cost of personal sacrifice; from finding success and public acclaim to entering into true sonship with our heavenly Father.

God designed us as men to be initiators, to use the substance of our maleness to enter our world as He would enter it and in a way that reflects His character. We are to enter with gentle but aggressive strength to be creators, bringing life out of death and light out of darkness.

That is God's plan, but sin sabotaged that divine design. And we men, instead of entering our world in a creative, life-giving way, have become disruptive, distorted, perverted, destructive, dominating and abandoning. Our manly desires are sinful and enslaving. A deep terror keeps us from strongly entering into the mystery of our world. We despise and hate mystery because entering mystery exposes our demanding, enslaving, sinful spirit. It shows up our desire to remain in control in order to function independently of our God.

This truth needs to disrupt and offend us. If God has not offended us as men, then we have not yet met the God of the Bible and of creation. It is the purpose and very passion of God's heart to make us into His design. Unfortunately, we have inherited the design-disrupting virus of Adam. Our sin offends God; it grieves Him and fills His heart with pain. But before we can deal effectively with this proneness to sin and offense, we need a fresh understanding of how this spiritual dilemma all came about. Join me as we move through the locker room of the male soul and enter into the joys of our redeemed manhood.

This is a book for men about male issues. For an explanation of the paradigm (analogy) used throughout this book, the reader may wish to read through the abbreviated explanation in the Appendix.

CHAPTER 2

Eve's Role in the Fall

When God created Adam, He was up to something, something good. He designed him as a male with the capacity to strongly initiate and enter, to create life, to bring light out of darkness for the glory of God and the good of others.

When God created Eve, He was up to something a little different. He designed her as a female with the capacity to actively respond by freely inviting, by richly nourishing and helping and by offering the substance of her soul in order to provide rest for the good of others and the glory of God.

Into this beautiful mystery of gender identity and harmonious interdependency came Satan in the form of a serpent. Through his scheming subterfuge, Adam and Eve fell into sin, and the rest is history.

Those may be the facts, but they leave some crucial questions begging for answers. Why did it happen? How did it happen? How did sin manage to barge into a perfect setting and wreak havoc? What transpired that created such spiritual shock waves that we today are still reeling from the impact? Let's begin our search for the answers by looking first at Eve and her responses, though she is by no means the sole culprit in this tragedy.

Eve's Temptation

The story line that presents Eve's temptation and fall is filled with a dynamic reality. She is not presented as a cardboard figure, but a real flesh-and-blood person interacting with others—Eve with God, Eve with Satan and Eve with her husband, Adam. There is in this process, as recorded in Genesis 3, a truly feminine context and flavor. Unfortunately for mankind, by the time Eve is through, the relational oneness that was there when she started is tragically shattered!

Genesis 3 begins with some very ominous words: "Now the serpent was more crafty than any of the wild animals the LORD God had made" (3:1). These words burst on the scene as a shocking intrusion into an otherwise glorious account of God's majestic creative work. With the declaration, "Now the serpent," the whole atmosphere of the biblical account radically changes. A sudden, chilling sense of foreboding enters the story.

This wild creature was created by the Lord God as subtly deceitful and cunning, descriptive qualities that also paint the biblical picture of Satan. He said to the woman, "Did God really say, 'You must not eat from any tree in the garden'?" (3:1).

The story makes it clear that the serpent initiated the conversation with Eve. He chose to speak directly to her as the *active responder,* avoiding the man, Adam, who was the strong initiator. This is significant, and perhaps needs further explanation. The male image-bearer of God—*the strong initiator*—expresses his essence in strong initiatory involvement that enters to bring life. The female image-bearer of God—*the active responder*—expresses her essence in active, inviting responsiveness that receives to nourish life. Together they are one image of equal parts, dignity, value and worth, reflecting one humanity for the glory of God and the good of others.

As the one created after Adam, Eve was the latecomer in the garden. She was not as qualified to deal with Satan's challenge. The moral prohibition about the tree had been given to Adam before Eve had come into existence. Through this instruction from God, Adam was prepared to face the tempter. Yet Eve took it upon herself to act in Adam's place and therefore she was deceived.

Eve's Disobedience

Eve's disobedience followed hard on the heels of her deception, and it came through a relational interchange with Satan. Paul wrote, "But I am afraid that just as Eve was deceived by the serpent's cunning, your minds may somehow be led astray from your sincere and pure devotion to Christ" (2 Corinthians 11:3).

Eve's deception was not an indication of some inherent flaw or of some inferiority of value in her constitutional, female-gender identity, but was instead a reflection of the guile and craftiness of Satan. As well, it reflects the truth that Eve was the active responder, that she was created as a suitable helper. By her taking Adam's male role as the strong initiator, Satan now had her in a vulnerable position. Through his wiles, he had tricked her into the first temptation and moral dilemma.

By so manipulating her, he caused her to violate both God's order of creation—the belief that there is significance in the order in which God, who is a God of order, created the world and people—and the roles their sexual identity were to play in reflecting God's image and design. Through the creation order and mandate, Adam was the first to have functional dominion. It was in this very violation that Eve became vulnerable to deception.

The serpent knew about God's command to Adam but twisted the truth as he conversed with Eve. Very cunningly he raised the issue of God's credibility, His trustworthiness, dependability and goodness—"Eve, are you sure God said this?" In those few words are voiced the core issue of all temptation—"Is God really good?"

> The woman said to the serpent, "We may eat fruit from the trees in the garden, but God did say, 'You must not eat fruit from the tree that is in the middle of the garden, and you must not touch it, or you will die.' " (Genesis 3:2-3)

At this point, Eve is in over her head. Taking functional dominion was to be a mutually interdependent responsibility, but here on her own she is strongly initiating with the serpent to defend, discern and reason the truth. She obviously knew about God's command, probably because Adam told her once they became one flesh. And she was accurately representing the truth, but the problem is she is doing it alone, not in partnership as God planned.

" 'You will not surely die,' the serpent said to the woman" (3:4). Here the serpent contradicts the truth, God's direct words to Adam—"[B]ut you must not eat from the tree of the knowledge of good and evil, for when you eat of it you will surely die" (2:17).

This is the first insidious shift from truth to error in the dynamic process of Eve's deceit. Through subtle manipulation, he is moving her toward doubting God, Adam and herself, and believing Satan instead. The powerful implicit message given through the serpent to Eve was basically, "Your husband and your God are neither trustworthy, dependable nor good." The explicit message was equally attractive and powerful— "You will not surely die!"

God had provided them with life. He had told Adam that in the middle of the garden was the tree of life. "And the LORD God commanded the man, 'You are free to eat from any tree in the garden' " (2:16). Yet after both Adam and Eve sinned, God said, "He must not be allowed to reach out his hand and take also from the tree of life and eat, and live forever" (3:22).

Satan, through the serpent, offered Eve "forever life" apart from any moral attachment to or dependency on God, her Life-giver and Sustainer! "Eve, shift your trust, your dependency to me! I will become your life-giver and sustainer," Satan intimated.

In a secondary way, Satan tempted Eve to leave her human relationship and experience of being one flesh with her husband and become autonomous. In so doing, he was asking her to give away her interdependence and mutual involvement with Adam for an independence and form of control that would relationally isolate her from him. This, I believe, is at the root of why fallen female image-bearers want to take control and live independently of fallen male image-bearers—the males have shown themselves to be untrustworthy, undependable and lacking in goodness. Like Eve, today's women struggle with a deep fear of insecurity in the presence of Satan, temptation and untrustworthy men.

The serpent then increased the payoff for disobeying God. He said, "For God knows that when you eat of it your eyes will be opened, and you will be like God, knowing good and evil" (3:5). This final argument was the telling blow to Eve's resistance. Satan was offering her not only life, but also power. By inference, he said, "You can be in control of good and evil because your eyes will be opened and you will have knowledge just like God. Come on, Eve! Sit in the throne room. Be like God. Take control over good which provides pleasure, and over evil which produces pain."

Eve's Fall

The prospect of being like the Almighty was too much for her to resist. "When the woman saw that the fruit of the tree was good for food and pleasing to the eye, and also desirable for gaining wisdom, she took some and ate it" (3:6).

At last, success! The serpent's temptation had achieved its intended results. Despite the fact that she was surrounded by "trees that were pleasing to the eye and good for food" (2:9), her attention was firmly riveted on the forbidden tree. Here was fruit that was not only good and pleasing and desirable, but could also provide her with all the wisdom she would ever need to live life successfully.

What was there about this tree that was so appealing? What form of goodness, pleasure and wisdom from the tree of knowledge of good and evil became so alluring to Eve that she would disobey God in order to have it? Did this one single tree produce a quality and type of fruit so good and pleasing that none of the other fruit in the garden could compete? Is it possible

God actually created this tree to overpower Eve and Adam with its promise of knowledge and wisdom?

The answer to these last two questions is an emphatic, "No!" The garden was full of trees that pleased both palate and eye, and one tree, the tree of life, that would allow them to enjoy a God-life forever. God designed it all for the enrichment and good of Adam and Eve, not as a means to trip them up. There was absolutely no issue of allurement or temptation until the serpent entered the garden and gave Eve a counteroffer.

But what about the nature of that tree of the knowledge of good and evil? What made it so appealing, so irresistible? I believe the answer lies in what it offered. By eating, Eve would not only have knowledge and wisdom, but also power and control. She would become like God.

This must have stirred in her a deep passion. The forbidden fruit would enable her to control her place of order and responsibility as the helper. With it, she could choose what was good for her, what gave her pleasure and what would make her wise and knowledgeable. She would no longer need to be dependent on her God. Nor would interdependence with Adam be necessary any more to jointly carry out their purpose of being fruitful, filling, ruling and subduing the earth. The prospect was overwhelmingly appealing. "[S]he took some and ate it" (3:6), the Bible says, and in so doing, Eve partook of the first "power-lunch" in the history of mankind.

Subsequently, "she [Eve] also gave some to her husband, who was with her" (3:6), and thus completed her part in the fall of mankind. This principle of sinning and sharing was highlighted in Romans by the apostle Paul, who wrote, "Although they know God's righteous decree that those who do such things deserve death, they not only continue to do these very things but also approve of those who practice them" (Romans 1:32).

Sin exposes the moral bankruptcy of our souls and always has consequences for both the sinner and his associates. It is like the ripple-effect of a pebble tossed into a pond; the circle of impact keeps growing ever larger. There is no such thing as sinning in isolation because sin severs one's relationship with God and others, and a severed relationship always brings an experiential taste of relational death.

Eve's Deception

Eve's act of sinning through disobedience was not a matter-of-fact, mechanical response. She was masterfully deceived by the Father of Lies. He took her God-created longing and passion and used it for evil. His outwardly friendly conversation was filled with truth and falsehood so cunningly interwoven that she was caught before she knew there was danger. Without intending to, she found her deep inner womanly passions stirred and aroused in ways that impacted her ultimate choice in giving in to the temptation. Her desires as a female image-bearer and as life-giver and mother of all humanity would from that time forward be predisposed to seek fulfillment outside the boundaries of the order and purpose that God ordained in creation.

Because Eve chose not to submit to God, she reversed the divine creation order, abdicating her function as the suitable helper. She chose to eat the fruit of the tree of knowledge of good and evil independently of Adam, thereby refusing to submit to him. Thus she was the one who was deceived by the serpent. "Then the LORD God said to the woman, 'What is this you have done?' The woman said, 'The serpent deceived me, and I ate' " (Genesis 3:13).

Satan seemed to be very aware of God's intended order for maleness and femaleness and how He wanted it expressed in fulfilling the creation mandate. Satan also seemed to be well aware of what would deeply stir Eve in her femininity. He appeared to know what longings and passions to provoke in order to deceive her into disobeying God's command. He also seemed to know enough about her femaleness to be able to entice her to step outside God's designed place and purpose.

The process that the serpent used to seduce and deceive Eve has profound implications for men and women, enabling them both to understand something of the feminine nature. And lest you think I'm suddenly writing a woman's book, not a man's, I hasten to assure you, I am not. The stated purpose of this book is to confront men with the sin and pain of their hearts and to call them to godliness. But it is impossible to talk about men and sin without bringing women into the picture since a large percentage of our sin is either with or against them.

Four Godly Desires of Women

From our position as men in the divinely created order, it is our God-given responsibility and privilege to love, minister to and serve the women in our world. To do so well, we need to better understand their femininity, to know what makes them tick. Perhaps a study of four of the godly desires of women evident in this text will help us improve our effectiveness as men.

1. The godly desire to listen to and obey God. The serpent knew what female desires to stir and entice. He appealed to her legitimate longing to listen to and obey God. Consider their conversation.

Satan said to the woman, "Did God really say . . . ?" (3:1).

The woman said to the serpent, "[B]ut God did say . . ." (3:3).

Eve, as the helper in the creation mandate, did her best to stand up and represent God to Satan. She tried to protect, defend and obey truth on her own. A woman deeply, passionately thirsts for intimacy with her God. She longs to obey Him and not give in to her vulnerability to Satan's deception.

2. The godly desire to live and not die. The serpent also appealed to Eve's passion for living. She was destined to become the mother of all humankind. Her very name means "living."[1] In the garden, she knew life more abundant. It tasted good and was pleasurable. She was full of the knowledge of life and did not want to lose it. She legitimately longed to live and not die. Knowing this, Satan picked up on it. " 'You will not surely die,' the serpent said to the woman" (3:4).

Femaleness is life. A woman has been designed by God to bear and nourish all aspects of life—physical, relational and spiritual. Women thrive on bearing and nurturing in all its many dimensions. Recognize that as their place in God's divine order; it's their assigned function in fulfilling the creation mandate. Destroying life in any form is diametrically opposed to a woman's passion to conceive, bear and nourish. We need to defend, protect and support this passion at all cost.

3. The godly desire to have legitimate knowledge, power and control within the boundaries set for her by God. A woman, in expressing her femaleness as a suitable helper, longs to have legitimate knowledge, power and control within the boundaries set for her by God. This frees her to reflect God's likeness, as an image-bearer, in carrying out her responsibilities to His glory and for the good of others. Satan took Eve's legitimate longing to reflect God's likeness and twisted it by tempting her into believing she could become like God.

Both men and women need to understand this deep feminine longing and protect it from the abuse of knowledge, power and control that comes apart from God. James warned us about this danger:

> But if you harbor bitter envy and selfish ambition in your hearts, do not boast about it or deny the truth. Such "wisdom" does not come down from heaven but is earthly, unspiritual, of the devil. For where you have envy and selfish ambition, there you find disorder and every evil practice. (James 3:14-16)

Satan first appealed to Eve's legitimate, God-designed longing to reflect God's likeness by expressing her femaleness as a helper to Adam. Now, the deceiver suggested that she could have all of this and more. "You can also have knowledge that will allow you to become like God, with enough power to control pleasure and pain. You can have all this by usurping the male's assigned responsibility and purpose in the creation order and mandate," Satan said.

This temptation has become appealing because it allows a woman a sense of power and control over life without the threat of male domination and rule. She can find soul-life outside of the God-ordained boundaries set for her. Satan always tempts us by offering us more than God does, in terms of what is good, pleasurable and knowledgeable.

Male domination over women violates their God-designed passion to reflect God's likeness in their femaleness. This domination, whether aggressive or passive, stirs in them a deep fear. It often provokes an urgency to take control over their own source of pleasure and pain outside God's designated boundaries.

Women, as well, need to take responsibility for how this legitimate longing has become twisted. It has infected their female soul like a virus. This is the virus of Eve which is part of a woman's particular sin problem that needs to be brought back into submission to God.

4. *The godly desire to enjoy the good, the pleasing, the desirable.* One final, general area of female innate longing revealed in this text is the deep desire that God has placed within her to enjoy that which is good, that which is pleasing to her eye and that which is desirable for gaining wisdom (see Genesis 3:6). Satan again preyed on these legitimate desires to lead Eve outside God's boundary for what was good, pleasurable and wise.

These longings for that which is "good" were to be used for the glory of God. This is how "good" was used throughout Genesis 1. Each time God made something, He judged it good. Satan could only work with what was legitimate in Eve because God had judged her as good. So he tempted her by twisting her legitimate longings, and thereafter influencing men to do the same.

Women need to allow God to take all of the legitimate longings, desires and passions that are such an in-

tegral part of their female essence and use them to glorify Him and not their own sense of self.

In summary, men, we need to understand what God
created as legitimate longings and abilities within the
female image-bearing soul. As the suitable helper, she
was designed by Him to actively and invitingly respond in order to warmly conceive, bear and nourish
life. This was her responsibility in the creation order
and mandate. She was to do it together in a partnership of mutual interdependence with the male image-
bearer. Practically, that longing is lived out in a carnal
passion to take relational dominion of multiplying and
filling the earth. This is substantiated by the specific
fit of God's judgment on the woman. He said that He
would greatly increase her pain in childbearing and in
birth. As well, her desire for her husband would now
be distorted and the man would rule over her, making
a relationship of oneness difficult and unsafe (see
Genesis 3:16).

A secondary longing for the female is to take functional dominion of ruling and subduing the created
world. This does not imply it is of lesser value to the
female or to God. It is just a lesser innate constitutional
longing and passion than is her primary longing to take
relational dominion.

We are partners together in this creation mandate.
Understanding, encouraging, edifying, supporting and
prizing these longings and abilities in a female image-
bearer are vitally important. It will help protect her
from the deceitful work of Satan, other fallen sinful
men and from her own misuse of these inner realities
of beauty.

What a holy calling we have as men in fulfilling our
creation mandate!

Endnote

[1] John D. Davis, *Davis Dictionary of the Bible*, 4th ed. (Grand Rapids, MI: Baker Book House, 1980), 234.

CHAPTER 3

Adam's Role in the Fall

Returning to the dynamic yet tragic story of man's fall into sin, we find the male image-bearer now entering into the process of temptation and disobedience. The setting is already clearly in place. We have looked at the roots and reasons for Eve's sin. Now the question comes, "Why did Adam sin?" What was the nature and process of Adam's disobedience to God's direct command?

God gave to the man alone the most important commandment—he was not to eat from the tree of the knowledge of good and evil. Disobedience to this command would lead to certain death (see Genesis 2:16-17). The assigning of this responsibility to the man made him better prepared to face the serpent and implies the greater responsibility of function entrusted to him by the Creator. The woman was created to be a helper which clearly implies a supportive function. Eve's responsibility was to support Adam in defending their obedience to this commandment (see 2:18).

Eve was deceived; Adam was not. So what was Adam's sin? Adam's sin is evident by two choices he made. Adam was *not* without blame. In fact, the story

33

of the fall of man makes it very clear that God addressed Adam first for disobeying His commandment. It seems to indicate that Adam was more culpable because he was created before Eve and it was to him that God specifically gave the command.

Adam's guilt comes as a result of the first of his two choices. His decision is made clear in these specific Scriptures:

> She also gave some to her husband, who was with her, and he ate it. . . . [The Lord God said,] "Have you eaten from the tree that I commanded you not to eat from?" The man said, "The woman you put here with me—she gave me some fruit from the tree, and I ate it." . . . To Adam he said, "Because you listened to your wife and ate from the tree about which I commanded you. . . ." (3:6, 11-12, 17)

The Sin of Commission

The nature of Adam's sin of disobedience and rebellion involved first the sin of commission. Adam, like Eve, was also "deceived"; she by Satan, he by his wife. There are some elements of deception in all acts of sin. God said it best—"Because you listened to your wife and ate from the tree about which I commanded you . . ." (3:17). Adam made a choice to listen to his wife and ignore the Lord. God had spoken to Adam clearly and specifically, yet somehow Eve's offer of the fruit of the tree of knowledge of good and evil was more tempting and alluring.

This interchange between Eve and Adam reveals a very obvious dynamic. First, there is Adam choosing to be relationally passive by becoming the active responder. Then there is the relational reality of Eve choosing to be the strong initiator. It was she who took the fruit, ate and then shared it with her husband. Adam, as the responder, likely watched the actions of his wife, because when she offered him the fruit, he was ready to take it.

In this brief scene, there is a clear violation of God's created order. Both Adam and Eve forsook their assigned responsibility to express their maleness and femaleness according to God's design, but not without consequences. Their sinful choices—to live in rebellion against God and independently from Him—had tremendous impact. Through their willfulness, the glory that God had crowned them with was shattered and their sense of oneness with each other was destroyed. God created them with the capacity to choose: to obey or disobey Him, to listen or ignore Him, to experience their deep, legitimate desires and longings and be able to satisfy them with His resources or to seek their own sources of satisfaction.

The Sin of Omission

Adam's culpability before God becomes clear in the second choice which he made within himself and before Eve and Satan. This can be called the sin of omission, which is reflected and demonstrated in what Adam chose *not* to do. One could argue that the order of his choices in how he disobeyed God could be reversed. In reality, both these choices were likely happening within Adam at the same time. He probably experienced the immediate introduction of some degree of self-consciousness and tension when faced with the choice to do something.

Adam's sin of omission was his choice to remain silent. He said and did nothing about something that mattered most to God, to Satan, to Eve, to himself, to mankind and to the physical, created world. By contrast, the woman, Eve, sinned not by silence, but by her words as she sought relational involvement. The man, Adam, sinned by both silence and passive, non-relational involvement. Thus they both sinned by their unique deeds and were held accountable to God, and both received the death penalty.

The legacy of Adam that all males have inherited is the gene of silence, of doing nothing functionally or relationally about what matters most to God, to others and to the earth. This is a generational trait passed on by Adam. We received it from our fathers and we passed it on to our sons.

Whether Adam was actually there with Eve during the entire temptation by the serpent is up for discussion and not all agree that he was present. My reading of Genesis 3 seems to indicate that he was there—"She also gave some to her husband, who was with her . . ." (3:6). However, this could mean he was there with her only after the serpent was finished with his actual temptation. The text is not absolutely clear, but it does seem to strongly imply that Adam was with her during the entire process of temptation and deception. If that position is true, then there are major implications for us as males.

Adam clearly made a choice in the presence of the serpent and his wife to refuse to take his God-designed responsibility to be the strong initiating man and husband. Let's face it, men. Adam did not resist Satan. He did not offer the created world to God by carrying out his responsibility of the creation mandate. And, as the man, Adam did not protect his bride, Eve. This has been the ongoing struggle that males have had since Adam's sin.

We see this sinful male pattern of avoidance also illustrated later in the Old Testament with Aaron. He
was supposed to do the same things as Adam, but he
also failed. While Moses was up on the mountain meeting with God, Aaron was down in the valley supposedly looking after the Israelites. But when the people
became impatient because Moses did not return and
demanded an idol to worship, Aaron gave in. He failed
to offer the world—symbolized by the sacrificing of
animals—to God. Instead, he sacrificed to the golden
calf. He did not protect God's people.

This whole issue of order and function in male-female relationships is on more than just the human
level. There is a greater design to be lived out in God's
plan and program for mankind. We dare not distort
and pervert it, either at the human or supernatural relationship levels.

As men, we all face time and time again the choice
to do something about what matters most to God, to
others and to creation. We, like Adam, choose to do
nothing, and the consequence of our sin of living out
our own rebellious will, independent of God, often has
drastic consequences. These consequences break our
sense of oneness in our relationship with God and with
others—instead of taking dominion, we dominate; instead of mutual interdependency, especially with the
opposite sex, we abandon. This choice of living and relating becomes evident in how we fail to live out our
God-designed expression of maleness.

Godly Desires of the Male

Some of the deep longings that God placed in the
male image-bearing soul become evident through the
dynamic process of Adam's sins of commission and

omission. As men, we need to recognize and take ownership of our legitimate desires or longings that make us passionate, alive, male image-bearers. Women, as well, need to seek to gain a deeper understanding of a male's deep longings so that they can know better how to minister, support and be suitable helpers in their partnership in fulfilling the creation mandate.

1. The godly desire to enter into his responsibility in the creation mandate in interdependent partnership with the female image-bearer. Designed into every male soul by God Himself is the longing to strongly, firmly and tenderly enter into his responsibility in the creation mandate and to do it together in a partnership of mutual interdependence with the female image-bearer. Practically, that longing is lived out in a stronger passion to take functional dominion, ruling and subduing the created world. This is substantiated by the specific way the curse of the ground was going to impact the man (see Genesis 3:17-19).

2. The godly desire to take relational dominion in multiplying and filling the earth. A secondary longing for the male is to take relational dominion in multiplying and filling the earth. This does not imply it is of lesser value to the male or to God. It is just less strong than is his primary longing to take functional dominion.

So Adam was designed by God to tend and keep the garden, to provide for and protect the helper. In the story of the fall, Adam's ability to express this legitimate longing became corrupted by his choice to disobey. He chose to satisfy these longings by not living responsibly before his God and before his wife. He opted for the path of least resistance when it came to matters of utmost importance.

The implications at a general level are that men seem to have a difficult time taking themselves and their relational intimacy with God seriously. Men find it takes little effort to avoid spiritual conflict and dealing with issues of spirituality. They more effortlessly enter into matters of doing, which are functional and less of a threat to their sense of maleness, rather than entering richly and personally into intimacy in relationships. By choice men would much rather do something to prove their sense of maleness than deal with the inner realities of the mind and heart. This happens when we take our sons to a hockey game and only talk about hockey, or take our wives shopping and never talk about personal issues, or fix the heater in our home but never sit by the heater with our family to relate personally.

As males, we long to do what God has designed us to do. But even deeper is the longing to be who God designed us to be in our identity as His image-bearers. Adam violated who he was by choosing to disobey God. At this point, Adam's sinful, fallen male identity replaced that which God had given him.

The fall of Adam and Eve into sin and out of relational oneness with their God and each other had disastrous consequences. The perfectly fitted male-female relationship and expression of sexuality in fulfilling the creation mandate was now reversed and became a misfit, a poor reflection of God's design and image. Their sin indeed destroyed their glory!

The remainder of the chapters of this section will address the results of sin in the male soul. His glory is now shattered. The shape of his male soul is now twisted and bent. His ability to express his male longings has been perverted and his image of God is distorted.

Solomon, the wisest man on earth, summarized it well: "This only have I found: God made mankind upright, but men have gone in search of many schemes" (Ecclesiastes 7:29).

CHAPTER 4

Retreating into Destruction

The adrenaline rush is over. Sin has been committed. Adam stands there very much exposed and vulnerable. He's trembling with shame and guilt, fearful of what God will say when He comes to walk with them in garden.

If Adam had a journal back then, and we had access to it, I can imagine it was filled with a mixture of fear and defiance. Perhaps it might read like this:

> Am I ever glad for fig leaves! Just being able to hide behind something gives me a great sense of relief and soul rest, and that's exactly what my shattered sense of maleness needs right now.
>
> I'm scared. I don't know what is going to happen to me for disobeying God. He shouldn't have saddled me with looking after the garden and that woman anyway.
>
> I have this awful sense of dread in the bowels of my soul. I wish there was some way to get rid of it. The only relief I get is from shifting the blame to someone else. I don't have what it takes to pull the thorns out of the earth and out of our

marriage. This business of taking dominion turns me off. I'm much more passionate about dominating and abusing my authority. The sense of power I experience in ruling over Eve and in abusing my function in carrying out the creation mandate is what fills this void of male emptiness inside me and seems to validate my manhood.

But what am I going to do? God has banished us from the garden. The tree of life is now beyond our reach. And there is that terrible foreboding sense of death that hangs over me.

Enough worrying. I'm young and I'm strong. I'll find my own sense of life. If I work hard enough, I can make it happen. I'm young and I'm strong. I may be outside the garden, but I can still make life work the way I want it. There is no way death is going to creep up on me. (see Genesis 3:7-24)

Admittedly this is purely fiction, but the essence of that scenario is very much fact. Corrupting, enslaving sinful desires, energized by Adam's disobedience, became the unnatural rhythms of life and passions of his male soul. These were fueled by his now idolatrous heart, since he had now become like God knowing good and evil.

Before eating of the forbidden tree, Adam and Eve had no consciousness of sin. They had the capacity, but it was not yet realized. The Scripture says it was not until they ate that their eyes were opened and they realized they were naked. Because of their sinful choices, suddenly they could see good and evil and experience it.

In the aftermath of transgression, a self-consciousness appeared in them and they became aware of not being dressed, of needing some form of covering. Disobedience moved them from a soul posture of strong God-consciousness and other-centeredness to having an immediate sense of self-consciousness and self-centeredness. From being consumed with dependency on God and an interdependence with each other, they become idolatrously independent from God and enslaved to selfishness. They now experienced immediate separation from the God-life they had been given. Cut off from Him, they tried to cope with the consequences on their own. Exerting their self-will, they sewed fig leaves together to cover themselves (Genesis 3:7).

Jeremiah speaks of this same twofold process of sin found in every human heart: "My people have committed two sins: They have forsaken me, the spring of living water, and have dug their own cisterns, broken cisterns that cannot hold water" (Jeremiah 2:13). Once mankind forsakes God, the idolatrous passion from within will be to drink from their own broken cisterns.

After God allowed them to come up with their plan to cover their nakedness, He initiated a meeting. This was what they feared, so they hid from Him among the trees of the garden (Genesis 3:8). Their sinfulness filled them with terror of a holy God, and they sought to hide from His presence.

David tells us that it is impossible to escape the presence of God:

Where can I go from your Spirit?
　　Where can I flee from you presence? . . .
If I say, "Surely the darkness will hide me
　　and the light become night around me,"

even the darkness will not be dark to you;
the night will shine like the day,
for darkness is as light to you.
(Psalm 139:7, 11-12)

Like Adam, we men, in our state of depravity (our sin
nature), are filled and energized by sinful, enslaving desires, desires that are evil and corrupt! Paul describes the
sin nature in this way: "Those who live according to the
sinful nature have their minds set on what that nature
desires. . . . The mind of sinful man is death . . . [because]
the sinful mind is hostile to God. . . . Those controlled by
the sinful nature cannot please God" (Romans 8:5-8). Peter also wrote about these evil desires when he said,
"[Y]ou may participate in the divine nature and escape
the corruption in the world caused by evil desires" (2 Peter 1:4).

Let me bring the reality of these sinful desires closer
to where we live today. The beginning of Genesis has
several examples.

Old Testament Examples

Adam's son, Cain, followed in his father's footsteps
and also expressed these sinful desires. When God rejected his offering, Cain became downcast and very angry. No doubt his mind was filled with thoughts like
these:

What I have as a man to offer God and others is
never good enough. What is the use of doing
what is right? Sin keeps ambushing me, provoking powerful evil desires in me that I can't seem
to master. One time, in an overpowering fit of
angry passion, I murdered my only brother.

Then, when God confronted me and exposed my sin, I lied and refused to take responsibility. The consequences were more than I could bear. My spirit became restless and I had a hard time settling down. What was hardest to live with was that there was no longer a sense of the presence of God. I felt so alone. (See Genesis 4:4-16.)

A group of men who moved to a new location in Babylonia also demonstrated this sin nature when they said, "We want to build a city with a building so high that it will guarantee our own security" (see Genesis 11:1-4).

In the city of Sodom, a group of men surrounded Lot's home and asked for the two "male" visitors, who were in reality angels. "We prefer these men over your virgin daughters," they cried. "Bring out those visitors so we can have sex with them" (see Genesis 19:5).

Contemporary Examples

Though these incidents took place very early in the history of man, there is a certain ring of familiarity with what men struggle with today. Pride, sexual lust and murder have become trademarks of both ancient and modern men who live outside the garden.

A man recently told me, "I feel beat up by life. I have no close friends, nobody I can relate to. The only thing that really brings me alive is pornography. I'm really hooked! How can I find something that is more inviting and less controlling to my life? What could possibly compete with this stuff that seduces me into a cesspool of alluring sensuality mixed with guilt and shame? I feel alive and dead inside at the same time."

Another Christian man said, "When I'm feeling like I have absolutely nothing else to give to my job, my wife or my three children, it feels like I keep sacrificing my salvation for ten minutes of soul rest that sexual fantasizing and masturbating bring me. I know David in Psalm 23 said that the Lord as my Shepherd would lead me beside still waters and restore my soul. I have tried that. It has not worked for me. Besides, I have no idea how to let the Lord do that. This Christianity stuff just doesn't work for me!"

John sells cars. He is good at what he does. Of course, there are some down months in the year where his sales drop off, but he says, "I just work harder and soon things change for me and I'm back on top personally and financially. When I make a sale, the personal rush I get from deep inside puts me in touch with a passion and desire so real and consuming that nothing else can compare. So what's the matter with that? Sure, I work sixty hours a week, but it's worth it!"

These men are in touch with something alive, something gripping that enslaves them just like Adam, Cain, the men at the tower of Babel and the males in Sodom. Our desires are alive, filling us with a sense of passion. But what are these manly passions, these often controlling desires that erupt from seemingly hidden pockets in our male soul and ambush us without concern for the consequences that follow? When are we most aware of these deep visceral feelings of being male?

For me, as a young boy, it happened over a two-week period of time. Two other ten-year-old boys and myself set out to take dominion over the forest about one-half mile from our homes. Our intention was to subdue, to rule over these woods by building our first tree house. I will never forget building the foundational frame twelve to fifteen feet off the ground. We had to somehow hang on to a two-by-four, shinny simultaneously up the trees, hold the hammer and pound in the nails.

Once the four two-by-fours were secured, we climbed up onto the small framed square between four trees and laid our floor. Then came the walls, the roof and behold—our tree house. I can still feel that sense of risk, the challenge and accomplishment that overwhelmed us. We had conquered the dangers, the obstacles and the task! The rush of male passion was as real as the blood pumping through our veins.

When I was a young man, during a football game, I collided with an opponent during the first half of the game. His teeth hit my ear and almost severed the top of it. Since this was the championship game and I was playing quarterback, I chose to carry on. The adrenaline triggered by the closeness of the contest easily numbed the pain of my injury. But when the game ended, there was plenty of pain as they took me to the hospital for stitches. The adrenaline rush from excitement and competition, thoroughly mingled with the pain and blood from my wounded ear, stirred in me a sense of manliness that I will never forget.

A friend of mine had a similar experience. "Steve," he said, "when I finally challenged the grade seven class bully and literally beat him physically into submission, that was the first time I had ever felt like a man and not just a little boy."

Another man spoke of a similar response from a hunting incident. He said, "When I shot that ten-point buck from the tree platform with my hunting bow after sitting for six hours, I felt like a million bucks. I don't even remember climbing down the tree to get to him. That surge of passion inside me was worth the hours of waiting in the cold autumn wind."

One more story comes from a man who writes, composes and plays his own music. "When I pick up that classical guitar and play my music through perfectly, I just feel like I'm in another world. I lose track of time. The experience is like no other I ever get as a man— better than what I get from my family, from church, even better than my personal time of worship with God."

What kind of fantasies—and I mean manly, not sexual—do you have that put you in touch with the substance and essence of maleness? What is it that ignites your manly passions and draws you out of your moods of indifference, apathy, boredom and deadness?

A man in his thirties responded to this question this way: "When I am most apathetic and down in my spirit, I find myself fantasizing about being in a four-wheel-drive Jeep with huge, oversized tires and driving into downtown traffic, crushing cars at stop lights."

I will never forget a twenty-four-year-old man telling me about one of his most stimulating fantasies. "I get this picture of being a rock star in front of 25,000 teenagers," he said. "I am stripped to the waist; sweat glistens over my body. The security men surrounding the stage are fighting off the frenzied fans as they try to touch me."

These stories reflect both corrupt passions and good desires. We were designed by God to take the substance of our maleness and enter into our world and its people. We are to reflect His character and nature, entering with bold initiative to pour out the essence of our maleness in order to bring about life. But instead, we fantasize about crushing cars with oversized four-wheel-drive Jeeps, or impacting thousands of people to the point of crazed idol worship. Or we work sixty hours a week in order to maintain a rush of passion that we can't seem to get anywhere else. We conquer in the trees, create music that results in an inner response that not even God can compete with and wonder why we are such driven men. Why are we never fully satisfied and content? Why are we constantly crying for more? We must have more of this same response we get from taking dominion by ruling and subduing! Give me more! There is life outside the garden. I have found it! But . . .

The Shattered Glory

Something glorious inside of us as men has been shattered, twisted, broken, bent! Our initiative to enter has now become unsafe and dangerous and often brings death to our world and to other people. The stench of death coming from our enslaving, sinful desires only grows as we get older. There is a dark side to our desires that is evil, corrupting and enslaving. It seems to lay fallow in the unplowed soil of the back forty acres of our souls. We often struggle with these monsters that lurk in the loins of our maleness. And like men throughout the ages, we cry out in moments of desperation, "How do we understand, how do we tame and replace these sinful enslaving passions with that which is godly and upright?"

Like Adam, we dread entering into a situation that we have never faced. We hate mystery. We despise the groaning of creation. And at the deepest level of our souls we rage at our God for giving us this woman who started it all! As a result, we become desperate, passion-driven men trying to prove our manhood for selfish purposes instead of freely expressing it for the good of our world, of others and for the glory of God.

All this is true, but don't give up the ship, men. God has not left us to flounder and sink. Through use of the plumb line of the Word of God and the indwelling presence of the Holy Spirit and through the company of others (especially men), we can unmask these enslaving, sinful desires that have corrupted our male souls. Once we identify the enemy, half the battle is already won. I strongly believe that if women want to better understand maleness, they should take a look at these desires. The same holds true for us as men. If we want to better enter into the lives of mothers, grandmothers, wives, daughters, friends, fiancées, employees and employers, then we need to better understand the enslaving desires of their female souls.

Who we are as males, no matter our stage of development, can be linked back to the virus of Adam that has infected us down through the generations of time. Since that is where it began, that is also where we need to begin in getting to the root of the passions that enslave us.

CHAPTER 5

Enslaving Desires That Corrupt

Let's start at the point in Adam's fall where his eyes were opened so he could recognize good and evil. In that fateful moment in history, there were at least four significant, enslaving desires that erupted in Adam's male soul, four desires from which these corrupted passions proceeded. These four enslaving desires are not all male-specific. There is certainly some overlap with the female's sinful, enslaving desires. What is significant in setting them apart is that they are distinctly influenced by the gender involved. Our sinful, enslaving desires are colored by our maleness, just as women's desires are shaped by their femininity.

Sinful Desires That Corrupt and Enslave

1. *I must choose to hide who I really am behind whatever fig leaves I can create.* "Then the eyes of both of them were opened, and they realized they were naked; so they sewed fig leaves together and made coverings for themselves. . . . [Adam] answered, 'I heard you in the garden, and I was afraid because I was naked; so I hid' " (Genesis 3:7, 10).

51

There is no personal experience more fearful and shameful than that symbolized by nakedness. For the first time, Adam and Eve recognized they were physically bare. However, since complete nakedness is both encouraged and blessed by God within the boundary of a monogamous, male-female marriage relationship, the nakedness of Genesis 3 would appear to symbolize a nakedness of soul. For the first time they felt guilt, shame and fear. God's moral righteousness no longer provided a covering for their inner consciousness. Masking their nakedness with fig leaves was their human attempt to cover their experience of immorality, of relational infidelity to God.

Adam now was determined to hide his unfaithfulness from God by hiding behind the covering of fig leaves and the trees of the garden. There is a day coming when all mankind will stand before God to be judged. This sense of soul nakedness before a holy God who will execute a holy justice fills fallen, sinful mankind with a fear and dread of the Almighty. John spoke clearly of this awful day: "Then I saw a great white throne and him who was seated on it. . . . The dead were judged according to what they had done as recorded in the books. . . . If anyone's name was not found written in the book of life, he was thrown into the lake of fire" (Revelation 20:11-12, 15). The writer of Hebrews also warned of this coming judgment when he said, "It is a dreadful thing to fall into the hands of the living God. . . . [F]or our 'God is a consuming fire' " (Hebrews 10:31; 12:29).

Adam now stood naked of soul and faced this God. No wonder he tried to hide. We, like Adam, fear God at this deep level. We seek to hide from Him behind our covering of fig leaves and our own groves of trees whenever God walks into our lives. It is even more frightening when He calls our name: "Steve, Adam, Moses, Gideon, George, where are you?"

My point is simple and profound. As a man I am terrified to stand soul-naked before God and to have Him personally call my name! And so is every man. So you and I, with a fervent, stubborn passion, try to hide who we really are from God. To do so, we each develop our own fig-leaf covering, our own ways of hiding who we are, tailored to our own sense of terror of God. Perhaps you will see your fig leaves in the stories which follow.

Moses

"Moses said to the LORD, 'O Lord, I have never been eloquent, neither in the past nor since you have spoken to your servant. I am slow of speech and tongue. . . . O Lord, please send someone else to do it' " (Exodus 4:10, 13).

Moses hid behind his perceived inability to speak well in public. Even after the Lord promised to help and teach him, Moses would not accept God's call. In his heart he believed God was untrustworthy, so he argued for someone to take his place.

Are we any different? I'm not. I remember when God asked me to begin to speak as a youth pastor and then as a college professor. I literally got nauseated before and during every public appearance. I pleaded with God to give me something less intimidating. "Let me do something," I begged, "that will not expose my deep fear of failing. Please, God, don't expose my inadequacies in public!"

God gives us all opportunities to speak for Him. For some, it is with sermons and lessons. For others, it is with skillful hands that can create books or music, construct buildings or repair broken things. When those opportunities come, do we accept them or do we hide behind our excuses? What form do your fig leaves take? What do they look like?

Gideon

Israel was at the mercy of the Midianites, when God called Gideon to deliver them. In spite of divine promises of help and victory, Gideon resisted. " 'But Lord,' Gideon asked, 'how can I save Israel? My clan is the weakest in Manasseh, and I am the least in my family' " (Judges 6:15).

Like Moses, Gideon was hard to convince. God personally asked him, affirmed him and helped him, but Gideon still asked for a sign and two more fleeces. He found that from deep within him arose this sinful desire to cover his own fear of failure, his own inability. His fig leaves took the form of an impoverished family and an insignificance of birth order.

Our passion is to hide behind our weaknesses, our lack of position and power. We sew fig leaves of excuses and try to put God off, demanding that He stop calling our name. "Go pick on someone else, Lord, someone who is better educated, has more money or power or prestige." When it comes to ruling and subduing and God calls our name, like Adam, we hide and look for fig leaves to cover our exposed soul. This passion runs so deep that we will argue with God even in the face of His personal promise to empower us, to teach us and to be with us. How deep is our terror! How futile our ways of hiding! How flimsy our covering of fig leaves before a holy God!

A Contemporary Father

Consider one final story that illustrates how desperate we are as men to hide what is really going on inside, even from those closest to us.

The speech was finished and the audience had been generous with its applause, and in the car on my way home my fourteen-year-old son turned to me and said, "I really admire you, Dad, being able to get up there and give a speech like that. You always know what to say to people. You always seem to know what you're doing."

I smiled when he said that. I may even have blushed modestly. But, at that moment, I didn't know what to say at all.

After a while I thanked him and assured him that some day he would be comfortable speaking in front of an audience, that he would always know what to say to people, that he would always know what he was doing. But what I really wanted to say to my son was that his father was not at all what he appeared to be and that being a man is frequently a facade.

It has taken me a long time to admit that—even to myself. Especially to myself. *My* father, after all, really *had* always known what *he* was doing. He was strong and confident and he never felt pain, never knew fear. There wasn't a leaky faucet he couldn't fix or an engine he couldn't manage to get running again. Mechanics never fooled him, salesmen never conned him. He was always calm in emergencies, always cool under fire. He never cried.

For a long time I wondered how such a man could have produced such a weakling for a son. I wondered where the self-doubts and the fears I felt all the time had come from. I wondered why the faucets I fixed always dripped twice as fast after I got finished with them, why engines that sputtered before I started to work on them went stone-dead under my wrench. I dreaded the thought that some day my father would see me cry. I didn't realize that fathers are not always everything they seem to be.

It's different for fathers than it is for mothers. Motherhood is honest, close to the surface. Mothers don't have to hide what they feel. They don't have to pretend.

When there are sounds downstairs in the middle of the night, a mother is allowed to pull the covers over her head and hope that they will go away. A father is supposed to put on his slippers and robe and march boldly down the stairs, even if he's pretty sure that it's the Manson family waiting for him in the kitchen.

When the road signs are confusing and the scenery is starting to look awfully unfamiliar, it's perfectly natural for a mother to pull over to the side of the road and ask for directions from the first person who comes along. A father is supposed to know exactly where he's going, even if he has to drive two hundred miles out of the way to prove it.

When the electricity goes out, no one questions a mother who simply lights a few candles and waits for the repairman to get there. But everyone wonders about a father who doesn't

pick up a screwdriver and head for the basement, even though he doesn't know his fuse box
from his sump pump. Mothers can load a broken
bike into the rear of the station wagon and drive
it to the repair shop. Fathers are supposed to be
able to fix it on the spot.

Mothers can sit in the stands at a football
game and cover their eyes and worry that it's
their kid who's going to be dragged out from underneath the pile of players with his arm broken
in eight places. The father's job is to pace the
sidelines and shout, "Let's hit somebody out
there, son," and never let anyone know that he
holds his breath every time the pile winds up on
top of his kid.

Mothers can admit to the real estate agent that
they don't know a thing about fixed-rate interest
and balloon payments and second mortgages.
Fathers are supposed to nod their heads and pretend that it all makes perfect sense.

Mothers can bang a new jar of peanut butter
on the floor until the lid is loose enough to turn.
Fathers are supposed to twist it off with their
bare hands—without getting red in the face.

Mothers who lose their jobs are unfortunate.
Fathers who lose their jobs are failures.

There are a lot of things a mother can do that
a father cannot, a lot of roles fathers are expected
to play without ever having been asked if we
care to play them. As men, we have come a long
way, but we still have a long way to go.

Those are some of the things I know now I
should have said to my fourteen-year-old son in
the car that night. I should have told him that

his father, like lots of fathers, often doesn't know what he's doing and sometimes is scared and every once in awhile wants to sit down and cry for no good reason at all.

I should have told him that the only reason his father, like lots of fathers, doesn't admit his weaknesses is because he's afraid that someone will think he is not a real man.

More important, what I should have said to my fourteen-year-old son in the car that night is that someday, when he's a father, he'll feel fear and self-doubt and pain, and that it's all right. But my father never told me, and I haven't told my son.[1]

Not only is this sinful enslaving desire to hide who we are all pervasive in each man, it is profoundly generational. We pass it on to our own sons just like Adam did to Cain, just like this father did with his fourteen-year-old son. In terms of relational dominion, we males are stubbornly enslaved to avoiding entering into relationships, especially with a female, and offering the essence of ourselves. As men we hide behind the fig leaf of function, of doing, of creating things, rather than investing our male substance in relationships. We deeply fear entering into the mystery of femaleness, of sonship with our own fathers, of friendship with other men, of fathering our own sons and daughters. So we hide behind busyness, ideals, our visions or our inadequacies and weaknesses. Refusing to acknowledge the sinful, enslaving desire of our heart, we choose to clothe our mortality with fig leaves of our own making.

Generally, males hide parts of their real self to avoid relational intimacy. A woman hides parts of her real self, often by silencing the self, in order to preserve and protect relational intimacy. Males fear relational closeness. Females fear relational distance. Both hide but for a different, sinful purpose.

What does your enslaving, sinful desire to hide look like? How does it impact your relationship with your heavenly Father? What stench of death results from your hiding who you really are from your own wife, your own children, especially your sons? What does your modeling of fig leaves do to your sons' sense of maleness? How are you impacting other men and young males around you?

These are hard questions that can only be answered if you will respond to your heavenly Father when He calls your name. "Adam, Moses, Gideon, Steve, George, where are you?" God isn't fooled by our hiding. He knows where and what we are. He simply calls as a means of encouraging us to step out and be the men He intended us to be. To keep on hiding is to be like Adam, who chose to do nothing about what mattered most to God and to Eve, his wife.

2. I will choose to abandon my God-designed and assigned creatorial responsibility by blame shifting to ease the dread in my male soul. "The man said, 'The woman you put here with me—she gave me some fruit from the tree and I ate it' " (Genesis 3:12).

Hiding one's soul nakedness breeds the enslaving, sinful desire to shift the blame to someone else. When God confronted Adam first—because of his created order and the accompanying assigned creation mandate—He was calling him to give moral account. God refused to treat His first-created, image-bearing male as a victim. In replying, Adam exercised his capacity to choose. He did this by giving a victim-focused response. "It was not my fault! In fact, if it was anyone's fault, it was Yours, God! This woman, Eve—You put her here with me. She gave me the fruit so I ate it!"

In his victim mentality, Adam arrogantly blames not just Eve, but God, his creator. This same expression of passion flowing out of our choice to live out of our victimization, enslaves and corrupts us as males. It literally soaks up any image-bearing substance of our maleness that is still there. It seems to drain our identity and leaves us functioning as impotent, emasculated, uninvolved men. Instead of life-giving, we become life-taking.

This virus has so infected our sense of maleness that we are incapable of reentering our world and the lives of others with any kind of redemptive, God-glorifying potency and purpose. Our male souls hang flaccid, limp, unable to enter our world with the glory we were once crowned with. The male potency we were designed to manifest has indeed been shattered. We live by drawing life from our false gods.

One of the most obvious stories of blame shifting comes from the life of Aaron:

> When Moses approached the camp and saw the calf and the dancing, his anger burned and he threw the tablets out of his hands, breaking them to pieces at the foot of the mountain. . . .
>
> He said to Aaron, "What did these people do to you, that you led them into such great sin?"
>
> "Do not be angry, my lord," Aaron answered. "You know how prone these people are to evil. They said to me, 'Make us gods who will go be-

fore us. As for this fellow Moses who brought us
up out of Egypt, we don't know what has happened to him.' So I told them, 'Whoever has any
gold jewelry, take it off.' Then they gave me the
gold, and I threw it into the fire, and out came
this calf!" (Exodus 32:19, 21-24)

Aaron went to absurd lengths to avoid taking responsibility for his actions. When he is confronted by
God through Moses, Aaron directly blames the people
and some apparent magical metamorphic process by
which collected jewelry changed into a golden calf of
its own volition and power. Aaron refused to face the
sin of his own idolatrous heart. It was he who had
abandoned his function as a spiritual leader and had
passively given in to the people.

Because of our alienation from God, we are terrified
of Him as Adam and Aaron were. We don't want to
face God's anger. When Moses burned with anger and
threw the Ten Commandments to the ground, shatter-
ing them, he reflected God's wrath. Aaron was not
man enough to face that wrath of God expressed in
and through Moses, so he blamed the people of God.

When we don't want to face a holy God, whom we
can't manipulate and whose wrath burns against the
idolatry of our hearts, we dream up other gods to
worship—safe gods, nice gods, convenient gods that
we can control, gods that have no standard of righteousness, no morality to hold us accountable. We
create a god in our own image that has no character
worthy of our total commitment and worship. Ultimately, this form of false worship leaves us dependent on our own schemes. For some men, this scheme
manifests itself in blame shifting as a primary form

of self-centeredness. The sinful consequences are abandonment of our initiative to enter into life and relationships with others.

If I were to put my finger on one of the most devastating sins of our hearts it would be our unwillingness to be the primary initiator in our homes and in our churches. In this, Satan has achieved an amazing tactical victory. Through him, society has accepted the politically correct notion that male initiatives as leaders in carrying out the creation mandate is born of male arrogance. Nothing could be farther from the truth. In fact, our pride and selfishness are what influence and often prevent us from taking initiative in a way that reflects the character of God. It is not the upsurge of interest in women's ministries that is the problem today; it's the personal and spiritual aimlessness, weakness, lethargy and loss of courage among men that is so disruptive.

Adam's legacy of silence has become our legend and reputation as men. Our pride and self-pity, our fear and laziness, our confusion over our sexual identity are luring many men into self-protecting cocoons of silence. And to the degree that this makes room for women to take more aggressive initiative in the home and in the Church, it is sometimes even endorsed as a virtue. But I believe that deep down in the core of our sexual identity, men—and women—know better and long for God's design to be expressed.

One of the leading causes of the breakdown of the family is the functional and relational abandonment of spouses and children by men who have ceased to celebrate their manhood through the roles of husbands and fathers. God's wrath burns against us because we have replaced Him with safe gods of our own making.

Bill's Story

Bill was a single man who was afraid to take initiative. He was attracted to Doris, a single woman in his office complex, but every time he saw her, his stomach knotted up with fear. He seemingly could not force himself to enter into her world and personal life. For eighteen months, he fought an internal battle between a relational drawing to Doris and a dread that paralyzed his male initiatory passion to enter. Then one day, he came to work and found her office empty. She had been transferred to another city.

As Bill reflected over his past eight years, he began to recognize a pattern in his relationships, not just with women, but with his own parents, siblings and friends—a refusal to initiate. Sure, it silenced the inner dread of his male soul, but it also left him lonely and feeling that he would forever be single because of a lack of courage. He sensed that in all his relationships, those closest to him felt like they never received anything of substance from him, that he had in effect emotionally abandoned them.

Roger's Story

Roger had a different problem. He kept moving from one job to another. His marriage was about to come undone because he was unable to give Sandy, his wife, and his two daughters any sense of security. Every time he settled into a job and it became routine and lost its challenge, he quit and moved on to another. This often required moving.

Roger was like his father, who had a similar pattern of handling the creation mandate of ruling and subduing by providing—he could never stay put. The harder Roger tried to avoid his father's pattern, the more he became like his dad. He refused to deal with this en-slaving, sinful desire of abandoning God's assigned or-der and responsibility by passing the buck—blame, blame, blame! He was stuck as a passionate victim.

Bill and Roger, like Adam, are idolaters who were unable to celebrate their manhood. What does your pattern of blame shifting and abandoning look like in your pilgrimage of manhood? If you don't see yourself here, perhaps you will in the next chapter when we look at sinful desires three and four.

Endnote

1 D.L. Stewart, "Why Fathers Hide Their Feelings," *Redbook* (January 1985), 32.

CHAPTER 6

Life Outside the Garden

We've looked at sinful desires one and two—hiding behind our fig leaves and blame shifting—but they are only half the problem. To get a complete picture of our inherited sinful desires we must look at three and four—proving our maleness and finding life outside the garden.

Am I Really Man Enough?

3. I will choose to dominate in order to prove I am a male with enough of the right substance.

To the woman he said,

". . . Your desire will be for your husband,
    and he will rule over you."

To Adam he said,

". . . Cursed is the ground because of you;
    through painful toil you will eat of it
    all the days of your life.
It will produce thorns and thistles for you. . . .

By the sweat of your brow
    you will eat your food."
        (Genesis 3:16-19)

God brought judgment on the serpent, on the
woman, on the man and on His created world. God
cursed creation, specifically the ground out of which
He created Adam. "By the sweat of your brow you
will eat your food until you return to the ground, since
from it you were taken; for dust you are and to dust
you will return" (3:19).

What God is saying to Adam essentially is this:
"Until the day you die, you will have to fight a war
with your earthiness, your humanity. Your separation
from Me will result in a permanent groaning of death
that runs so deep within your male soul and within the
bowels of creation that you will never have rest from
the painful toil of wrestling with thorns and thistles."

This is illustrated in the two chapters that follow the
account of the fall of man, where the Lord speaks to
Cain:

> What have you done? Listen! Your brother's
> blood cries out to me from the ground. Now
> you are under a curse and driven from the
> ground, which opened up its mouth to receive
> your brother's blood from your hand. When you
> work the ground, it will no longer yield its crops
> for you. You will be a restless wanderer on the
> earth. (4:10-12)

Noah's father Lamech said of Noah, "He will comfort us in the labor and painful toil of our hands caused
by the ground the LORD has cursed" (5:29).

Paul told us the same truth about creation and about us:

> For the creation was subjected to frustration, not by its own choice, but by the will of the one who subjected it, in hope that the creation itself will be liberated from its bondage to decay and brought into glorious freedom of the children of God.
>
> We know that the whole creation has been groaning as in the pains of childbirth right up to the present time. Not only so, but we ourselves, who have the firstfruits of the Spirit, groan inwardly as we wait for our adoption as sons, the redemption of our bodies. (Romans 8:20-23)

Noah's building of the ark is a picture of salvation in Christ. After the flood, Noah built an altar to the Lord and sacrificed some of the clean animals and birds. "The LORD smelled the pleasing aroma and said in his heart: 'Never again will I curse the ground because of man, even though every inclination of his heart is evil from childhood. And never again will I destroy all living creatures, as I have done' " (Genesis 8:21).

Something about Noah's sacrifice pleased the Lord and He said He would never judge the earth or the animals again by flood. Possibly this is how Noah comforts us in the labor and painful toil of our hands. It was the aroma of his sacrifice that led God to make this promise: "As long as the earth endures, seedtime and harvest, cold and heat, summer and winter, day and night will never cease" (8:22). There is comfort in this.

God's judgment of Adam by cursing the ground

with thorns and thistles, leading to painful toil and
sweat, had a male fit that deeply impacted him and all
men. Work now shifted from fulfilling, joyful caring
for the garden to the reality of pain and sweat.

Moving from Dominion to Domination

In his soul, Adam moved from taking dominion over
creation as God's representative to dominating creation as God's enemy. Domination now suited what
man had become. Why? Because creation would fight
back with groaning like the pain of childbirth. This
meant that man would forever be in conflict with creation. Adam now could see! His eyes were open to evil
and its fruit—thorns, weeds, thistles. "Adam, you will
sweat and hurt to provide food to eat. Being a man will
never be like it was before you sinned. In order to survive, you will rule and subdue the earth in a dominating way to prove you are a man, rather than to express
your manhood with joy."

The personal battle involved in the work of ruling
and subduing the earth triggers a male's sinful desire
to prove his manhood by dominating. I will find a
way to handle the thorns, weeds and thistles in my
life at everyone's expense, including my own. So I
become a driven man, not a free man. I will be the
best farmer, mechanic, teacher, dentist, fisherman,
athlete, preacher, missionary, musician, artist that I
can be.

Sounds noble! But will I be the best for God's
glory—or is it for my glory? For God's pleasure, like
Noah's offering—or for the pleasure of my well-being?
Do I have the right stuff that proves my manliness?
You bet! Look at the size of my wheat fields or cattle
farm, my business clientele as a mechanic, dentist, doc-

tor, lawyer! My music sells! My artistry is gaining in appraisal and popularity! No question about feeling like a man. I have proved it over these long, tough years of painful, sweat-filled toil! And you can't tell me otherwise. Look at my house, my barns, my estate!

But men, God is not impressed when our agenda is to make a name for ourselves. How can we prove our manhood by dominating God's creation through the expression of our enslaving, sinful passion? We can't. In Genesis 11:8, God dealt with this passion of arrogance: "So the LORD scattered them from there over all the earth, and they stopped building the city."

Haggai the prophet spoke what was in the Lord's heart about this issue. In Haggai 1 he reminds them of their fruitless efforts to get ahead and then explains the cause: " 'You expected much, but see, it turned out to be little. What you brought home, I blew away. Why?' declares the LORD Almighty. 'Because of my house, which remains a ruin, while each of you is busy with his own house. Therefore . . . the heavens have withheld their dew and the earth its crops' " (1:9-10).

Jesus said it in similar but even stronger language: "Watch out! Be on your guard against all kinds of greed; a man's life does not consist in the abundance of his possessions" (Luke 12:15). Then He told the crowd the story of the rich farmer who was only concerned about building bigger barns and ended it with this warning: "This is how it will be with anyone who stores up things for himself but is not rich toward God" (12:21).

God's Word has given us some very clear evidence of how this sinful desire corrupts the male soul. Dominating functionally, by ruling and subduing creation to prove one's manhood, is a sinful passion that expresses itself outside the boundaries of God's design and assignment to take dominion. This is evident when a man stops expressing his maleness with freedom and pursues function as a primary source of personal power. The sinful fruit of this power pursuit can manifest itself in greedy arrogance, where creation is abused to satisfy a man's thirsty demand for more and more. Dominating can produce the sinful consequences of mismanagement of the resources of creation, of time and of people. Loving things and using people becomes the trademark reputation of male selfishness and self-centered domination.

Paul said it best when he confronted us head on about this sin:

> The acts of the sinful nature are obvious: sexual immorality, impurity and debauchery; idolatry and witchcraft; hatred, discord, jealousy, fits of rage, selfish ambition, dissensions, factions and envy; drunkenness, orgies, and the like. I warn you, as I did before, that those who live like this will not inherit the kingdom of God. (Galatians 5:19-21)

As men, we sinfully spill our male substance in bouts of uncontrolled idolatrous self-worship. We invest ourselves with a passion in forms of functional domination that isolate us from relationships of substance, intimacy with our heavenly Father and with other significant people. Men who dominate, for the most part, crucify their relational longings on the cross of selfish ambition—power, accomplishment, glory. We become too focused on what we do best, at the expense of friendship, fellowship and love.

We rule over women in relational forms of domination that leave them feeling unsafe and unloved in our presence. We sacrifice them on our altars of academic degrees, crop production, sermonizing, evangelistic outreach, clientele load, business achievement and sexual demands. The list goes on as Paul the apostle noted.

When we choose to invest all of the substance of our manhood in loving things and using people, we have only crumbs of our male essence left over for our spouses, our children, our parents or other male friendships. We end up bankrupt relationally, needing no one, using anyone to satisfy this enslaving sinful desire to dominate functionally and relationally to prove our manliness. Dominating makes us dangerous men.

How do you use power to dominate in order to prove you are a man? What consequences of death, from the expression of this sinful desire, do you see in and around you?

Life Outside the Garden

4. I will choose to find life outside the garden in order to get relief from the stench of evil, pain and death within and around me.

And the LORD God said, "The man has now become like one of us, knowing good and evil. He must not be allowed to reach out his hand and take also from the tree of life and eat, and live forever." So the LORD God banished him from the Garden of Eden to work the ground from which he had been taken. After he drove the man out, he placed on the east side of the Garden of Eden cherubim and a flaming sword

flashing back and forth to guard the way to the
tree of life. (Genesis 3:22-24)

Why did God have to set cherubim with a flaming
sword flashing back and forth to guard the way to the
tree of life? Why did the Lord God say the man must
not be allowed to reach out his hand and take also from
the tree of life and live forever? God knew the depths
of the depravity in Adam's heart and that his passion
would be to find life on his own. God took this sinful
desire in Adam so seriously that He used angelic
power to guard His way to life eternal. Only God's
provision of a way back could bring life eternal for
mankind. The shedding of the blood of animals took
place so their nakedness and shame could be dealt with
by God.

Like Adam, we cannot get back into the garden. Yet
our souls have an insatiable hunger for the fruit from
the tree of life. God's judgment was banishment from
the garden and painful, sweat-producing toil. Work
was not a judgment. But the curse of the ground and
being banished from the source and place of life left
Adam with an inner emptiness that now cried out for
refilling and relief. The loss of inner God-life in Adam
and the smell of death as the curse began to choke life
out of God's creation now drove Adam and his male
seed to rebelliously and stubbornly demand a way to
live outside the garden.

Men, when the pain of our labor and the weariness
from our sweat drain us of any remaining awareness
and experience of maleness, there is within our male
soul an eruption of a sinful desire that justifies any
form of selfish pursuit of life as long as it brings relief
and fullness. A glimpse into the lives of men who, like

you and me, cry out for life and relief outside the garden may help to bring flesh and bones to the point I am trying to make.

Leon's Story

Leon said, "I get sick and tired of trying to figure out my wife and how to satisfy her needs. No matter what I do, it never seems enough. Why do I feel this death-stench of dread in my gut every evening as I drive home from work? I hate that feeling. That's why I leave as soon as I'm through supper and head to the golf club, have a round of golf and a few beers with the guys. I feel a lot less pressure golfing than when I'm home with her. Being with the other men helps get rid of that dread and replaces it with a sense of relieved enjoyment."

Ken's Story

Ken told me, "There's no justice in life. Where was God when my father took me down to the railway track when I was eight? I thought we were going to watch the train go by. Instead, right before my eyes, he jumped in front of the train and killed himself. I can't seem to get close to God. I have no close friends. I'm hooked on alcohol and now I see my seventeen-year-old son going into drugs. Life and people expect too much of me and give nothing back. I'm thinking of ending it all!"

We all have a story of how we pursue life outside the garden. Somewhere between a Leon and a Ken—when life asks too much, when unemployment has sucked the passion of maleness dry in us, when boredom leaves us without a sense of passion and our souls are exuding the stench of death, when as a single man, I keep seeking to move into a woman's life, and she never responds and my sexual desires run out of control—we have all discovered a form of life, a corrupted tree of good, pleasurable, wise-looking fruit.

But Satan has deceived us! As a patterned response, we too quickly choose a busier work life instead of meaningfully relating with a male friend, spouse or child; a round of golf instead of a time of personal or corporate worship with God the Father; a hunting trip instead of some time off with our wives; a hockey game on TV instead of a phone call to a male friend to ask for intercessory prayer or to pray for him. Examples abound of corrupted fruit that dangles tantalizingly before us, heavily laden branches of the tree of the knowledge of good and evil waving before our opened eyes and naked souls. It looks so good, so pleasant and so fulfilling.

What fruit do you keep eating that justifies your idol of selfishness?

Our sinful desire to find life and relief to replace the stench of death can rule and control us. The Spirit of God, the people of God, the Word of God and the good things of life often have a hard time competing with this passion, especially when we try to find life outside the garden apart from God.

These four enslaving, sinful passions have corrupted our male, image-bearing souls, leaving us impotent to initiate entering into the mystery of life, our world and relationships. Sin has emasculated our maleness and now our substance gets spilled out in ways that damage and destroy God's creation and other image-bearers.

As men we are filled with passion! If we are going to begin to grow in our understanding of maleness, then we need to recognize and take full ownership of the enslaving, sinful passions that have corrupted the way we carry out God's creation mandate.

We, like Adam, choose to:

- Hide who we are behind our own fig leaves;

- Abandon our God-assigned creation responsibility by blame shifting;

- Dominate in order to prove our manhood;

- Find life outside the garden to provide relief from evil, pain and death.

These virus like, enslaving desires have infected and corrupted our male, image-bearing soul. Adam's legacy has left us agents of this sin-virus, infecting our world and others. We are in need of major heart surgery. But before we will ever cry out for a doctor, we must know in our hearts that we are sinfully sick. This virus is deadly! Jeremiah confirmed it when he said, "The heart is deceitful above all things and beyond cure. Who can understand it? I the LORD search the heart and examine the mind" (Jeremiah 17:9-10).

Let the Lord continue to examine your heart and mind as we press on through our shattered glory.

CHAPTER 7

Wounded Males Are Unsafe

A story is told of Yehiel Dinur, a Holocaust survivor, who served as a witness at the trial of Adolf Eichmann.

> Dinur entered the courtroom and stared at the man behind the bulletproof glass—the man who had presided over the slaughter of millions. The court was hushed as a victim confronted a butcher of his people. Suddenly Dinur began to sob and collapsed to the floor. But not out of anger or bitterness. As he explained later in an interview, what struck him was a terrifying realization. "I was afraid about myself," Dinur said. "I saw that I am capable to do this. . . . Exactly like he." In a moment of chilling clarity, Dinur saw the skull beneath the skin. "Eichmann," he concluded, "is in all of us."[1]

Personally, I cannot identify with Dinur at the level of his passionate recognition and response to the evil that erupted deep within when he saw Eichmann. I have never wept over the "Eichmann" in the "skull beneath my skin."

But I know it is there inside me. One night at my son's hockey game, the referee missed a call against what I saw as a flagrant high-sticking penalty. Once more, it was a potentially injurious act by the opposing player. I literally stepped down a full two rows in the stands, and getting as close to the referee as possible, I passionately shouted at the top of my voice, "Open your eyes, ref! Get in the game or get off the ice!"

If the intent and passion of my heart at that moment could somehow be measured on a scale of degrees of evil, I would be both ashamed and afraid at what you would see and think about me. As I reflect and write about what erupted from inside my heart, I can only get a beginning sense of how unsafe a man I was to that referee. My death-words carried the passionate evil message of relational revenge and murder to my human brother, who was doing the best he could. The safety glass around the ice was no shield for his heart.

Possibly you still can't identify with either Dinur's experience or mine. Maybe it's because you have never had to face an "Eichmann" of that magnitude, someone whose sin was so heinous, who wounded and killed so many. But all of us as men have faced another sinful human being and experienced the impact of his or her sin against us. We have all been wounded by looks, words or deeds. The pain in our hearts was real.

Now comes the choice. How do we manage both other people's sin and its impact of pain inside of us? If you identify, at least, with my hate-filled retaliation toward the referee, you know that an evil potential resides within you. As you face the one who feels like your enemy, at that very moment, a counterreaction of sinful passion ambushes your best intentions. You realize the "Eichmann" is there in you. He is an unsafe skeleton in the closet of your male soul.

As this evil surfaces and bears its sinful fruit, your relationship is interrupted. Your spirit has automatically closed into a silent fist. Even your ability to love is suffocated by this sinful, evil passion escaping from the "Eichmann" in your soul. At this point, you are no longer merely a victim of others' sin; you yourself have become a reactive, sinful agent, choosing to victimize the person who has just hurt you. This reactive response may be anything from a silent, passive, anger-filled withdrawal to an unleashing of death-words or physical acts designed to wound and inflict pain. In so doing, we have now become no different than our perpetrator.

The difference between Dinur's response in the crowded courtroom and my response at the hockey game was not one of degree of evil in our hearts, but how we chose to manage that evil passion. He sobbed in recognition and fear of the evil within him! I committed relational murder through the stabbing of my sinful, impassioned words.

Two Prevalent Myths

There are currently two prevalent myths that fuel our misperception of the depths of sin in our hearts and our potential to come across to others as an "unsafe man." The first myth is the insidious, politically correct, cultural assumption that *goodness is at the core of our humanity*. This world structure deludes us into thinking we are always victims, never villains; always deprived, never depraved. This myth always blame shifts. It focuses on a sickness of society, a dysfunctional father, mother or family system or a sickness of the mind. The consequence is that evil in subtle or more obvious forms is multiplied by denying its very existence.

But our rebellion against God has produced in all of us what theologians call "total depravity." This does not mean we are as bad as we could possibly be, because we can always find some new way to rebel against God. Rather, it means that we are depraved at the core of our beings and that our depravity affects every area of our lives. It also means that if unchecked, we get worse and worse over time, as our depravity works its way more deeply into our hearts. The "Eichmann" is inside us all. As unbelieving men do good deeds, they are not done with the right heart motivation because they are not done in a context of love for God. Even when believers in Jesus Christ do good deeds, we don't always do them with right motivation.

The second myth that pervades our culture and is perpetuated by the deceitfulness of our sinful hearts is that *men don't hurt*. Soul pain and heart wounds become, at worst, nothing but dead scar tissue. The worst that pain can become is an irritant, to be dismissed with four-letter words.

We have bought into this lie that grown men never sob over the sin or the groaning of their hearts; that it's hard to face the harsh reality of living outside the garden where the sin of weeds, the evil of thistles and the pain of thorns flourish. This lie has convinced us that we never need to cry out for help from God or from others. Somehow we see ourselves as a different male breed than the one God labeled as "a man after my own heart." We hold ourselves apart from David who cried out with anguish:

Be merciful to me, O LORD, for I am in distress;
  my eyes grow weak with sorrow,
  my soul and my body with grief.
My life is consumed by anguish
  and my years by groaning;
my strength fails because of my affliction,
  and my bones grow weak. . . .
  I am the utter contempt of my neighbors;
I am a dread to my friends—
  those who see me on the street flee from me.
I am forgotten by them as though I were dead;
  I have become like broken pottery.
      (Psalm 31:9-12)

Both the belief and practice of these two myths contribute to an unsafe spirit and acts of violence that left unchecked reflect the "Eichmann" in our souls. Both are hard for us to take full ownership and responsibility for.

The sin and anguish of our hearts are not strange bedfellows. When we deny their existence within, these two companions birth the fruits of sin. Often we are unaware of their impact on our world or the pain they cause in others and for the Spirit of the living God. The impact of insidious or obvious evil can so easily come about through either premeditated planning or in a sudden ambush of sinful passion.

Sin has deeply wounded us all. We, in turn, in our sinful reaction, have deeply wounded others. It was our sin that wounded the Lord Jesus Christ, the Son of God. Dinur's response was an offering of a broken and a contrite heart before the Lord. My response at the hockey game was one of unashamed evil that grieved the Holy Spirit living within me.

David confessed in Psalm 51 that ultimately his sin was against God alone. To be sure, David had sinned against Bathsheba, destroyed through murder the very life of Uriah, and in fact, had sinned against the entire nation of Israel. But what he had done was wrong only because it violated God's standards, not because Uriah or Bathsheba did not like it. Ultimately, God was the offended party, for David's actions violated God's holy standard of righteousness.

If our sin wounded the Lord Jesus—"and by his wounds we are healed" (Isaiah 53:5)—then we certainly wound others and are hurt by others. To deny our own personal inner pain is to deny the impact of someone else's sin on us. This in turn leads to our refusal to recognize that the pain we carry in our wounded hearts is the pain of the one who sinned against us. Diminishing our own wounding deadens the sense of personal passion for our sin and its deadly consequences on others.

But most of all, when we choose to live in denial of the pain of our own hearts, we are communicating loudly and clearly that our sin has no impact on God, that the cross on which Jesus was crucified was really not necessary. What conceit! That, I'm ashamed to write, is the difference between Dinur's and my heart response. His was one of humility; mine, arrogance! Both our sin and pain have divine impact on our God.

Remember God's response to man's wickedness in Genesis: "The LORD was grieved that he had made man on the earth, and his heart was filled with pain" (6:6). Hear the anguish of His heart as He laments in Hosea:

"When Israel was a child, I loved him,
　and out of Egypt I called my son.
But the more I called Israel,
　the further they went from me.
They sacrificed to the Baals
　and they burned incense to images. . . .
How can I give you up, Ephraim?
　How can I hand you over, Israel? . . .
My heart is changed within me;
　all my compassion is aroused.
I will not carry out my fierce anger. . . .
For I am God, and not man—
　the Holy One among you."
　　　(11:1-2, 8-9)

Do Men Really Hurt Inside?

John's story is not unlike stories we can tell of our own personal pain.

"It was obvious to me that, except for my good standing at school, I was in no way fulfilling my father's concept of what a son should be," John told me. "No matter what the circumstances, whatever I said disappointed him.

" 'Stupid' was the most common adjective I was branded with. 'Deaf,' 'dumb,' 'blind' were close second favorites. I hung my head in shame. The chambers of my developing male soul were filled with a sense of death. It seemed that the mere sound of my voice roused his contempt for my intelligence.

"When Jim, Dad and I were fencing one day at the bog end of the farm, we ran short of wire—just a few feet short. Dad sent me to the other end of the fence, a good quarter-mile walk, to fetch the piece we needed. Just so he wouldn't scold me if I brought too short a piece, I decided to bring a whole roll. It was quite heavy.

"He smiled sarcastically at me when I arrived. 'You know, John, I feel sorry for you. Not because you lugged that load all the way for nothing, but because you're so stupid.' "

Solomon verified the deadly damage that John experienced in his relationship with his father: "The tongue has the power of life and death" (Proverbs 18:21). David also wrote that what happens to a male like John can be devastating: "Scorn has broken my heart and has left me helpless; I looked for sympathy, but there was none, for comforters, but I found none" (Psalm 69:20).

Wrestling with the Father Wound

Of all the wounding of the heart caused by living outside the garden, nothing can damage and cripple the male soul as deeply as the father wound. I do not minimize the pain that comes from being laid off or even crippled to the point of not being able to work. Both can be devastating. However, when relational dominion is violated by a father through abandonment or domination over the years, then the sins of this father are passed on to not just his son, but to the third and fourth generations.

John's story of inner pain reflects this kind of creation-mandate violation. So also do the last two verses of the Old Testament when they refer to the incredible generational damage of the sin of fathers on their children and the resulting curse that comes into a nation or country: "See, I will send you the prophet Elijah before that great and dreadful day of the LORD comes. He will turn the hearts of the fathers to their children, and the hearts of the children to their fathers; or else I will come and strike the land with a curse" (Malachi 4:5-6).

When a father's heart is not turned toward his children, there are two obvious consequences. One, the heart of the child turns away from the father—and needs to return—and secondly, the land is filled with a curse or with death. The demise of righteous, holy living and an ever-increasing pervasiveness of evil breeds death in family relationships and leads to the breakdown of governmental authority. This downward spiral also impacts relationships with the living God, where religious life becomes a duty instead of a privilege. The loss of spiritual passion ends in a waning cultural influence for God.

God's own family, the Israelites, experienced His curse throughout their history when they were disobedient. "We have become orphans and fatherless, our mothers like widows. . . . Our fathers sinned and are no more, and we bear their punishment" (Lamentations 5:3, 7); "This is what the LORD says: . . . I will smash them one against the other, fathers and sons alike, declares the LORD. I will allow no pity or mercy or compassion to keep me from destroying them" (Jeremiah 13:13-14).

The Old Testament concludes with the promise to send the spirit of Elijah to turn the hearts of fathers and children toward each other. Then silence! God does not speak again for four hundred years. To put that in perspective for today it would mean not hearing from God since the late 1500s! Nothing but silence, more silence! I wonder what those four centuries were like, especially for father-son relationships.

Then God sends someone who fulfills this promise

after four hundred years of waiting—John the Baptist. As part of his threefold job description, he was to mend family relationships. "And he will go on before the Lord, in the spirit and power of Elijah, to turn the hearts of the fathers to their children . . . to make ready a people prepared for the Lord" (Luke 1:17).

Does history repeat itself? Is there a problem today with us sons being able to relate with substance, intimacy and redeemed purpose with our own fathers? With our own sons and daughters? The answer is "Yes! Yes!" Solomon verified this when he said, "Whatever is has already been, and what will be has been before; and God will call the past to account" (Ecclesiastes 3:15).

Paul wrote to Timothy, warning him of the same symptoms that come when fathers do not hold their children in their hearts.

> But mark this: There will be terrible times in the last days. People will be lovers of themselves, lovers of money, boastful, proud, abusive, disobedient to their parents, ungrateful, unholy, without love, unforgiving, slanderous, without self-control, brutal, not lovers of the good, treacherous, rash, conceited, lovers of pleasure rather than lovers of God—having a form of godliness but denying its power. (2 Timothy 3:1-5)

When fathers do not turn their hearts toward their children, a process of death, a curse, begins to bring decay in human relationships. This is especially true between fathers and sons. Let's explore several father-son relationships from Scripture to see why this is so.

Isaac Patterns His Father

Isaac, as a man of faith like his father Abraham, provides us with an example of doubting the God of his father. God told Isaac to stay in the land of Gerar during a severe famine and that He would bless and be with him. But when Isaac got there, the men were attracted to his beautiful wife, Rebekah. For self-protection he told them she was his sister (Genesis 26:7).

Deception is often used in biblical narratives by powerless people like Isaac. He knew God promised to be with him (Genesis 26:3), but he chose to handle this potential problem by lying to the authorities and other men. His deceitfulness was passed on generationally to his son Jacob, who with his mother—he was her favorite (25:28)—elaborately deceived Isaac for Esau's blessing. Later Esau—he was his father's favorite (25:28)—came in from hunting to find his blessing had been stolen. You can feel the pathos in Esau's response: "When Esau heard his father's words, he burst out with a loud and bitter cry and said to his father, 'Bless me—me too, my father!' " (27:34).

Do you sense the drama? Isaac trembles violently when he realizes his son, Jacob, has deceived him and now he cannot give his blessing to Esau, his firstborn. Esau cries, weeps for his father's blessing. Something deep is stirred in these two men. Despite what has happened, Isaac blesses Esau with a different blessing: "Your dwelling will be away from the earth's richness, away from the dew of heaven above. You will live by the sword and you will serve your brother. But when you grow restless, you will throw his yoke from off your neck" (27:39-40).

Let me bring this deceitful event into our setting. It would be like your younger brother getting the family farm and you, as the older brother, being told to go out and be a migrant worker, possibly at best doing custom combining for other farmers. What sinful desires would that wound inflame in your male soul? Listen to Esau's sinful passion, fueled by the sin of his brother Jacob, and the deep wounding of his spirit. "Esau held a grudge against Jacob because of the blessing his father had given him. He said to himself, 'The days of mourning for my father are near; then I will kill my brother Jacob' " (27:41).

This sounds a lot like Cain's response to Abel. Esau is in effect saying, "As soon as my father dies and the funeral is over, I'll get revenge. I will dominate by killing him. He deserves death for how deeply he has hurt me by deceiving my father and robbing me."

The Problem with Unattended Pain

When we choose to leave our soul pain unattended, unhealed and denied, we, like Esau, become unsafe men. Let me review the process that makes us dangerous, manipulative males. True manhood is boldly entering into our world and relationships with initiative that is gentle and strong, that reflects how God would enter. Our manly initiative has become unsafe because we have inherited the legacy of Adam. This capability to strongly enter in order to spill our life for others and God's glory has been emasculated.

God's curse on the ground leaves males with a soul-dreaded questioning: "Do I have the right substance to pull the thorns and thistles out of life and relationships?" This triggers a frantic search for answers, medication for this virus, proof that the legacy doesn't really bother us outside the garden! In all of this, we get beat up by the weeds, thorns and thistles of life.

When life spills all over the back forty acres of our male souls we feel pain; we groan deeply. This is exactly what God said would be the natural consequence of male sin. When we don't manage the dread, the soul pain, the physical hurts in a God-ordained manner, then our groaning and pain will energize our sinful, enslaving desires and passions. Note I didn't say our deep groaning and pain create these sinful desires; our rebellion against God did that. What makes us unsafe and dangerous males, whether that's an eleven-year-old or a maturing man, is the reality of our enslaving, sinful desires that we often energize by the unhealed wounds of our souls.

We, like Esau and John, experience deeply the impact of our fathers' sin. Not only do we become generational carriers of Adam's legacy, we also carry the sins and soul pain of our fathers. Their unhealed wounds, in turn, wound us. If we do not deal with both the sin and pain of our hearts, we become unsafe to the degree that we pass that sin and pain on to our children and spouses. For example, Esau was carrying his own sin, plus the consequences of both the sin of Adam and Isaac. This is compounded by the consequence and impact of his father's sin through Jacob. That's a tremendous load for anyone to carry. No wonder Esau became unsafe to Jacob and to his world.

We need to take seriously what kind of damage we do, especially to women and children, by being unsafe. So often they don't feel soul-safe in our presence. God help us! We need His help and hope! Women in general long to be held in our hearts, to know that our hearts are toward them. That is when they will feel soul-secure and relationally safe in our presence, in our homes, offices, schools, cities and country.

Residual soul pain (i.e., that which has not been dealt with) leaves a wide-open door for our sinful, enslaving desires to run rampant. Self-control, as a fruit of the Holy Spirit, is hard pressed to compete with residual soul pain and unchecked, sinful passions. Some of us men try to control these enslaving passions through legalism—rules, regulations, self-energized discipline. When we try this, we become self-sufficient, arrogant men, in that we project the image and message that we need no one.

Men who dominate become relationally hardened. Our spirit becomes closed like a tense, clenched fist. When we try to handle our sinful passions and soul wounds by blame shifting and abandoning our responsibilities as men, we become relationally dependent, passive males who suck soul-life from everyone around us. We are then pitied and ridiculed.

David's Sin Goes Generational

Let me share one final story from Scripture about the impact of a father's sin on his son and the pain that it brought. King David committed the sin of adultery and murder. David's choice to sleep with Bathsheba is a good example of his giving in to the sinful, enslaving desire of finding life for his soul outside the garden. The choice to murder Uriah, the husband of Bathsheba, was an expression of his passion to dominate in order to take control over the consequences of his previous sin.

One of the results of his transgression was the generational sin and pain passed on to one of his sons.

This is what the LORD says: "Out of your own household I am going to bring calamity upon

you. Before your very eyes I will take your
wives and give them to one who is close to you,
and he will lie with your wives in broad daylight. You did it in secret, but I will do this thing
in broad daylight before all Israel. (2 Samuel
12:11-12)

What we often do in the secret places of our souls,
behind the walls of our homes, gets shouted from the
rooftop by our children. In public they carry the impact of our sin and residual pain into the schools,
churches and streets. God often uses the consequences
of our sin upon our own children to discipline us as
men, husbands and fathers.

The story is fulfilled when Absalom, David's son,
betrayed him by attempting to overthrow his leadership as king. Absalom asked an advisor for counsel in
this takeover. His advisor answered: "Lie with your father's concubines whom he left to take care of the pal-
ace. Then all Israel will hear that you have made
yourself a stench in your father's nostrils, and the
hands of everyone with you will be strengthened" (2
Samuel 16:21-22).

A father's sins clearly wound and impact his children. Sons are especially affected as they develop a
sense of how to be men and how to manage their enslaving, sinful desires and soul pain in godly ways.

Endnote

[1] Charles Colson, "Making the World Safe for Religion," *Christianity Today*, November 8, 1993, 32. Reprinted by permission of
Prison Fellowship, P.O. Box 17500, Washington, DC 20041-0500.

CHAPTER 8

How We Wound Our Children

As fathers, we sinfully mismanage our soul pain, thus generationally wounding our sons and daughters. In the next chapter, I will develop more fully the sinful patterns that we choose in relating to our world and others. (Reminder: Part II presents the exciting answers/solution to the problems of sin and pain which are defined in this section, Part I.) For now, let me generally explain how this dynamic of sin and pain gets transmitted from father to children, resulting in a curse of death on their developing maleness and femaleness.

Sinful Patterns of Relating that Wound

As men, our emasculated way of entering into our world and relationships takes one of two directions: We either abandon or dominate.

We are all different personalities, some quiet, some outgoing. We all can move both ways on the continuum of relating, sometimes being more dominating, other times more abandoning or passive. However, there is a primary pattern of how we initiate entering and a secondary style of relating. It could look something like this:

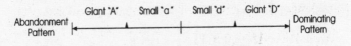

Abandonment Pattern — Giant "A" — Small "a" — Small "d" — Giant "D" — Dominating Pattern

Sinful Initiative Pattern of Relating

What establishes my primary relational pattern is which end of the continuum kicks in when I feel most threatened as a man. When my soul nakedness is about to be exposed, when I need to hide, find life apart from God or prove my manhood, do I dominate or abandon? These sinful desires, fueled by residual soul wounds, powerfully influence my most strategic weapon. I will either abandon you—flight, or I will dominate you—fight. Rising from the shadowy depths of our male souls are these dangerous images of abandonment or domination which represent the denied aspects of the self we refuse to look at. Soul nakedness before God and others stirs up a deep dread.

But for us there is much to be faced here: the truth about us, yes, but also the lies we believe about ourselves but don't want to admit. Defensiveness won't do us any good; the realities of abandonment and domination must be confronted.

No one is eager to initiate these painful, dread-filled encounters with our inmost being. Most of us—and this was and often still is true in my marriage, with my four children and son-in-law and with my male friends—must often be forcefully confronted by the consequences of our behavior. Eventually our wives, children and male friends must stop protecting and taking care of us. And if we are fortunate, as I was and still am, they will confront us.

Let's look now at some of the familiar images of maleness that we reflect as we relate to our world.

Men Who Abandon

Small "a" abandonment pattern

Fathers who fit the small "a" abandonment pattern provide the physical necessities of life—food, clothing, housing. They work hard, often sacrificing much of their own wants and personal needs for the sake of the family. They are "functional" fathers who fulfill their duty to provide. They are dads committed totally to the functional creation mandate of ruling and subduing.

The strength of function of such fathers, unchecked by any relational involvement with their sons or daughters, leaves them highly unbalanced and void of the relational substance of their father's soul and heart. This wounds our sons and daughters, slowly and silently. While these men honestly believe they have been or are presently being good dads, their sons never receive physical or verbal affection from them. Such a father never speaks words of life and encouragement into their lives. He is too busy, too weary to give the demonstrative affections of his heart. This father abandons by neglecting to give his time and heart affections to his sons and daughters.

Sons who are neglected by fathers who fit this pattern generally grow up with a similar, sinful initiative pattern of relating to their spouse and children in the next generation. They become the nice guy. Such a man may seem to be his dominant wife's victim, but he has a hidden mean streak and may ultimately rule his controlling partner and/or children. His inability to take a stand or to be there for his family drives his wife and children to distraction. They may also have a silent, hidden fear of him and his rage. These are sons who had very little fathering and at best fathering of a similar pattern. So now in marriage and family life, the women and children become relationally overbearing and the man, as husband and father, becomes relationally under-involved. He becomes a little boy in relation to them.

While growing up, this pattern is most evident in the father-son relationship. The father gives functional involvement to his son—working together, playing ball together, fishing together—but giving him little, if any, of the good and bad stuff (substance) of his heart. Typically, sons (or daughters and spouses) grow up not knowing their father (or husband) other than by the function or work he does.

This father's major sin is one of omission—the legacy of Adam—not giving of the rich realities of his soul; doing nothing about what matters most to his wife, sons and daughters. This major wounding leaves a question in the soul of a son: "Am I really loved and held in my father's heart?" And the daughter wonders, "Am I really loved and prized by my father?" His wife asks, "Am I really treasured as the apple of his eye?"

Men Who Give Nothing

Giant "A" abandonment pattern

Fathers who fit the giant "A" abandonment pattern provide neither the functional necessities of life nor the relational substance of love, affection and personal soul involvement. These fathers abandon their sons and daughters by choosing to take no initiative to fulfill either creation mandate. They are creation parasites. This type of men who become husbands want a mother, not a wife. They are still little boys who refuse to grow up to face the thorns, thistles and weeds of life. They refuse to father by choice of the sin of commission.

Like Adam, they passively take and eat the fruit of life that someone else picks and works so hard for. These men physically abandon by leaving their spouses and children. They leave by blame shifting and go into substance abuse—alcohol, drugs, gambling. They deaden the pain in their wounded, sinful soul in any way possible.

Why are there so many of these addicted men? What forces in their family life, or lack of it, have created such personal, emotional soul emptiness, such human desolation that their only access to emotional warmth and male soul intimacy is through a chemical or sexual simulation of the experience? Their loneliness touches every one of us. The ultimate way they abandon is to commit suicide, leaving behind a widow and fatherless children. Reeling from gaping wounds of betrayal, the wife and children believe the worst:

"I'm not loved!"

"I'm not and never have been held in his heart as a son!"

"I've never been prized by my daddy!"

"My husband has only used me and never treasured me."

Listen to this son's story of wounding from his father who grievously sinned against him by abandonment.

"I remember the day twenty-five years ago like it was only yesterday. My father took me in his old beat-up 1960 Chevy pickup to head an hour's drive from the house in the country to the city. Just to be alone with my father raised my expectations that he and I could do something special. He told me it was a business trip and we would be staying in a hotel with a swimming pool, that he would take time with me on the weekend, going out for pizza and then for a swim.

"I was ten years old. My father had never taken me anywhere with him; I thought we would talk all the way to the city. The farther he drove, the more the silence made it obvious that he didn't want to talk or maybe he didn't know what to talk about. In hindsight, it was probably more that he didn't know how to talk to me. I remember, he turned the radio on and some western songs were playing.

"We arrived at the hotel and checked in late Friday evening, and then had something to eat in the hotel restaurant. That was a thrill because Dad was an alcoholic and he rarely came home to eat. His pickup usually was parked at the local pub in the small town about a mile from our house in the country. After we ate Dad took me to the room. He left saying he would be back before the pool closed, and then we could go for a swim together. I quickly put on my swim trunks and began to wait.

"The time for the pool to close came and went. Around 11:30 p.m. there was a knock on the door. I went and opened it, hoping it was Dad. It was a woman asking if a man by the name of my father was in the room. I said, 'No,' but I thought he had gone down the hall to a room filled with some other men.

"I took her down to the room I thought he was in and she knocked. A man with a bottle of beer answered the door. I could see past him and I noticed a bunch of other men and several ladies with very little on in the room. He went and got my Dad. I could tell he wasn't expecting me to be there at the door. He saw me and growled, 'Get back to your room and don't tell your mother,' as he took this woman's hand and closed the door.

"Then it hit me, My father wasn't here to do business, nor was he here to spend any time with me. I went back to my room, crushed in my spirit. And I sobbed! I cried so hard I thought I would convulse with stomach pain. He never came back till late Sunday afternoon. His eyes were swollen and glazed. To this day I'm not sure how we made it home.

"Several months later Dad moved away and I've never seen him since. I wished I would never have had a dad than to have one who was there and then left and never came back. The ache finally turned to numbness. The inside of me as a thirty-five-year-old man feels frozen. I have no feelings. I act like a living corpse."

CHAPTER 9

The Perils of Power

In the last chapter, we looked at the small "a" and giant "A" abandonment patterns of entering into our world and relationships. We turn now to the other end of the continuum to examine the patterns of domination.

The Take-Care-of-Me Man

Small "d" dominant pattern

Fathers who fit the small "d" dominant pattern have some similar characteristics to the small "a" pattern of abandonment. The subtle difference is in the need of these fathers to misuse their male initiative in entering their world and their sons' and daughters' lives. There is a sharper, demanding, more noticeable edge to their male spirit. By contrast, the small "a" father has a more passive expression of power with a subtle demanding spirit of "take care of me" when the thorns and thistles are too hard to pull, or "I'm too weak to enter."

The small "d" father is dutiful without passion. He is the dad who comes home, having worked hard providing functionally and dutifully for his children, but inside he is still at work. His body is present, but his spirit (who he is) is preoccupied with functional dominion—his work, ministry, self-centered leisure activities, hobbies or service organizations. The light of his "male front porch" is on, but there is no one at home for his son or daughter. As a father, he demands respect from his children, though he doesn't know how to earn it. He lives a more rigid and legalistic lifestyle. What he gives of himself to his children is like the mannequin that is well kept and dressed appropriately in the shopping mall window. This man is unfaithful in how he relates as a friend, husband and father. He may betray his male friends and his wife in the name of ambition or in the interest of freer sexual expression. He may betray his children for almost any reason. There is a self-focus that consumes him, a narcissistic habit of dominating that he is blind to, but is condoned by his culture, church and society at large. He cannot seem to transcend self-interest. Self-achieved submission seems an unlikely hero role in his life.

He is a self-sacrificing man. He denies his own emotional needs, depletes himself for his company, business, farm, students, people groups in missionary service, patients or art. But all too often, the sacrifice of himself is in a self-aggrandizing manner. He comes home drained and depleted and expects others to take care of him.

It is an issue of selfishness to sacrifice those nearest you while giving to those outside the family to an extreme degree. This pattern of small "d" domination is really a reflection of his negative feelings, the motivational lie about himself that he chooses to live by.

So what happens to a boy that makes it so difficult for him to grow up to be a faithful father to his children? Often he was betrayed by his childhood father, who functioned as he does, though it is usually difficult to see him as anybody's victim.

This father can also come across like the computer-man. He can be as ominous as Darth Vadar or as humorous as R2D2, but he is mechanical, and he was not born that way. The decision for him to choose to live within the narrow zone of the intellect was created in his childhood by experiences that made him feel terrified of emotion and intimacy.

Several years ago, Jerry, a forty-four-year-old father of four, sat with me in my office. He told me his story.

"My dad is a successful missionary in central Africa. I grew up in the tribe of nationals our mission was committed to. My father spent all my childhood years absolutely sold out to this tribe. I took correspondence courses for my schooling until grade seven. Then I went off to the missionary boarding school until the end of my grade twelve year. Nothing changed when I came back into the tribe and was home for school holidays and breaks. The people were always at our door and dad was always there for them seven days a week."

All of a sudden Jerry burst into quiet crying. Then it began to build into deep, gut-wrenching sobs. Suddenly before I realized what he was doing, he was up out of his chair and in my arms, clinging and holding onto me in desperation. I will never forget the words that came from deep within him: "Will you be my father?" With this his uncontrolled sobbing became even more pain-filled as he literally wailed in my arms. Both the boy and the man inside him were grieving the loss of a father who was a "successful missionary" but a colossal failure as a father. Even at forty-four, Jerry was still longing and crying out for his father's heart to turn back to him. In desperation he was turning his heart toward me as a surrogate father.

Small "d" dominating fathers wound deeply with a dutiful heart. Jerry's father needs no one, including a relationship with him. What fathers like this feed on and are sustained by are the shots of power generated and experienced through their functional performance. Their male identity is rooted in work, service, ministry—in DOING!

Possibly Jerry was acquainted with some of David's pain from his relationship with his father, Jesse: "Though my father and mother forsake me, the LORD will receive me" (Psalm 27:10).

The Unsafe, Violent Man

Giant "D" dominant pattern

Fathers who fit the giant "D" dominant pattern of initiating toward their sons are twisted and contorted with passionate, angry power. Rage and power make for a very unsafe, violent man. As a father, he is intimidating. From the style of a despotic army general to the soft-voiced accountant who makes his wife count even her pocket change, this guy is everywhere. He is in charge of most of the world's overt power and wields the domestic power in his home.

Like all authoritarians, he rules from fear of being dominated again like he was by his own father. He erupts into a rage against anyone who tries to control him, including God. His wife and children are bound to him in a way that squelches their spirits and protects himself from experiencing the soul rage and dread of any further loss. He is often violent because he feels isolated from his father and from his own children. This father crushes his son's spirit with his emasculating use of male power. The male presence exhibited is full of wrath and malice. Perhaps Solomon was speaking of him when he wrote: "A hot-tempered man stirs up dissension" (Proverbs 15:18).

When he was eight, Jimmy went downstairs one Saturday morning. There he saw the remodeling project of his father, three-quarters complete. As a twenty-seven-year-old man he told me this story about what he did as he longed to take dominion and create and to help and please his father.

"I went over to the one-quarter-inch paneling piled in a corner of the basement and, with great effort, managed to drag a four-by-eight sheet across the room. It took me a while to stand it on end. After pushing it against the bare insulated wall of studs, I began to hammer nails. It took me a while to finally get one nail through the paneling and into a stud. I was elated! My sense of accomplishment filled me with a male pride and satisfaction that I know is the way God made us to be.

"Then I heard his car drive in the garage. I ran upstairs, grabbed his arm, which I never did, and half-running pulled him along with me to the basement. 'Daddy, Daddy,' I said with a mixture of satisfied passion and pride, 'look!' And as I pointed to that lone sheet of finished paneling, I saw the streaks of red shoot up the sides of his neck. I knew I was in serious trouble.

"With beat-red face, he charged the panel, like an enraged bull going after the matador. He literally tore the paneling sheet in pieces as he ripped it off! Then he back-handed me across the face. Blood from my nose and cut lip began to shoot all over the floor. Then he pushed me down and with a loud bellow said, 'You useless, good-for-nothing _____, you nailed that sheet over an electric outlet! Are you blind or dumb, or both? If I ever catch you trying to do anything like this again, I'll break your fingers!'

"Physical and verbal abuse were all too common in my life as I grew up.

"You know, I've never gotten over that or other times like it. Maybe that's why every time my six-year-old boy makes a mistake I'm all over him. Jessie, my wife, called me on this last week. She asked me if I'd ever hugged James. She said she wonders if I'm an abuser. Did that ever set me off. I yelled and swore and, to be honest, I felt like hitting her. It was all I could do to control this rage inside of me."

I believe that our culture has gradually divorced itself from God because fathers have stopped patterning their parenting after the fatherhood of God. It reminds me of the prophesy of Hosea, when the kingdom of Israel was in the darkest hour of its entire history. The land was polluted with the consequences of the curse—greed, oppression, robbery, falsehood, adultery and murder. The fathers of the nation had failed in their responsibility. Hosea gave us this perspective by summing up the tragic situation: "My people are destroyed from lack of knowledge. Because you have rejected knowledge, I also reject you as my priests; because you have ignored the law of your God, I also will ignore your children" (4:6).

There is no hope for the children of this country unless we fathers return from the exile of self-centered, self-enhancing, self-protective behavior and choose to offer our souls to the mercy and grace of our heavenly Father who created our sons and daughters. As fathers, we must come to know God as Father, as our passionate, primary agenda, so we can grasp His fatherhood as the pattern for our own.

In entering back into the Father-heart of God, we must not ignore the wounds in our souls, the pain we carry as sons that is also our father's pain. This is an important part of our pilgrimage as men and sons—to examine how we have managed our woundedness.

In this examination we need to recognize that the wounds which produce male pain in our souls and bodies can be highly motivating in serving two opposite purposes. This happens when one or more of these three conditions take place: 1) We experience physical and personal soul wounding when someone else sins against us; 2) We experience physical suffering or agony in our hearts as a result of choosing to live sinfully; or 3) We experience calamity which comes upon us outside our control, and our sorrow and loss create physical or soul pain.

At this point, we can choose to manage our pain and suffering of body and soul in one of two ways: sinfully and selfishly or redemptively and other-centered.

Handling Pain Sinfully and Selfishly

The deeper, more continuous the soul wound, the greater the agony. Therefore the motivation for some form of relief and healing intensifies within us. Not just self-preservation kicks in, but also some form of selfish protection.

We say, "No one will ever get close to me again."

"I will trust no one with what's going on inside me as a man."

"I will never let myself be needy and loved deeply by another human being."

"You think I would take on that kind of responsibility? I could never do that!"

Self-centeredness will also motivate me to find some form of self-enhancement to deaden my inner pain, quiet the deep male dread of failure in my soul and make me feel good about myself. I will become the best at what I do, not as a glorious expression of my manhood for the good of others, but as the major soul prop of my well-being to prove my manhood.

"I will be the best marathon runner in my community."

"No other dentist in our town will have a better reputation and more clients."

"No other farmer in the area will be better known for his production of quality seed grain."

More power, more financial success, more prestige and position, and more pleasure from leisure, sex and substance abuse. High octane self-centeredness fills up the male sense of well-being and covers the soul wounds with Band-Aids.™

Managing soul pain in sinful ways needs to be closely examined. When we choose to sinfully manage the pain of our hearts without God's intervention, help, healing, restoration and repentance will not be able to compete with whatever form our self-centeredness takes. Unhealed wounds leave easy access for our sinful desires to enslave and corrupt the way we live and move and have our being. This results in the stench of soul death which is like the aroma of the curse on who we are and on what we do. Our male souls become passionless for God and relationally bankrupt. Needing no one at a deep level, we end up loving things and using people.

Handling Pain Redemptively and Other-Centeredly

The deeper the soul wound the greater the pain of the heart. Therefore, the motivation to enter into the Father-heart of God as His son intensifies within us. To find and know God and to experience His knowing of us becomes a burning passion in our souls. This redeemed desire frees us in our suffering to move beyond a demand for God to always heal us to the deeper hunger of wanting to know Him more intimately.

Choosing to manage our soul wounds in a redemptive way begins a pilgrimage of righteousness that brings about God-honoring, other-centered expressions of our maleness. This second option for managing soul pain is a journey into righteousness, one that is often not inviting because of the disruption and destabilization it brings.

Such a redemptive journey is thoroughly scriptural. Solomon writes: "Blows and wounds cleanse away evil, and beatings purge the inmost being" (Proverbs 20:30). In Job's story we read this perspective on God's purpose for suffering: "Blessed is the man whom God corrects; so do not despise the discipline of the Almighty. For he wounds, but he also binds up; he injures, but his hands also heal" (Job 5:17-18).

Hosea's plea to God's people reflects God's heart for our wounds: "Come, let us return to the LORD. He has torn us to pieces but he will heal us; he has injured us but he will bind up our wounds" (Hosea 6:1). In Hebrews, God puts it in a redemptive perspective that is very helpful: "God disciplines us for our good, that we may share in his holiness. No discipline seems pleasant at the time, but painful. Later on, however, it produces a harvest of righteousness and peace for those who have been trained by it" (Hebrews 12:10-11).

Like Adam, we have a choice. We may cover our sin, pain and male dread of God with our own fig leaves and eat our own fruit from the tree of knowledge of good/pleasure and evil/pain, or let God come and clothe our sin, wounds and dread of Him with the garments of His righteousness.

When we choose to ignore our woundedness, especially the father wound, our souls will stagnate under old, callous scar tissue. This opens us up to a subtle, downward spiral into forms of passive violence that create not life, but death around us. Or for some, the trek into violence becomes more noticeable and terrifying. Looking at the violent nature of our sinful male souls is not an easy exercise, but it is essential if we are to journey out of the locker room and into the heart of God.

CHAPTER 10

The Violent, Terrifying Male

The fastest growing male crime in our culture is domestic violence. At the root of it is one of our best-kept/unkept male secrets—the "Eichmann" that is in all of us. Though we don't always express our violence in dangerous ways, it is there beneath the surface, an evil passion that is both a potential and actual killer of our relationships and world.

On December 6, 1990, the world was shocked by the massacre in which Marc Lepine shot and killed fourteen engineering students at the University of Montreal simply because they were women. Vern Grey, an advocate for women's rights, spoke out against this crime which is part of a social trend:

> We have to start listening to the facts of the *Statistics Canada* report that found fifty-one percent of the women in Canada have experienced physical or sexual abuse. There seems to be something innate in men that they need to show their power over women. I think it would be fair to say most men have the potential to be violent.[1]

The absent father is the curse of our day. Homes without dads are creating a male who is confused about his identity. Modern men are under a great deal of sexual-identity stress. Males are therefore lashing out in forms of violent frustration. North America is becoming increasingly filled with enraged, isolated young men who no longer know who they are. With confusion and a lost sense of male sexual identity comes a loss of power. That loss is often expressed in uncontrolled and violent ways.

In 1994, 407,140 women were raped or sexually assaulted and over one million child victim cases of substantiated maltreatment and neglect were reported. Another national study revealed that a woman is physically abused by her husband every nine seconds in the U.S.[2] And because of self-contempt and self-hate, men in our culture are destroying themselves also. Of the 31,100 Americans who committed suicide in 1993, eighty percent were men. By year end 1994, our nation's prisons held a record 1,054,000 inmates of whom roughly one million were men. All this has resulted in a life expectancy for U.S. males that is 6.7 years lower than that for females.

This trend toward violence is also evident among teenagers. In 1993, of the 1.5 million offenses committed by U.S. juveniles, eighty percent were attributed to males seventeen years of age and under. This included violent acts of murder, armed robbery and rape.[3] J.M. Makepeace, in his groundbreaking work on dating violence, notes that the pattern of violence between dating high school students resembles that of both college-age students and married couples. It is his opinion that high school students may, indeed, be establihing patterns of violence that can persist into marriage.[4]

The Roots of Violence

What is causing so many young males to commit such violent, serious crimes in our country? The key factor is the absence of a father.

Ten years after these statistics were posted, the world was shocked by some sordid photos of a Liverpool infant, two-year-old James Bulger, who had been critically beaten and left on the railway tracks to die. The culprits were two eleven-year-old boys, Jon Venables and Robert Thompson. Venables' parents were separated at the time of the crime and his father was out of work. Thompson's father had abandoned his six children. They were both convicted of murdering two-year-old James Bulger.

Where does the violence of murder come from in two eleven-year-olds? Reporter Victoria McDonald of the *London Daily Telegraph* considered that question in her coverage of the Liverpool tragedy. She offered an interesting perspective on our predicament. Here are some comments by Oxford sociology professor, H.H. Halsey, that were included in her report:

> What should be universally acknowledged is that the children of parents who do not take on personal, active and long-term responsibility for the social upbringing of the children they generate are thereby disadvantaged in many major aspects of their chances of living a successful life.[5]

Put simply, according to Halsey, crime is connected with the diminution of social control by mothers and fathers. "We have got to get a moral grip on the next generation," Halsey says.

In a 1993 report, Norman Dennis and George Erdos of Newcastle Upon Tyne University wrote, "To an increasing extent, young males are being inadequately socialized. The consequences are that youths turn to anti-social behavior, varying from unruliness through criminality to swarming and street rioting, and are ill prepared to become good fathers in their turn."[6]

The prevailing sociological view of this century was that violent crime is caused by environmental factors—poverty, racism, oppression, lack of opportunity to be properly educated. If the cause of violence and crime is the external environment, then violence could be cured by changing the environment. But this does not seem to be the case.

In the 1950's, psychologist Stanton Somenow and psychiatrist Samuel Yochelson, sharing the conventional wisdom that criminals and violence are spawned by their environment, set out to prove their point. They began a seventeen-year study involving thousands of hours of clinical testing of 250 inmates in the District of Columbia. To their astonishment, they discovered that the cause of crime cannot be traced to environment, poverty or oppression. Instead, it is the result of individuals making, as they put it, wrong moral choices. In their 1977 work, *The Criminal Personality*, they concluded that the answer to crime and violence is the conversion of the wrong-doer to a more responsible lifestyle.[7]

Life Outside the Garden

Right from the beginning violence in men was let loose not by environmental influence, but by that which generated these conditions—life outside the garden! All of these factors were introduced by the fall when Adam and Eve chose to believe Satan rather than God. Within a generation of that fall, Cain had murdered Abel.

Any approach to understand and deal with the violence that lies within us as men cannot ignore the reality of our ongoing battle with the power of sin for we are fallen humanity. We dare not pass over the moral dispositions of our inner self. To do so is to ignore our moral culpability and character.

Malcolm Muggeridge expresses it this way: "When mortal men try to live without God they infallibly succumb to megalomania, or erotomania, or both. The raised fist or the raised phallus and the contemporary world bears it out."[8]

December 2, 1993 was "World AIDS Day." Around the world many events were staged to put the global spotlight on AIDS. Music fans rocked with Princess Diana at London's Wembley Stadium to raise money for the project. In Paris, a giant pink condom covered a fifty-foot-tall downtown landmark. This pink, fifty-foot condom could symbolize the upraised phallus before God.

In our culture we see that when sex runs outside the controls of moral standards and boundaries, violence follows. Psychiatrist Dr. John White says:

Muggeridge is right, first the erect phallus, then the raised fist. The rampant pursuit of pleasure eventually on a national level breeds murder. Right from the time of the fall, history portrayed through the Old and New Testaments has made the connection between sexual sin and violence.[9]

It's time we stop ignoring the biblical explanation for that which is tearing our nations apart.

A perversion, a twistedness, a bentness in our male sexuality was the first consequence of the fall. Prior to that, God had prescribed the appropriate authority—and the necessary physical and personal resources—for the male to carry out his assigned responsibility in both areas of the creation mandate. Functionally, he was to rule and subdue the earth; relationally, he was to be fruitful, multiply and fill the earth. His sin resulted in a loss of the right use of these inner personal and moral resources. His authority became enslaved to his sinful desires. Abuse of this authority has resulted in a misuse of resources and people ever since.

The trend of thinking we can become like God has resulted in us becoming our own gods. We have become power hungry and power abusers for we are under the direct influence of our enslaving, sinful desires. Add to this the energizing of unhealed wounds and soul pain and it is not hard to see how we have managed to corrupt our sense and expression of our God-ordained order, authority and responsibility. This inner reality breeds and fuels violence that churns and smoulders beneath the surface of our male souls, waiting to erupt.

Authority is the appropriate use of power assigned by God to the male to carry out his part of the creation mandate. Since the fall, it has been impossible to morally harness and channel this power. There is no formula that guarantees that men will use it totally for God's glory and the good of others.

Scripture and reality bear this truth out: The more a male perceives a loss of personal power, the more he will resort to an intensified, escalating, passionate pursuit of it. This pursuit of power results in a growing expression of violence.

Violence, simply defined in this context, is the misuse and abuse of any expression of power that goes beyond God-ordained moral and personal boundaries and that is not energized and motivated by love for God. Violence is the sin-energized, flipside of the aggressive passion God gave the image-bearing, pre-fall male. God created men to be energized with an appropriate amount of aggressive passion. He did this so the male could initiate entering the created world to rule and subdue, and enter into relationships to multiply and fill the earth for the glory of God. Everything God designed about maleness was stamped "good" by the Creator. But Adam's sin struck a deathblow to all the passions unique to the male design. Pre-fall, image-bearing, male aggression out of control becomes the passion of violence.

A current illustration may help. Tracking many young adolescent males today will find them congregating in their "place of worship." All the trappings for the pursuit of power and the experience of irresponsible male impact and violent domination are provided there through high-tech development.

This place of power for young men is the video arcade which beckons everywhere—shopping malls, bars, convenience stores, motels. A casual study of this environment will reveal some disturbing facts. Males outnumber females ten to one in on-site locations. If any females are present they are there primarily to meet males. Few young women are drawn to playing these violent games.

Many of the most power-addicting games for the

males are violent in design, demanding a passionate outpouring of male potency. Those involved have a single-minded focus. Many stand there for hours of uninterrupted game after addictive game, without so much as a single break until they lose, win or run out of money. Bodies moving, arms stiff, hands in staccato jerks wreak mayhem, killing and violence on their computer-controlled competitors. The arousal of male power in the depths of their souls leads to a soul orgasm of masculine potency.

These young men feel alive in ways they rarely do anywhere else. They are taking dominion in this world with a form of impact that can't be matched elsewhere. Whether it's a video game in the family room, a portable game in a boy's back pocket or one of the idols lined up row after row at the arcade altars, the addiction is the same. Video games provide males with a source of impact, outside God's moral boundaries, that supplies an experience of male potency and power with absolutely no responsibility to clean up the blood and bodies of the maimed and dead. That is outright idolatry!

The greater our experience of loss of power as males, the greater our acts of violence. We are driven to restore our personal sense of male potency. If we in our inmost male identity know we have been designed to initiate entering into a fallen sinful world, then we will passionately make entrance at whatever cost to our environment, to other people and to ourselves. Personal soul impotency is as shame-producing as physical and sexual impotency.

Terms like "losing face," "fragile male ego," "chicken" and "wimp" are expressions for the dreaded experience of soul impotency. No man will live in the horror and shame of male powerlessness. Even the male form of passivity is as potent an expression of power as dominating male behavior.

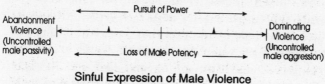

Sinful Expression of Male Violence

Passive Forms of Violence

Passive forms of violence usually get all kinds of rewards for the male without his having to pull any thorns and thistles out of his world. If he pouts, complains, grumbles, makes promises he never keeps, verbally or mentally abuses or the big one—blame shifts and leaves relationship—then in a perverted way he is relationally violent. By these schemes he can receive relational attention if he wants it or keep others away from him. He can get ongoing handouts from spouse, parents and government. No weed-pulling for this male.

Passive violence is a violation of male responsibility in the creation mandate. Just look at the sense of perverted power this gives to a man. Unfortunately, it results in a form of death to the marriage relationship, the turning of children's hearts from their fathers and a major negative impact on the economy.

Suicide is the ultimate expression of personal power. The choice to take one's life by males far outnumbers the female population. When other forms of power wane, men turn their violence on themselves.

The male misuse and abuse of power moves along the continuum from passive abandonment forms of violence to dominating violence, depending on the degree of threat or actual loss of male potency/power.

Dominating Forms of Violence

Dominating forms of violence work just as well for some males as passive forms do for others. Acts of male violence do exactly what the perpetrator wants. It gives him a sense and experience of power—male potency! Labels such as "macho," "jock," "redneck," "tough," "hunk," "stud," "aggressive" and "competitive" are all expressions that essentially define a male's attempt to experience his male potency.

This form of abuse manifests itself in violence of a more heinous nature. In the realm of functional dominion, ruling and subduing become dictatorships in government, work places, home and in the outright destruction of the environment through greed. In the realm of relational dominion, where man is to be fruitful and multiply and fill the earth, the thoughts and deeds of dominating males move into physical and sexual abuse and even murder.

National forms of male violence are always bred in the sinful, pain-filled heart of the individual who infects first his home and family, his work and leisure world, and then his community. Communities become villages, towns and cities. Cities strongly influence the cultural trends of the nation.

Let me get very pointed. Domestic violence is Satan's special triumph. Christian men, like non-Christian men, batter their spouses and children. Uncontrolled rage and frustration surge up within all of us. When it erupts in this form of physical abuse, it is *always* our responsibility. No woman or child deserves to be mistreated with this form of violence simply so we can retrieve a sense of male potency and power. Many batterers have been childhood victims of this form of generational sin. Often these men seem unable to control their actions, apologizing and groveling for forgiveness. But the bottom line is this: If the home is not safe, if wives are not safe from the brutality of husbands, children not safe from their fathers' violence, old people not safe from their offspring, then men, we have "hell" on earth!

The Danger of Unrestrained Indulgence

Sexual power and violence that erupts out of our male pursuit of potency is more than a psychological, sociological or cultural problem. Our lack of self-control is rooted in our sinful, unhealed male souls. Sexual power and violence indicate that individually and nationally as males we are coming under diabolical rule and divine judgment. This happens to us not only when we fail to worship the living God in spirit and in truth, but also when we men have too little of God in the passion of our souls. When we reach that point, He gives us over to *lust* and murder.

Romans 1:21-32 gives a very graphic description of this "giving over." Three times in this passage, the words "God gave them over" are used. Paul seems to be indicating that this is the form God's judgment takes on an individual and on a nation—to give us over to the consequences of our sin. Once a man tries to run his life without God he gradually loses protection from sexual lust, violence and even murder. The Old Testament bears witness to this fact as well. One of the strongest condemnations the prophets made to the sex-saturated, idolatrous people of their day was that they were guilty of violence and abuse of the fatherless, the widow, the aged and the poor.

This sequence is also evident in the lives of some men in the Old Testament. One such man was David, who as

king had sex with Uriah's wife—the raised phallus.
Then, after doing his best to hide his sin, he arranged to
have Uriah murdered—the raised fist of violence! Then
there was Solomon, to whom God gave wisdom beyond
any other. Here was a man consumed with sexual power
and his life ended in his trying to murder God's next ap-
pointed king (see 1 Kings 11:1-9, 40). Samson is another
man who exhibits this pattern of pursuing power
through sexual lust and violence (Judges 15:1-8).

Common male patterns of sexual violence today
move all the way from date rape to marital sex without
loving consent to power rape. Pornography and sexual
abuse of children and younger females have led to the
worship of the phallus and the bodies of youngsters
and women. Illicit sex such as date rape and fornication—sex outside of marriage—has led to unwanted
pregnancies, then abortions, a disturbing modern example of sex leading to violence.

The relationship of sex and violence is not a simplistic one. The individual male who seeks power through
this form of sexual sin does not automatically become
violent in the sense of murder. The process is much
more a community and national social consequence,
not necessarily an individual direction in every case.

However, once a male chooses to enter into sexual
sin, he can no longer be assured that he has the protection of God over the inclinations of his heart to do violence. God says, "Watch out!" Loss of control in one
area can lead to the other. First, erotomania, then
megalomania. The raised phallus, then the raised fist
in the face of God. Without God or enough of loving
Him, lust and murder will escape our hearts, produc-
ing the fruits of death in our families, our communities
and our nation. Male violence curses our land today,

Powermaking this country an ever increasingly dangerous place to live.

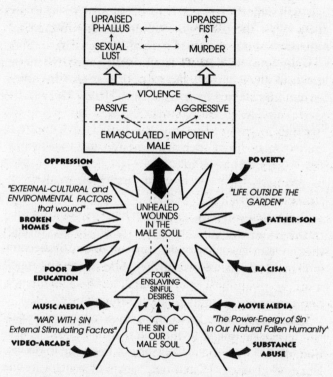

Violence is an unpredictable passion that always lies just below the surface of male civility ... WHY?

Male Violence: The Sinful Pursuit of Personal Power

Men, we need fathers with the spirit of Elijah to turn the hearts of our sons, young and old, back to our God. Before that will ever happen, we must continue the inner look at our own sinful ways of relating to others, especially to our loved ones and specifically to our sons and young males.

Jude's exhortation needs to be kept in mind as we press on for the final two chapters relating to the consequences of our shattered glory: "Be merciful to those who doubt; snatch others from the fire and save them; to others show mercy, mixed with fear—hating even the clothing stained by corrupt flesh" (Jude 22-23).

Endnotes

1 Vern Gray, "War Vet Fighting for Women," *Winnipeg Free Press*, Nov. 23, 1993. Used by permission.

2 The Commonwealth Fund, "First Comprehesive National Health Survey of American Women Finds Them at Significant Risk," NY, 1993 as reported by Pennsylvania Coalition Against Domestic Violence, Harrisburg, PA.

3 Unless otherwise cited, the figures given were gleaned from the following sources: *Sourcebook of Criminal Justice Statistics 1995* (Albany, NY: The Hingleang Criminal Justice Research Center, 1996); *The World Almanac* and *Book of Facts 1997* (Mahwah, NJ: World Almanac Books, 1997); and U.S. Deparment of Commerce, Bureau of the Census, *Statistical Abstract of the United States, 1996*.

4 J.M. Makepeace, "Courtship Violence Among College Students," *Family Relations*, 30, 97-102.

5 Geoff Still, *Newsletter* (Vancouver, BC: Focus on the Family, Sept. 1993), 1.

6 Ibid.

7 Ibid., 2.

8 Malcolm Muggeridge, *Christ and the Media* (Grand Rapids, MI: Eerdmans, 1977), 61.

9 Dr. John White, "Sexual Sin, Violence Inextricably Linked," unpublished article, 1993.

CHAPTER 11

Relating without Substance

Relationship is the only reality of substance we can take to heaven. At the head of the list will be our sonship with our heavenly Father, but there will also be many other relationships in which we have invested over the years. The giving away of who we are as males to someone else is an investment that carries eternal dividends. How we choose to relate to others will be the indicator of the value of our investment and the nature of our reward! The way we invest the very substance of our maleness is of prime importance to God.

Let's go back to the first male, Adam. When he faced a problem he had a choice, a moral choice. This choice mattered most deeply to the One who had breathed soul-life into him, for God had made Adam to worship and enjoy Him. Ultimately at stake was the deepest issue of eternal reality—who was to be enjoyed and worshiped? Choosing God would bring great glory and enjoyment to the Creator.

Can you picture the interest in heaven, the focused attention? There was the Godhead, the Father who ordained the Son to create, the Son who had designed and orchestrated the creation of man and the Spirit

who brooded over the formless void. Then there were
the legions of heavenly and satanic angels watching in
breathless anticipation for this crown of creation's very
first moral choice.

Alas, the hurrahs were not in heaven that day as
Adam made a choice to respond instead of initiating.
He refused to strongly and firmly enter into God's reality of order, creation and relationship. Retreating, he
passively took the forbidden fruit of knowledge of
good and evil. He chose to do nothing about the serpent's temptation and deception. He refused to protect
the place of vulnerability in which Satan put Eve.
Adam's choice had an eternal impact on mankind. The
nature of how Adam related as a male to his God, to
Satan and to his wife moved heaven and hell.

The Lord God immediately carried on His relationship with Adam and Eve by strongly entering and responding. He exposed their sin and brought immediate
judgment upon Adam and Eve and the earth. He also
brought judgment to Satan.

> Cursed are you above all the livestock
>   and all the wild animals!
> You will crawl on your belly
>   and you will eat the dust
>   all the days of your life.
> And I will put enmity
>   between you and the woman,
>   and between your offspring and hers;
> he will crush your head,
>   and you will strike his heel.
>   (Genesis 3:14-15)

There are serious implications of immense eternal

consequences because of how Adam related. Adam and Eve's relational choice infected all earthly human relationships. Supernatural relationships were strongly affected as well—Satan would strike the Son of God's heel at His crucifixion and Christ would crush Satan's head through His death, resurrection and ascension to the right hand of the Father. Since we as males have inherited Adam's legacy, our pattern of relating is no different than his. Infected by the virus of Adam's sin, we continue to relate in ways that also influence heaven and hell, as well as all our earthly relationships.

The Law of Human Relationships

The fall and its consequences brought a law of human relationship into existence. This law is as real and powerful in its existence today as it was the moment the eyes of Adam and Eve were opened. This law of human relationship can best be expressed in this manner: *All human relationships are constantly spiraling away from intimacy and substance to separateness and function.*

To be gender specific in its application, let us take a look at the impact of this law on male and female sexuality.

Male dread moves us to fear relational closeness and pursue safety in function alone. We hide our substance of soul reality in order to avoid relational intimacy, closeness and oneness. Our primary fig leaf to hide behind is to make function our soul mistress.

Female dread moves women to fear relational distance and pursue safety in a web of relationship. They tend to hide by silencing parts of their soul reality in order to avoid relational loss, distancing and separateness. Their primary fig leaf to hide behind is to make relationships their soul lover.

Both male and female are enslaved by the desire for power. You may wonder in our day if women are just as enslaved to the primary function of ruling and subduing as men are. On the cultural surface this appears to be the case. However, let me suggest that there are at least two significant internal realities that make women different from men. First, when all attempts to make relationships work break down, especially between women and men, women feel driven into function, either to survive or to find soul power, life and meaning as a primary form of existence. Second, even when women make functional dominion their primary focus in life, they pursue and use power to establish or re-establish a web of relationships in order to nourish and nurture a sense of soul security for themselves.

To women, function serves a deeper, female longing—safe relationships! To men, functional dominion serves the purpose of avoiding oneness of relationship and squeezing as much sense of dominion as possible out of what they do—impact. Both male and female long for impact, a man for functional impact and a woman for relational impact. Both long for intimacy, a man for functional intimacy and a woman for relational intimacy.

A male will use relational intimacy with a woman in order to get a sense of dominion, an experience of power and impact in his world. One example of functional intimacy for males is described by Paul Sachdev, professor at Memorial University's School of Social Work:

> A female's motive for sexual activity is entirely different from a male's. Sex for a man is a sign of male prowess and superiority, a status

among peers. . . . But for a large majority of women, sex is related to emotional security, expressing or obtaining love or filling a void in their lives. They want closeness and tenderness; which is much more important to them than the physical aspect of sex.[1]

Under enslavement to sinful desires and the choice to live with untended soul wounds, males live with a corrupted form and purpose for relating. This is compounded by the deepening threat of facing relational realities that we know absolutely nothing about. Faced with this dilemma, like Adam, our rebellious choices are translated into one of two sinful ways of handling life—the selfish relational patterns of abandonment and domination. Most men relate between these two extremes. The following diagram will help explain how male dread of soul nakedness before God and significant others motivates him to relate in self-centered patterns that ultimately bring a sense of drudgery and death to his soul.

Selfish Male Patterns of Relating

Male Abandonment

Listen to the inner worldview with which Tom looks at life and relationships:

"I don't want to be required to pull the thorns and thistles out of God's groaning creation or creatures. Someone else ought to pull them for me. It's unfair for me to have to enter into painful, physical and relational toil and sweat physical or personal perspiration. I'm really afraid to suffer physically or personally. If I suffer in these ways, I will perish. I just can't take the blows of life. I feel so unsure of myself, so inadequate, so weak. I have next to no awareness of what it is like to be a man. In fact, to be honest with you, I don't want to be manly. Something in me does want to grow up, but a bigger part of me wants to be taken care of. It feels safer to be given life than to be a life-giver. Even though living this way seems easiest for me, I often feel strong self-contempt. I hate my maleness!

"I am a fear-driven man in bondage to finding some form of solace to take away my fears. My greatest struggle is to initiate entering into the world around me. Life and people are such an unknown. When I get anywhere close to life and people I retreat and hide. I feel out of control. I demand that others give me life, to provide me with some form of pleasure, without my taking any responsibility. If others won't give me what I want, then I search for and find some relief, some pleasure, anything to make me feel some inner passion and life without having to be responsible for the consequences. I just won't take any personal risk if I sense this awful dread inside from some form of threat. This is the idolatry of my own heart.

"Let me be even more specific about my motivational lie. My motivational lie is what I believe deep inside is the truth about my male identity and sexuality. Listen carefully. I really have nothing to offer life or any human being that is of any substance or value. I firmly believe and feel I am incapable of being someone or accomplishing anything that is worthy of respect as a male. Whatever does spill out of my life is only like a dribble and brings about no fruit whatsoever. When I stand with my soul naked before myself, what hurts the most is that I have become convinced that who I am would not matter to you or to God because I really do not matter to myself.

"Based on these powerfully felt, personal convictions, I have made a vow that motivates the way I choose to live life. If I could put words and feelings to my motivational vow, it would sound something like this: I will never let myself feel like I matter to anyone. I will never give any part of who I really am to life or people. I will only reach out and take whatever life and others will give to me, or whatever I can get without any physical or personal risk or responsibility. I'm a life-taker, not a life-giver.

"The idolatry of my empty, lifeless, male soul is my worship of what life and others must do to nourish me. Whenever I send off this message to others, to take care of me by nourishing my inner being with some form of life, I make them feel a tremendous burden and pressure. I can tell people soon don't like being around me. They try to avoid me. They either feel sorry for me and pity me or they get disgusted with me. Sometimes I can tell they feel bad that they can't make me feel better and that they think it's their fault.

"I'm not an enjoyable man to be around."

Some examples of how worldviews like Tom's are lived out by other abandoning males may help to clarify this type of response. Although there are many ways a male avoids responsibility, there are two which stand out more directly.

The Absent, Uninvolved Male:
The Passive Wimp —Manipulatively Compliant

The absent, uninvolved male is covered over by a

layer of denial that is maintained by his own unproductivity, inactivity and relational impotence. To fill the huge hole of soul emptiness, he often resorts to substance abuse—mainly alcohol, drugs, food or all of these. The use of sexually perverted activities is another source of male pleasure. The more passive sexual perversions are more appealing because of the low personal risk or threat to his maleness. Sexual fantasies, pornography, masturbation, voyeurism and transvestitism are some of the low-threat forms of sexual pleasure that he uses to nourish whatever sense of maleness he can stir up.

He is a very lonely man, but is in terror of relational intimacy. Therefore, he feels trapped in a pain-fear cycle. It hurts to be so lonely and friendless, but he is afraid to enter into any meaningful relationships. When he does, he is so fear-driven that he usually abandons. Divorce is very high with these men. Fatherless children are a normal way of life. Among younger males, sexual involvement without responsibility for any children born or for the young woman involved is the common pattern.

The only fraternity of relationship that exists for these males is gangs, which become the replacement for family and a father relationship. Violence often becomes the only impact they know to experience male potency and power.

Then there are the men who have entered into life and have failed, men who have tried marriage and family life and left for good. These men often end up joining the company of other homeless men in our urban centers. This is their last hope for any relational and physical survival.

His own sense of maleness and any uniqueness is

nonexistent. He has no awareness of how demanding his selfishness is in getting others to take responsibility for him. When anyone asks for anything personal from him he runs by becoming quiet, or he clams up and his male spirit simply shrivels up. So he is personally impotent, unable to give anything of substance to a friend, a parent, a woman or his children. His relationships rarely endure over a lifetime.

This male will avoid interpersonal conflict at the cost of all innerpersonal integrity. He will lie to avoid telling you what he really thinks and feels.

He uses the power of his passivity to control others. You can try to fill this man up with all the forms of responsible help you can come up with, but he simply absorbs them into a soul wound so deep and painful, and into a sin nature so rebellious that you become the one who feels helplessly powerless. He is your consummate male wimp.

The posture of this man's heart toward God is very much one of total unbelief. He does not believe God is powerful nor personally caring. James describes a man like this when he writes, "[H]e who doubts is like a wave of the sea, blown and tossed by the wind. That man should not think he will receive anything from the Lord; he is a double-minded man, unstable in all he does" (James 1:6-8).

Let me tell you John's story that reflects the sinful desires and woundedness of a man who never changed his cowardly, passive way of relating.

"I never even imagined ending up homeless and living with other men on the streets. I was a shell of a man. Broken in spirit, aimless, relationally destitute and without a flicker of hope. The only solace I ever experienced was the taste and warmth of a hot bowl of soup when I could get one from a soup kitchen. The rest of the men all had stories full of different circumstances than mine but all with a common theme. It seemed strange that the most I had ever been able to relate to someone was now with these other men. One shell of a man to another shell of a man. Exchanging stories of hopeless pain, tragedy and immorality never uplifted any of us. But at least on occasion someone would relate.

"All my life I had been a loner. Dad tried mining, trucking and never could stick with a job. When I was eight he hung himself in our garage. I remember coming to get my bike to ride to school. As I walked into the garage I remember brushing against something and looking up—I saw my father. You are the first one I have ever told this to since it happened. I could never talk about it with anyone. Mom blamed Dad. She had a breakdown and they put her into a mental institution. I went from one foster home to another. People tried to love me but something in my spirit was closed so tight that no love got in.

"I met this girl when I was nineteen and she was eighteen. She seemed to find a way to make me feel better about myself. We married and had two daughters and a son. I tried to stick with a job, but the boss always seemed to lose confidence in me and my abilities. You see, the harder I tried the worse my mistakes were. The pattern was the same, job after job. Either laid off or fired.

"I could never seem to talk to anyone about it. I was demoralized most of the time. I never could relate to my wife or three children. The more I tried the worse the fighting and arguing became. I will never forget the day I faced two choices: one, do what Dad did, or two, leave my wife and family. I chose to leave. From there it's been all downhill into hell. I can't even remember how long I have been on the streets.

"I'm trapped in a cycle of despair. It's just physical survival from one day to the next. I have not seen my wife and three children in ten years. I tried the best I knew how to make something of my life. It never worked. I have no hope of it ever changing for me. I'm thirty-nine and already in hell. The next one can't be any worse than this."

Every man's life is a story of pilgrimage. We need to tell our stories as a way to let the Spirit of God get access to the pain and sin of our hearts. Most men who share their stories with me, like the one above, tell me that the main reason they don't talk about the inner reality of their souls is because they are convinced no one really makes the effort to listen or care. Even their own fathers fail at this, if they still have one. Beyond the longing as sons to exchange stories with their own fathers, men tell me that they believe other men just don't care.

Men who never tell their stories become dangerous men. The sin and pain of their hearts result in a pattern of relating that leaves a mark of death on creation and on people. Abandonment is a curse. Passive avoidance is a way of relating that needs to be exposed, faced and changed by the story of good news brought by Jesus, the second Adam.

The Absent, Involved Male: The Nice Man—Manipulatively Dutiful

The absent, involved male is involved only in function. He does find a job, but it carries little or no passion for him. When something else comes along he usually quits and hops on the next opportunity. He moves around a lot and is restless. Work never seems to do it. It never is the right fit for him. When he is laid off or fired, he has no qualms about living off unemployment for as long as he can before seriously looking again. Or he will use welfare if he can qualify. He doesn't depend on these resources out of a desperate need of poverty, but rather because of a restless fear that he can never seem to quiet. He tries to provide for his family, but does so without passion or enjoyment.

He appears more together on the surface. He is a faithful follower of others' desires, ideas, convictions. His soul motto for relating to others is something like this: "I will give you what you want if it is not too threatening or inconvenient. But I won't give you what little substance I do have. I will be involved without becoming personally attached to anyone."

His personality tends to be somewhat bland, often relationally boring unless you get him going on one of his selfish interests. As a son growing up or as a husband and father, he is home as little as possible. If he is home, he is into function, doing only what is of interest to himself—TV, computer, golf, puttering endlessly.

As a husband or father he is not relationally engaged with his wife or children other than through activity that he prefers or enjoys. He has no sense of what his wife's or children's legitimate needs or desires are, especially those that relate to a desire for meaningful involvement with him as a husband and father. Even more tragic, he has no awareness of what God has given to him as a male to give away to others, whether that is a friend, his wife, his children or as a son to his own father and mother. Most painful of all is that this man passes this relational pattern on to future generations.

His selfish relational style leaves him with little experience of his substance of maleness. What he is in touch with is a gnawing pain from his unhealed wounds. His soul pain is like a low-grade fever or headache. He mostly feels his enslaving, sinful desires pressing for expression and satisfaction. He quiets his soul pain and satisfies his sinful desires by more acceptable forms of activities.

In the secrecy of his own life, he is given to struggling with some powerful sexual passions and fantasies, lust patterns and other passive forms of sexual perversions. If he chooses to use sexual perversions, no one knows, including those closest to him. He is often a closet masturbater, voyeur, secret exhibitionist, obscene phone caller or is into computer pornography.

If he is a Christian male, his soul posture toward God is one of lukewarmness. God's feeling for this heart attitude is expressed in the words of John:

> I know your deeds, that you are neither cold nor hot. I wish your were either one or the other! So, because you are lukewarm—neither hot nor cold—I am about to spit you out of my mouth. You say, "I am rich; I have acquired wealth and do not need a thing." But you do not realize that you are wretched, pitiful, poor, blind and naked. (Revelation 3:15-17)

The Most Common Complaint

The most common complaint I have heard from married women during my twenty-five years of teaching and counseling is about absentee husbands and fathers who do not connect with their wives and children. Here is one such story from a wife of a Christian man that reflects some of these relational abandonment characteristics. He's a nice man who is still evil.

The kids are in bed. There's nothing on TV tonight. I ask my husband if he minds if I turn the tube off. He grunts. As I walk to the set my mind is racing. Maybe, just maybe tonight we'll talk. I mean have a conversation that consists of more than my usual question with his mumbled one-word answer or, more accurately, no answer at all. Silence—I live in a world with continuous noise but, between him and myself, silence. Please—oh, God, let him open up. I initiate (once again; for the thousandth time). My heart pounds—oh, how can I word it this time? What can I say that will open the door to just talk? I don't have to have a DEEP MEANINGFUL CONVERSATION. JUST SOMETHING!

As I open my mouth—he gets up and goes to the bedroom. The door closes behind him. The light showing under the door gives way to darkness. So does my hope. I sit alone on the couch. My heart begins to ache. I'm tired of being alone. Hey, I'm married. I have been for years. Why do I sit alone? The sadness undergoes a change slowly—then with increased fervor I get mad. I AM MAD. I am sick and tired of living with a sissy. A wimp—a coward. You know, he's afraid of me!

Hostile, you say. You better believe it. I'm sick and tired of living in a world of passive men.

My two sons like sports. They're pretty good. They could be a lot better if their Dad would take a little of his precious time and play catch with them. (I'm sorry, catch once a year at the church picnic doesn't quite make the boys into great ball players.) But Dad's too busy. He's at work. He's at the health club. He's riding his four-wheeler. He's working on the car. He's playing golf. He's tired. He's watching a video movie. So who plays catch with my boys? Me. My husband says, "You shouldn't be playing men's sports." So who's going to do it? He *says* he will. But he doesn't. Remember? *He's* too busy. Satisfying himself doing what he likes. . . . So my poor sons have to be second-rate in sports. They could have been good. Really good. Yeah—I'm mad.

My daughter is a teenager. She likes boys. *They* notice her. *They* pay attention to her. She responds. I know what's coming. I try to talk to her. But it's not me she wants. It's Dad. Yeah, Dad! If he'd just hug her, notice her, talk to her—just a little—she wouldn't need those boys so much. But no . . . so she turns elsewhere for attention and love. And there's nothing I can do.

A mom isn't enough. Kids need a father. And not just a body, a passive, silent presence.

And here's the killer. My husband's father did the same number on him. Didn't hug him. Didn't take him to anything, let alone watch his baseball games. And he HATES his father. Now my husband's doing the same thing. Will our sons grow up to be passive? Will they be cowards?[2]

You may not relate to the circumstances of this story, but some will be able to relate to Tom's pattern of passivity. We need to come to understand that the sin in our hearts is more than just some outward act; its pervasiveness influences the way we relate to others and how we enter into life.

Sin for Tom goes much deeper than being interested in his four-wheeler, driving over rough terrain to go deer and moose hunting. The stench and aroma of death in his passive pattern of relating to his wife and children is obvious to them. But like so many men, Tom is oblivious to his impact. His sinful, enslaving desires, mixed with and energized by his unhealed soul wounds, keep him preoccupied and self-centered. His self-awareness is typical for a male, very shallow and superficial, if not nonexistent.

Endnotes

1 Paul Sachdev, "Professor Says Sexes Differ Widely on Sex," *Winnipeg Free Press*, Nov. 8, 1993. Used by permission.

2 Weldon Hardenbrook, "Where's Dad?" *Recovering Biblical Manhood and Womanhood*, John Piper and Wayne Grudem, eds. (Wheaton, IL: Crossway, 1991), 379-380.

CHAPTER 12

Males Who Dominate

Y ou may be one of those who cannot identify at all
with the abandonment pattern of relating. In fact,
you may possibly feel a certain degree of pity or contempt for men like this who come across as wimpy and
without a backbone of maleness. You are probably
thinking, "Why can't they be men like us?" While you
hold on to these possible reactions, let's move along the
continuum and examine the description and characteristics of the dominating male pattern of relating.
Perhaps you will find some familiarity there.

Let's listen to the inner worldview of males like Jim
who live and look at life and relationship in a dominating way.

"Better you than me that hurts! I will wound you,
get one up on you before you wound or get the best of
me. Life outside the garden is hard. Everything you
get or want is by the sweat of your brow. Work is
tough, painful, and if you don't get the best of the
thorns, thistles and the weeds in life, then they will get
the best of you. That won't happen to me! I don't care
how hard I have to work or what I have to do in life; I
won't let life or people beat me up!

"Life is brutal, out of control. Any means of making it work is legitimate. I'm not required to give anything of myself to you because you are so deplorable. I know that is something of how Adam may have thought and felt toward God and Eve—'God, I'm not required to take responsibility for doing anything about the serpent's coming and deceiving Eve. You made her the way she is. It's not my fault she's weak and easy to talk into something.'

"Yes, I know my strength sounds and feels defensive to others, but that is just who I am. It's not my problem! If you have a problem with me being more aggressive or pushy then that's because you are too weak to be real upfront. I despise people who won't stand on their own two feet!

"Life is unfair; just look around you. If you're not on guard, the injustice of life can get to you. When it gets too close to me, or hurts someone I'm responsible for, I feel something deep inside me well up and I come alive as a man. My motto in life is 'I don't get back; I get even!' Power for me is a must. Weakness will only get you run over by life and others. I suppose if you could take a picture of my male soul, you would see it in the shape of a clenched fist.

"I hate the mystery of life and people. Confusion makes me mad. I certainly would never let on to anyone that when I don't know what to do, I feel a deep dread inside of me or I feel powerless. When I ever get close to those thoughts and feelings, I just work harder, longer and try harder. With people, I simply come on stronger and become more verbally and/or physically overpowering. I won't back down to anything or anyone.

"If you listen deeply to the rebellion of my soul as a

male it would sound like this: 'I will empower myself
without God, without you, without being responsible
to ever have to move into what I can't control. I will
use things and people as my source of power.' This is
what the idolatry of my heart looks like.

"This passion to dominate instead of taking dominion gets to feeling like a lot of pressure. Pressure to be
successful, to not fail, to never be weak. When the
pressure gets to be too much I get awfully angry and
push you away. My anger also helps to move me away
from this deep dread that surfaces and from past or
present hurt. I really lose touch with myself. It feels
like my soul goes numb and I can't feel anything or
anyone. Oh well, back to work!

"Let me be very honest, which is something new for
me. Here is what I believe is really true about my male
identity and sexuality. Unless I have something to offer life or others besides the substance of who I really
am, you would never want to enjoy me, be with me or
respect me. What I do is all that matters! Who I am
means nothing in a dog-eat-dog world. Besides, it
won't put bread on the table or get you anything nice
in life. This sums up the motivational lie that drives
me.

"Based on the core belief that soul life and power are
derived in function, in what I do and not in who I am,
I have made a strong commitment to live by the following vow: 'Since it feels like there is nothing of real
substance in me for you to enjoy, I will never stop
functioning. I'll give you what I have, my hands, my
voice, my mind, but not my soul. No one gets that!' I
get very passionate about this. I will have impact in
life! I will feel potent and alive, powerful! That is my
motivational vow. I'm a life-user, not a life-giver.

"This idolatry of my heart leaves me objectified as a success object. Whenever I send this message I make others feel unsafe in my presence. I'm not a safe male to be around. People feel used, disposable, objectified, ugly, not good enough, undesirable—and worst of all—unwanted.

"Women especially feel unenjoyed for who they really are, that they are only wanted for their body and sex. They don't feel cherished and protected by men like me. I provide them with things, but not with the security of relational love and commitment. I don't know how to sacrificially lay my life down for what really matters most to them and to God. Sounds like I'm just like that first image-bearer, Adam, who seriously messed up. I'm definitely not a safe man to be around."

The Dynamics of Domination

Here are some examples and characteristics of males who, like Jim, avoid relationship by the way they sinfully dominate. Out of the many, we will examine two general types together with some of their identifying characteristics.

The Dominating, Involved Male:
The Distant Man —Manipulatively Involved

For the dominating, involved male the sinful, enslaving desires energized by the pain of his unhealed soul wounds create a passion that expresses itself in aggression. It is corrupted but controlled, overpowering yet insidious. This passion can flow out of any personality type.

His sense of manhood is derived from how hard he works and how successful he is at accumulating things and providing for those for whom he is responsible. In fact, he is unaware of his selfishness because of the growing sense of self-righteousness that comes from being such a good provider. He does not have time or energy to give any substance of his soul. He finds himself unable to enter into verbal or physical affection, into the joy or pain of others or letting anyone into the inner realities of his own soul.

He does relate to others through activities, whether that is work or pleasure or both. But no one gets his heart. He never uses function as a vehicle to enter into the deeper reality of relationships. So he uses activities and people to give him a sense of well-being—that he is really doing OK as a man. His friends, children, wife and family describe him totally by what he does. He's a computer expert, works for IBM! He likes racketball, goes camping with us, takes us to the symphony. He's into gardening and flying radio-controlled airplanes. No one speaks of him in relational terms— "he's my best friend"; "he's angry most of the time, impatient"; "he talks to me, lets me see his struggles"; "I can pray with him and for him."

His life vocation is what he does best. Move him outside his world of work into relationship and he is lost. Stop him from doing something with you and instead interact on a relational level and he is out of his league. Ask most sons, "When you went fishing with your dad, what did you talk about?" Many will answer, "about fish and fishing; or we never talked; hours of silence." Now is that real substance—fishing, hockey, field work, crop yield, bio-ethics, law? The point is obvious, I hope. The distant man is involved and relates only on the level of function; rarely, if ever, on the level of relational substance.

A young man told me, "While riding home from the

arena, Dad rarely or never asked me about why I was starting to get so angry and taking such undisciplined penalties. Was there something bothering me? It was simply, you played a great—or a lousy—game. Then silence the rest of the way home. It was like we never had anything else in common."

This man engages in his work with passion. He lives and moves and has his being in his job. When he is not at work, he is involved as an elder, board member at church, doing community work, heading up fund drives for this cause or that cause. He is an out-of-state man. When he is home, he's not really home. His attention and soul passion, even while in the house is still on his work or another function. His male presence shouts loudly to everyone, "I'm an important man because I have important things to do." He is your classic workaholic who says, "I will give you my sweat, but not my soul. I have slaved fourteen hours a day, son, so you could go to college. What more do you want from me?"

This man is hard to get to know. He only engages in relationship if it is to his advantage. When he is with you, his agenda is always self-centered, not other-centered. To him relationships are a nuisance, a bother, a hindrance to his self-serving agenda. His lifestyle announces in a clear, silent message, "I don't need people!"

This man is driven to always compensate in some way for his dread of failure and loss of power. Another investment, one more trophy fish, one more season in professional sports, one more degree, another of this, one more of that. The dread and pain of his heart run deep, leaving a bottomless hole in his soul that not even power can fill or eradicate. He ends up very busy at what he does best so he can avoid what he dreads most—a naked soul that knows that if life or even God takes from him what he does best, he has nothing else to offer you.

The distant man's soul posture toward God is an indifferent heart that shouts, "I don't need You, God." Solomon said it well: "There is a way that seems right to a man, but in the end it leads to death" (Proverbs 16:25).

Here are two real life stories to put some flesh on the characteristics of this type of maleness. Never will I forget this first story and its impact on my soul.

A Successful Failure

A Christian leader went to the hospital as the result of an emergency. He was fifty-one years of age, a successful pastor. His present church attendance had multiplied from 225 to 650 in five years. All of the previous three churches had flourished under his pastoral leadership. Teaching the Word of God was his first love. On average he put twenty-five to thirty hours of preparation a week into his Sunday morning sermon which was given at three repeated services. He spent at least that much time in administrative work, and another ten hours every week in visitation. Sixty to seventy hours had paid tremendous dividends for the kingdom of God, or was it for the kingdom of Tom?

Now he lay dying of a sudden heart attack. He called the only man he thought might really care about him As this humble man took his friend and pastor's hand as he lay slipping into the valley of the shadow of death, he heard this confession.

"Last week my wife of twenty-seven years left me for another man. She said, 'I have not loved you in years. You have been there for everyone in your church, but you have never been there for me. I have found a man who cares about me and not just about his job.' My church doesn't even know yet.

"A month ago my son wrote me after ten years of silence between us and asked if I was still as busy as I had always been. If I was, not to bother writing back because he would not bother to visit then. The people in the church just thought he had been working overseas and could never make it home."

He was sobbing then, with the little strength he had left. He never did finish telling his friend about his other son and daughter. His last words were "I'm a successful failure!"

Here is a man whose family abandoned him because his mistress was his ministry. He was living for function, not substance; a man whose source of soul-life came not from his identity in Christ, but from his identity in ministry; a man who took to heaven "successful churches," but left behind a broken family. What a tragedy!

Dynamic, Friendless Jim

Then there was Jim. He was a decisive man, single, on the move. From all outward appearance, he was flawlessly together. No cracks ever appeared in his armor of professionalism. He was twenty-nine, vice-president of his investment firm and much noticed by both the single and married women. It's not that he never noticed their attention, but he was too involved, too busy to get attached. He was like the typical North American male—friendless. Sure, he socialized, but there were no deep friendships in his life. When the president of his firm got the call from the company lawyer that Jim had been charged for date rape, he was as shocked as everyone else in this corporate world.

Jim, you see, was a man who derived power from his function and office, leaving his soul sterile and void of any relational involvement. Something in him craved intimacy and demanded gratification. His sexual desires went wild; they seemed untameable to him. It felt like he was a different man that night and couldn't stop himself. That's when he sexually entered the woman he had dated for the first time—without her consent.

Jim wasn't willing to enter into exploring the mystery of this woman's soul. That felt too risky, too out of control. He used his power without relational responsibility. And so he plundered and conquered the mystery of her body through nonconsenting sex. He was devastated, his career lost, his future in question. But worst of all, he robbed and stole something from this woman that she could never get back—her virginity. He not only raped her body, he raped her soul. She would forever live with this wound. And so would Jim, unless he turned for help to Jesus, the only Healer of sin and wounds, and to those who could incarnate the Lord Jesus to him.

The Dominating, Uninvolved Male: The Macho Man—Manipulatively Intimidating

The dominating, uninvolved male's sinful desires are fueled by unhealed wounds. He shouts, "I don't want relationship with anyone." The posture of this male soul is a tightly clenched fist in the face of others, especially women. He is a rage-driven man, bent on revenge because the injustices of life have beat his male soul into a pain-filled pulp.

He invests most of his passion fine-tuning a system of macho behavior that will give him a taste of his maleness. He is on red-alert to prove to his world and everyone that he is a man. He destroys relationships.

He is extremely threatened by relational intimacy. He often resorts to using his male potency in an abusive manner. He ranges from verbal/mental cruelty to physical and even sexual abuse. His male presence is experienced as relationally rigid, cold, authoritarian and fear-inducing. Others experience him as a male without boundaries. He lives out who he is in whatever way he pleases. And you do not confront him. He is not open to challenge, debate or feedback about his life. He is not interested in any self-disclosure. That would be an obvious display of weakness. His self-awareness of the painful, sinful way he impacts his world is nonexistent. He is only aware of how to get what he wants.

He is very dogmatic in his beliefs, convictions and opinions. He tends to come across as an authority on any subject. Rules in life apply to everyone else, but he is very arbitrary in following them. He is both subtly and outrightly intimidating in bringing anyone who threatens him under his control. Do not cross this man in any way as he is prone to outbursts of soul rage that are devastating in their consequence. He is a destroyer of life. Domination of creation and of others is his common mode of operation.

This man is terrorized by his powerlessness. Beneath the hardened, crusty, rough edges of his soul is a man who, somewhere in his past, felt the injustice and hardships of life and people. His soul bristles with unrighteous wrath against God, life and others.

The posture of his heart toward God is the upraised fist. God is not good, nor is He powerful! His male strength has become hardened. His heart is cold toward God. His soul cries out to heaven, "I don't want God!" You can find this man in the words of David, who wrote, "The fool says in his heart, 'There is no God.' They are corrupt, their deeds are vile; there is no one who does good" (Psalm 14:1).

Perhaps the humor of this short article by syndicated columnist, David Barry, will expose the foolishness of the macho male.

Road Warriors

Our topic today, in our continuing series on guys, is: Why Guys Act Macho.

One recent morning I was driving in Miami on Interstate 95, which should have a sign that says:

WARNING
HIGH TESTOSTERONE LEVELS
NEXT 15 MILES

In the left lane, one behind the other, were two well-dressed middle-age men, both driving luxury telephone-equipped German automobiles. They looked like responsible business executives, probably named Roger, with good jobs and nice families and male pattern baldness, the kind of guys whose most violent physical activity, on an average day, is stapling. They were driving normally, except that the guy in front, Roger One, was thoughtlessly going only about

65 miles an hour, which in Miami is the speed limit normally observed inside car washes. So Roger Two pulled up behind until the two cars were approximately one electron apart, and honked his horn.

Of course, Roger One was not about to stand for THAT. You let a guy honk at you, and you are basically admitting that he has a bigger stapler. So Roger One stomped on his brakes, forcing Roger Two to swerve onto the shoulder, where, showing amazing presence of mind in an emergency, he was able to make obscene gestures *with both hands*.

At this point both Rogers accelerated to approximately 147 miles per hour and began weaving violently from lane to lane through dense rush-hour traffic, each risking numerous lives in an effort to get in front of the other, screaming and getting spit all over their walnut dashboards.

I quickly lost sight of them, but I bet neither one backed down. Their co-workers probably wondered what happened to them. "Where the heck is Roger?" they probably said later that morning, unaware that, even as they spoke, the duelling Rogers, still only inches apart, were approaching the Canadian border. This is not unusual guy behavior. One time in a Washington, DC, traffic jam I saw two guys, also driving nice cars, reach a point where their lanes were supposed to merge. But neither one would yield, so they very slowly—we are talking maybe one mile per hour—*drove into each other*.

Other examples of pointlessly destructive or hurtful macho guy behavior include:

- Guys at sporting events getting into shoving matches and occasionally sustaining fatal heart attacks over such issues as who was next in line for pretzels.
- Guys on the street making mouth noises at women.
- Boxing.
- Foreign policy.

Why do guys do these things? One possible explanation is that they believe women are impressed. In fact, however, most women have the opposite reaction to macho behavior. You rarely hear women say things like, "Norm, when that vending machine failed to give you a *Three Musketeers* bar and you punched it so hard that you broke your hand and we had to go to the hospital instead of my best friend's daughter's wedding, I became so filled with lust for you that I nearly tore off all my clothes right there in the emergency room." No, women are far more likely to say: "Norm, you have the brains of an Odor Eater."

But the real explanation for macho behavior is not that guys are stupid. The real explanation is that because of complex and subtle hormone-based chemical reactions occurring in their brains, guys frequently *act* stupid. This is true throughout the animal kingdom, where you have examples such as male elks, who, instead of simply flipping a coin, will bang their heads against each other for hours to see who gets to mate with the female elk, who is on the sidelines, filing her nails and wondering how she ever got hooked up with such a moron species,

until eventually she gets bored and wanders off
to bed. Meanwhile the guy elks keep banging
into each other until one of them finally "wins,"
although at this point his brain, which was not
exactly a steel trap to begin with, is so badly
damaged that, in his confusion, he will mate
with the first object he encounters, including
shrubbery, which is why you see so few baby
elks around.[1]

Beneath this posture of heart is a man who dreads
nakedness of soul in the presence of a holy God. He
covers his dread with the fig leaves of a macho, sexist
spirit that is an abomination to the Lord. But God
searches out the spirit of a man like this because He
hungers to bring His Father-heart to him: "The lamp
of the LORD searches the spirit of a man; it searches
out his inmost being" (Proverbs 20:27).

Intimidating Jerry

Jerry's story sounded frighteningly familiar to me
when he came for counseling. It may ring true to some
of you who have found yourself identifying with the
characteristics of this last male who relates primarily
by intimidation.

"I'm afraid!"

"Of what, Jerry?"

"Of myself!"

"Are you ready to tell me about it?"

"Ya! If I don't, someone is going to get hurt. I'm a
cattle rancher. Been into livestock for twenty-five
years. My three sons have grown up. Two of them ran
away when they turned sixteen. Never been back. The
youngest just turned eighteen. He told me yesterday

he would be history from this place as soon as he graduates in June from high school. My wife has been in and out of the mental health care home. Says she's afraid of me. Especially around calving season she seems to always get depressed.

"Man, I don't know where to begin. This is a lot harder than I thought it would be. Six months ago you would never have caught me dead talking about myself to anyone. Especially the likes of you guys. What a soft life, sitting in a warm office in a plush chair, grunting at people, acting like you are listening and you care!"

"Something happened to get you past all that, Jerry, and bring you here."

"It sure has! Came to a head about a month ago when I was trying to move some cattle from one part of the stock pens to another. One of the three-year-old steers wouldn't go. I tried everything I could think of. Nothing was working. Then I lost it! I took an iron bar and I literally beat that steer to death. What scared me the most was not that I killed it—not saying that was good or anything—but when I was finished and was standing over the steer's body, I felt this rush of power and it tasted sweet. I mean, like a couple of shots of warm brandy that hits your gut! I enjoyed killing that animal!"

"Where's all that coming from, Jerry?"

"I don't much know. I have never let myself think about what goes on inside me. Only guys who are weak and into themselves do that kind of stuff. But this scared the _____ out of me!"

"Why did your two oldest sons run away?"

"I can talk about this steer, but I'm not sure I'm ready to talk about Billy and Ted, or my wife!"

"Have you ever physically beat them?"

"You sure get to the heart of things quick!"

"We are not at the heart of things yet, but that could get us going in that direction. No sense wasting time with a man like you. I'm sure you don't waste time getting your point across or getting others to give you theirs, do you?"

"Nope! My way of thinking is if you got something to say, spit it out! Don't stand there drinking a whole cup of coffee before you start telling me what you really have to say! Yes, I beat my sons, and my wife once or twice, but they had it coming! Let me tell you about the time just before my second oldest son, Ted, ran away . . ."

Jerry's story carried on. It took him much longer than he thought to empty the sin and pain and evil of his heart. He told me that coming to see me was like lifting the man-hole cover off the septic tank on his ranch. He had a pilgrimage to talk about, one filled with the dark desires of his soul.

God was beginning to shine His lamp on Jerry's inmost being. It wasn't pretty. It was ugly! The sin was covered by the stench of death. The scar tissue over unhealed wounds since boyhood left the male shape of Jerry's soul distorted and grotesque. No wonder he was becoming afraid of himself. Now he was also becoming aware of his fear of a holy God. Together, we both began to see that the fear of the Lord is the beginning of wisdom, and that the fear of the Lord is safe! It is the fear of man that is a snare.

Men, we need to talk about our inmost stories. We have all got a story to tell. Have you ever told your story to yourself, to God, to another? I invite you to tell your story! Remember, "God made mankind upright, but men have gone in search of many schemes" (Ecclesiastes 7:29).

Our relational pattern of relating is the outworking of our scheming, bent male souls. They are no longer upright in shape. We have all found a sinful pattern, a system, a formula of relating that keeps us hidden from the gaze of others. Our scheme of relating gives away our stubborn commitment to live as upright as we can without ever bowing our knees to God in radical trust and broken contrition of heart.

God assures us it won't work. It will only lead to death, the death of our human relationships. Death of oneness! Death of soul and spirit intimacy with others and with our heavenly Father. "There is a way that seems right to a man, but in the end it leads to death. Even in laughter the heart may ache, and joy may end in grief" (Proverbs 14:12-13).

Our relational patterns are real. They carry the passion and desires of our souls into how we live and handle life. Though no man has just characteristics of one type, we all have a relational pattern of protecting and enhancing our own position. Just let the level of threat to lift our fig leaves get high enough and it will quickly kick in. Up the soul-dread level, and like Adam, we will go into hiding, blame shifting through abandonment or domination, and find relief. In most cases, our relational response falls into a single, more identifiable pattern.

The sin of our hearts is most clearly visible and experienced by others in the way we relate. The closer the relationships, the more that which is hidden is exposed. This is especially true in the company of women, particularly our wives, and also with our children. Other men seem least aware of who we really are.

Let God the Holy Spirit convict you of more than

just the *fruit* of your sin—the symptoms. Let Him take you to the *root* of your sin. God is after the idolatry of our hearts. He is a jealous and holy God. He will not share His glory or our affection with anyone or anything else! Worshiping what our passivity does for us, worshiping what our domination does for us is what shatters His glory in us! That kind of self-worship gives us a false sense of control and power to handle life without ever needing to let God in to plow up the back forty acres of our souls.

Let the plowshares go deep. When we choose to keep God, His Word and others out of the underbelly of our souls, then the locker rooms of our hearts get filled with sin that enslaves us.

Men, there's one more mile to walk. Come with me into the stench of the locker room of the dark desires of our souls. A soul without substance, the right substance, grows empty on function alone. Being emptied of relational substance and bankrupt of function sets us up as men for a stronghold that is impossible to break in our own strength.

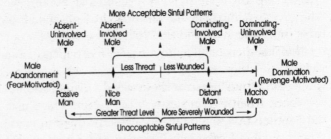

Selfish Male Patterns of Relating

Endnote

[1] Dave Barry, "Road Warrior," *Miami Herald* (January, 1991). Copyright 1991 by the author. Used by permission.

CHAPTER 13

From Dependency to Stronghold

J ason sat in my office one day and let me into the hidden places of his soul. It was his way of inviting me to enter into his pilgrimage.

"I have got a hole inside me. I'm not sure where it is, but I know it's there. It's deep, wide and ugly; and if God doesn't heal it or fill it, I'm soon going to be all hole and no me.

"My father helped dig the hole. He was a minister who loved his congregation and God more than his family. He wasn't there for me. Because of his relationship with his father, he probably would not have known how to love me even if he had been there.

"My mother helped dig the hole. She was alone while my father ministered, and I was cast in the role of her best friend, always there to keep her company.

"Once when I traveled with my father, I was sexually abused by the oldest son of the family with whom I was staying. I tried to tell my parents, but I was five and I didn't have the words. I dug the hole deeper. I was bad and dirty because I allowed the older boy to touch me.

"In early grade school, I knew I was different. I fol-

159

lowed boys I admired home just to find out where they lived. At school I couldn't look at them enough. If only, I thought, if only I could be like them in every way, maybe . . . just maybe I would be whole instead of a hole.

"I wanted to know why God didn't save me from my differentness and my desires. I tried to explain myself to our pastor; and he said I had to resist sin or else. My hole got bigger.

"As a young man, the hole was filled with pain. I knew I was a wretched sinner, and I had to keep up the appearance of being a nice guy. I landscaped my deep hole: tall trees, low shrubs, even a weeping willow. Everyone loves weeping willows.

"I kept on visiting forest preserves where I could meet others who were in pain. I would feel temporarily refreshed after these sexual encounters, but I knew they were wrong. When I tried to stop, the pain would become too much.

"One day a forest ranger caught me and called the police. I was arrested for indecent exposure. I knew I had to deal with my problem; I had a compulsive habit."

Jason's locker room! Your locker room! My locker room! What does the locker room of our soul look like, this place where the dark side of our desires lurk? Paul describes it in his letter to the Ephesians:

> So I tell you this, and insist on it in the Lord, that you must no longer live as the Gentiles do, in the futility of their thinking. They are darkened in their understanding and separated from the life of God because of the ignorance that is in them due to the hardening of their hearts.

Having lost all sensitivity, they have given themselves over to sensuality so as to indulge in every kind of impurity, with a continual lust for more. . . .

But among you there must not be even a hint of sexual immorality, or of any kind of impurity, or of greed, because these are improper for God's holy people. Nor should there be obscenity, foolish talk or coarse joking, which are out of place, but rather thanksgiving. For of this you can be sure: No immoral, impure or greedy person—such a man is an idolater—has any inheritance in the kingdom of Christ and of God. . . .

Have nothing to do with the fruitless deeds of darkness, but rather expose them. For it is shameful even to mention what the disobedient do in secret. But everything exposed by the light becomes visible, for it is light that makes everything visible. This is why it is said: "Wake up, O sleeper, rise from the dead, and Christ will shine on you." (Ephesians 4:17-19; 5:3-5, 11-14)

Jesus also did not mince words in describing our hearts.

"You have heard that it was said, 'Do not commit adultery.' But I tell you that anyone who looks at a woman lustfully has already committed adultery with her in his heart. If your right eye causes you to sin, gouge it out and throw it away. It is better for you to lose one part of your body than for your whole body to be thrown into hell. . . ."

Peter said, "Explain the parable to us. "

"Are you still so dull?" Jesus asked them. "Don't you see that whatever enters the mouth goes into the stomach and then out of the body? But the things that come out of the mouth come from the heart, and these make a man 'unclean.' For out of the heart come evil thoughts, murder, adultery, sexual immorality, theft, false testimony, slander. These are what make a man 'unclean'; but eating with unwashed hands does not make him 'unclean.' " (Matthew 5:27-29; 15:15-20)

Memories of the Locker Room

Most of us men remember the locker room as we grew up, that room where we as young males changed our clothes and lost our innocence. It was here where we were "educated" by jock-talk and ill-conceived peer wisdom. It was in this sacred male domain where the dark desires and realities of hearts, described by Paul and Jesus, were bandied about. The big difference between the two, however, is that our talk played in the darkness, while God's Word calls us to the light.

As we grew older the talk from the dark side continued to come out in the locker rooms of life. As men living in a pagan culture, our locker rooms are influenced and in most cases corrupted by the stench of sin. Like Jason, we have a hole in our soul—a hole of unwholeness, of incompleteness, because of our own sin, the sin committed against us and unhealed wounds that fester with pain. From the broken posture of our souls, we try to enter into our groaning, cursed world, and into the mysteries of unfairness and injustice with a pattern of relating that leaves us emotionally and morally bankrupt.

When we are quiet for a little while, we can feel it unmistakably. There is that missing substance of something that makes us driven men. We are vulnerable to the deepest yearnings of our souls being salved, silenced, satisfied by the idols of our hearts.

We always need more of whatever it is that temporarily quiets the inner turmoil of the soul. Some of us men resort to scratching this itch of incompleteness with addictive chemicals—alcohol, prescriptive or street drugs. Soon, there is the overpowering demand for another hit, another jolt, another fix. One of the greatest enemies of healthy manhood is substance abuse.

Jack said to me, "I only started to drink a little to help me unwind. I used to know where to stop. It's become more difficult of late."

Tim expressed real shame as he said, "I just eat! I love to eat! But look at me! The doctor warned me severely today that being so overweight made me heart-attack material! But I'm not sure I can stop even with the threat of a heart attack!"

Then there is Carl. "My wife keeps telling me I spend too much time working," he said. "She says I'm never around for her or the children. And when I am home, she complains I'm still not really there. So what does she want me to do . . . quit and go on welfare?" Carl was getting intense as he talked!

Many of us, like Carl, have resorted to the so-called "noble" approach for filling the emptiness inside us. We can stave off the inner gnawing of our itch for impact just by keeping busy—working, working, working. If we pause long enough, like on a statutory holiday, and begin to feel it again, we quickly get back to work driving the empty feeling of unwholeness underground once more. Workaholism is dominion gone wild; it's domination, without boundaries; it's man's frantic attempt to prove his wholeness.

Sex—An Enemy of Manhood

Another great enemy of manhood is sex. Male sexuality does not decorate our souls, but deeply defines who we are. Is it any wonder that we use this strongest component of our sexuality to define our experience of maleness?

Sex needs no help to be attractive, but the media has given it anyway. Their relentless indoctrination has led all levels of society to believe that life without sex is empty and passionless, that the male intimacy-itch can be dealt a deathblow by just enjoying more sex.

Ed became successful at marketing for his company that sells kitchen cupboards across North America. He said to me, "You know, Steve, after a long day of flying, business and interacting with other people, I feel emptied out. I'm not feeling down; it's more like I have given it my all and that feels good and right. But then, more recently, when I get back to my hotel room, I have started turning on the "skin" channel. Before I know it, I'm not feeling drained, in fact, I feel alive! It's not just sexually alive; that's there, but it's deeper I think. I'm in touch with something that's powerful and I want more! Can you help me understand what's going on? I'm too ashamed to tell my fiancée. I usually feel pretty guilty when I finally turn it off."

Jake was one man I had the highest regard for. He was older, in his mid-fifties. To me he qualified as a man after the heart of God. The other day he asked, "Can we talk?" So we met that evening. His story went like this.

"Steve, I love the Lord! These past several months have been a time of intimacy with Him like I have never known. Have I ever enjoyed my times of worshiping Him! But something else is going on. I'm embarrassed to even mention it; but if I don't I'm afraid it's going to get the best of me. It feels like the closer I get to God, the greater my sexual desires become. I always thought they would lessen when I enjoyed the Lord as much as I am these days. It's like there is another part of me that runs on a track that is parallel to this intimacy track with God. Is there such a thing? The temptation to masturbate overwhelmed me. And being a widower, it's been hard since Elsie passed away. I'm really confused! How in the world has God made us?"

In Search of a Remedy

Some of us men just itch, unconscious of what it is all about. We scratch ourselves with whatever works, mindless of the numbing state into which our male souls have drifted. Unable to control the sexual temptations, we struggle all alone as men!

Others of us follow the illusion that there is an actual remedy—richer relating with loved ones, more money, bigger barns, developing male friendships, better preaching, deeper faith, change of government, better physical conditioning, a more supportive wife, cooperative children, or even if I could just find a girlfriend or wife!

Let me shock some of you. There is no answer! The sin nature is never fully eradicated. The Lord Jesus invites us as men to let Him come and grab us around the shoulder and hold on to us while we scratch with meaningful worship and service to Him and love for others. Learning to enjoy and know Him in our struggles deepens our sense of aliveness as men.

Some men have been dramatically rescued from sexual perversions, alcohol dependency, workaholism, the love of money, and they won't feel the itch of emptiness or the desire to scratch with these same solutions again for a long time. You may even believe you have been permanently cured from the thirst of your soul. But eventually the inner hunger comes back. Heaven on earth does not yet exist. Living outside the garden will always give way to insatiable desires and cravings. The cure, Scripture says, comes later. For now we must put up with our groaning—waiting, hoping! Paul gave us this perspective:

> Now we know that if the earthly tent we live in is destroyed, we have a building from God, an eternal house in heaven, not built by human hands. Meanwhile we groan, longing to be clothed with our heavenly dwelling, because when we are clothed, we will not be found naked. For while we are in this tent, we groan and are burdened, because we do not wish to be unclothed but to be clothed with our heavenly dwelling, so that what is mortal may be swallowed up by life. Now it is God who has made us for this very purpose and has given us the Spirit as a deposit, guaranteeing what is to come. (2 Corinthians 5:1-5)

Most men I meet are under the illusion that we are powerful enough to diminish the reality of living outside the garden. They mistakenly believe that we can even topple God's memorial to our sin, the curse. We feign allegiance to needing God; but often in our hearts we are functional atheists. We refuse to accept that there is no complete solution to what drives us. This insatiable longing will not go away. So we remain chained and often imprisoned to our idolatrous dark desires, bound in a stronghold that keeps crushing our male spirit. Men like Jason, Jack, Tim, Carl, Ed, and yes, even Jake and you and I are in a battle against three very real enemies.

Men, we need to know our enemy. Reconnaissance is the first step in preparing to do an ongoing, lifelong battle with our adversaries. And like these down-to-earth fellow pilgrims whose stories I have shared, we need outside help to engage in the war and win the battles.

The Bible teaches us that we have three principal enemies: the world, the flesh and the devil. I invite you to enter into a deeper understanding of these adversaries so the strongholds that keep us imprisoned can be broken.

The Battle with the World

In the New Testament, the word *world* is used to sometimes simply refer to the earth as opposed to heaven. In this sense there is nothing bad about the world. But the New Testament also uses *world* in a moral sense. We see this where Jesus tells the Father that the world hates those who choose to follow Him: "I have given them your word and the world has hated them, for they are not of the world any more than I am of the world" (John 17:14).

> Do not love the world or anything in the world. If anyone loves the world, the love of the

Father is not in him. For everything in the world—the cravings of sinful man, the lust of his eyes and the boasting of what he has and does—comes not from the Father but from the world. The world and its desires pass away, but the man who does the will of God lives forever. (1 John 2:15-17)

Richard Lovelace suggests a very helpful definition of the *world*: "The *world* can be defined as corporate flesh—a pattern of drives and actions resulting from the interrelationship of all the individual flesh in the bulk of humanity."[1]

The world is that sphere or people group that has no affection for the things of God. In this sense, it exists in conflict with and fights against the kingdom of God.

Our culture, as an example, has fought this war from an entirely secular, pagan (godless) worldview. It is failing precisely because of its idolatrous worship of things and function. Since World War II, the West has followed the typical pattern that breeds idolatry. This was evident even of God's people, Israel: "When I fed them, they were satisfied; when they were satisfied, they became proud; then they forgot me" (Hosea 13:6).

We men enjoy our freedom to function without having to move into relationships or worry about finding meaning in our prosperity. But after years of worshiping self by focusing on things and function, our delight begins to diminish. We find ourselves empty, lonely and bored with our freedom. So we up the tempo to get more and do more.

This puzzles us because this sense of discontentment is still pervasive. Our pagan culture has become good at one thing—reducing life to the worship of things and function. What catches us off guard is the rampant epidemic of emptiness and boredom. We are relationally lonely. A pagan culture produces the curse of death over the deepest reality of the universe—truth lived out in relationship. God designed us to glorify Him and work for the good of others. Paganism leads us in the opposite direction. It is like a stinking, dying corpse writhing in drivenness.

This sickness of getting more and doing more seems so right, so meaningful. Sin does work! We should not be naive about it. The serpent offered Adam and Eve a source of life that he promised would sustain and empower them outside the garden. And it does. But Solomon, who ended up loving things, worshiping function and using people, said: "There is a way that seems right to a man, but in the end it leads to death" (Proverbs 16:25). How much better to have the testimony of Moses: "He chose to be mistreated along with the people of God rather than to enjoy the pleasures of sin for a short time" (Hebrews 11:25).

Our paganism, which worships the god of consumerism, promotes borrowing and spending rather than saving and sacrificial giving; self-indulgence rather than self-discipline; self-improvement and self-esteem rather than self-sacrifice, duty and following after righteousness. Our cultural brand of reality is focused on entertaining ourselves to the point of relational and spiritual death. The inflaming of our dark desires through the media has elevated and enthroned personal pleasure as the hedonistic goddess of our age.

This pagan world system is an enemy of God and therefore an enemy of man. It is one of the three powerful chains that creates a cultural context for the

strongholds that destroy our manliness. These chains
bind us to our sin, our pain and our patterns of relating
that choke out relational intimacy with others and with
God. As men we must remember and embrace the
truth in relationship. We are not ourselves by ourselves. We do not become more manly and human behind the wheel of our four-wheel drives and grown-up
toys, or when capped and degreed with one more academic plaudit. Our paganism is wiping out our manly
will to engage in relationships. When that infects who
we are, then we live as crippled males, hell-bent to live
as success objects and idolatrous functioners.

The Battle with the Flesh

Richard Lovelace also gives a helpful definition of
the concept of our *flesh*: "Flesh in its negative sense re-
fers to the whole human personality—body, soul,
mind, and emotions—as they function *apart* from the
presence or control of the Holy Spirit."[2]

The fierce struggle between the flesh and the spirit
in the Bible is not to be understood as some kind of
war we fight between our body and soul. Rather, what
the New Testament means is the war between the
power of our enslaving, sinful desires in our natural,
fallen humanity against the influence of God the Holy
Spirit in our lives. "For the sinful nature desires what
is contrary to the Spirit, and the Spirit what is contrary to the sinful nature. They are in conflict with
each other, so that you do not do what you want"
(Galatians 5:17).

For the man who chooses to accept Christ's pardon
and forgiveness, the ongoing struggle between his sinful and redeemed desires lies in the fact that his flesh
was not totally annihilated within him at conversion.

His flesh has received a deathblow that breaks its power, but it is still very much alive and struggling. Our flesh is not something superficial in our lives; it goes to the very core of our personality. Its influence is powerful; the war against it is both real and continual.

By scriptural definition, our *flesh* is not our physical being. It does, however, encompass physical acts—sexual perversions, drunkenness, workaholism, for example—as well as innumerable negative behaviors and attitudes: lying, envy, hatred, worship of money (greed) and other attitudes and dispositions of our inner male being.

The man who chooses to believe, who loves God and others, who is controlled no longer by his flesh but by the Spirit of God, is spiritual in this sense. "You, however, are controlled not by the sinful nature but by the Spirit, if the Spirit of God lives in you" (Romans 8:9). But at the same time, like Paul, the believing man commits sin and is still "carnal," meaning fleshly or unspirited. Paul testifies of himself, "I am unspiritual, sold as a slave to sin" (7:14).

Even the man who is saved is still partially enslaved to sin. As a result, he must struggle for freedom through the power of the Spirit. It is true that some Christians are by definition "carnal" or "unspiritual." However, it is not true that others have advanced to such a deep spiritual level that they are forever freed from this warfare. Every Christian is potentially both spiritual and carnal (unspiritual) and must, regardless of his experience, fight the good fight.

Men, no matter how passionately we love God and others, this fight against the flesh—our sinful dark desires—still rages on within our souls. We only deceive ourselves if we think we don't have to worry about the sinful, dark passions of our fallen nature that incline us to evil. "If we claim to be without sin, we deceive ourselves and the truth is not in us" (1 John 1:8).

Fighting the enemy of our flesh, our sinful dark desires, involves starving them by feeding and nurturing only our redeemed, spiritual desires.

> Dear friends, I urge you, as aliens and strangers in the world, to abstain from sinful desires, which war against your soul. Live such good lives among the pagans that, though they accuse you of doing wrong, they may see your good deeds and glorify God on the day he visits us. (1 Peter 2:11-12)

We have an enemy with whom we are in combat. The language of the Bible is passionate with zeal, vitality, strength and urgency. Conflict is not a passive term; war suggests casualties and death. We need to war against our sinful, enslaving dark desires of the flesh. Jason, Jack, Tim, Carl, Ed and Jake are in a war within themselves and surrounded by the enemy of God, the world system of pagan secularism and hedonism. Their "flesh" is another chain that becomes a part of a stronghold that binds their manliness.

There is one more enemy even more insidious than the first two. Failure to recognize this enemy often leaves us reeling, and we become casualties of our strongholds.

The Battle with Satan

The first man, Adam, faced the serpent energized by Satan and was left impotent and passive. By choice, he did nothing about what mattered most to God and to his wife, Eve. Since that time, satanic attacks of deception, accusation and destruction have often left us like they left Adam—bewildered, passive and impotent.

Many men will readily admit that they believe there is a God, or more personally even, testify they believe in God. Far fewer will admit to believing in the devil, despite the presence of so much horror and wickedness in the world. In spite of personal struggles that rob men of the virility of their soul, despite every effort to live without groaning, too many men live like Adam. Either men reject the idea of a powerful, personal spirit-being named Satan, or they become blind to the deceiving, destructive ways that his demonic emissaries carry out his purposes. It tells us that there is indeed a realm of fallen angels, and their chief is Satan, the devil. The Bible clearly supports such teaching.

The first disclosure we have about Satan is that he is clever, far more clever than Adam and Eve, who were living in the perfect environment of Eden. He is able to deceive us by presenting himself as an "angel of light":

> But I am afraid that just as Eve was deceived by the serpent's cunning, your minds may somehow be led astray from your sincere and pure devotion to Christ. . . . [F]or Satan himself masquerades as an angel of light. (2 Corinthians 11:3, 14)
> . . . in order that Satan might not outwit us. For we are not unaware of his schemes. (2:11)

Scripture also presents Satan as a formidable foe who destroys and devours. For the most part, it is Christ who is compared to a mighty lion in the Bible, the Lion of the tribe of Judah. However, Satan is also compared to a lion. He is not as powerful as the Lion of the tribe of Judah, but he is much stronger than you and I. "Be self-controlled and alert. Your enemy the devil prowls around like a roaring lion looking for someone to devour" (1 Peter 5:8).

Satan is also presented as the accuser. In the books of Job, Zechariah and Revelation, we see Satan standing before God accusing believers of their sins.

> "Does Job fear God for nothing?" Satan replied. "Have you not put a hedge around him and his household and everything he has? . . . But stretch out your hand and strike everything he has, and he will surely curse you to your face." (Job 1:9, 11)

> Then he showed me Joshua the high priest standing before the angel of the LORD, and Satan standing at his right side to accuse him. (Zechariah 3:1)

> Then I heard a loud voice in heaven say:
> "Now have come the salvation and the power
>   and the kingdom of our God,
>   and the authority of his Christ.
> For the accuser of our brothers,
>   who accuses them before our God day
>   and night,
>   has been hurled down."
>   (Revelation 12:10)

Satan also accuses us to ourselves. He makes us think our lives are ruined, that we have passed the point of forgiveness. He accuses us to other people too, so that those who serve and seek to live for Christ will always be lied about in the Church and in the world.

Paul says that we are called to make war against Satan. He tells us that though we must contend against the world system which is pagan, and our flesh, our battle goes beyond these, for it is also "against the spiritual forces of evil in the heavenly realms."

> Finally, be strong in the Lord and in his mighty power. Put on the full armor of God so that you can take your stand against the devil's schemes. For our struggle is not against flesh and blood, but against the rulers, against the authorities, against the powers of this dark world and against the spiritual forces of evil in the heavenly realms. (Ephesians 6:10-12)

In this chapter we have met Job, a wealthy but ordinary family man; Joshua, a man in leadership; and numerous common sinners who have become sons of the Father in heaven. Each of them was in conflict, being accused day and night before God. If you can identify with any of these men, then you too are in spiritual warfare.

Endnotes

[1] Richard Lovelace, *Renewal as a Way of Life* (Downers Grove, IL: InterVarsity Press, 1985), 86.

[2] Ibid., 72.

CHAPTER 14

Understanding Our Enslavement

The battle to be men after the heart of God rages on in a world that hates both God and us. It's fought in the locker room of our own souls where our dark desires war against the Spirit. It continues on in the heavenlies where Satan accuses us before God the Father. He attacks us by trying to deceive our thinking and perspective, and he does his powerful best to devour and destroy us in the context of our relationships. Paul explained this very well:

> For though we live in the world, we do not wage war as the world does. The weapons we fight with are not the weapons of the world. On the contrary, they have divine power to demolish strongholds. We demolish arguments and every pretension that sets itself up against the knowledge of God, and we take captive every thought to make it obedient to Christ. (2 Corinthians 10:3-5)

The Stronghold of Functional Dependency
When we as men are reduced to mere function and

robbed of the joy of relational intimacy with others and with our heavenly Father, there is no basis for true joy. The celebration of manhood is for those who live in sexual purity and treat women with honor, who husband their wives with the sacrificial cherishing of Jesus, who father their children with hearts turned toward them, who invest in ongoing friendship with other men. Strongholds keep us from this God-intended blessing.

Our strongholds can be understood in part from Paul's teaching. A stronghold is a warped philosophy that is perpetrated by Satan and a corrupt culture. A warped philosophy is a worldview that is made up of arguments—a set of beliefs—that are erected to stand against the truth of God. When we apply this to our personal worldview, it encompasses our "motivational lie and vow" which we have chosen to live by. The pattern of how we sinfully relate to others is the fruit of this kind of vow and lie that has set itself up against the knowledge of God.

I personally have been faced by God, who has exposed my motivational lie which operates as the protection for my naked soul. My lying core conviction is that "I'm not important to God and to others. Therefore, I don't really matter to anyone including God." My motivational vow grows out of this lie—"I will make myself important so that I will matter to God and to others."

A stronghold is also a warped philosophy which is made up of pretensions that set themselves up against the truth of God. A pretension is a false motive put forth to hide or excuse what is real in us as men. On a personal level, these are the emotion-laden, impulsive, sinful desires of our hearts. When fueled by our own personal pain and energized by Satan's deceiving, accusing or destructive involvement, there are generated within us motivational excuses for our way of relating and entering into life.

For me, believing I don't matter and having to live life proving I do meant that I was justified in excusing whatever self-centered way of relating and living that served to protect or enhance my sense of manhood. I have a deep dread of disappointing or failing anyone, which translates into saying "yes" to everyone's expectations and being as nice a man as I can be. When this way of relating won't work, because I can't please everyone all of the time, I choose to not live with personal integrity. That's a euphemistic way of saying I lie. I excuse my lying by not facing the sin of my own heart, by not entering into the impact of death and pain that it has on my wife, children and other friends. I will never forget a friend who confronted me with this rebuke: "You know, Steve, your niceness nauseates me!"

God has recently used my wife to expose my lack of personal integrity at this deep level. She said, "I feel deeply hurt by your betrayal of me and our level of relational intimacy. You purposefully choose to not tell me what you really feel or think or what I should know about something that involves us. That hurts me deeply."

So I find this law at work: When I want to do good, evil is right there with me. For in my inner being I delight in God's law; but I see another law at work in the members of my body, waging war against the law of my mind and making me a prisoner of the law of sin at work

within my members. What a wretched man I
am! Who will rescue me from this body of
death? (Romans 7:21-24)

I can relate with Paul's dilemma! He has described
to perfection my stronghold of sin and its fallout.

Paul tells us that these strongholds—our three enemies; the world system, our fleshly, sinful enslaving
desires and Satan—do not respond to world-tools, but
only to powerful God-tools. You and I as men cannot
smash or demolish these arguments—our motivational
lies, vows, pretensions, excuses—unless we take them
captive and become obedient to Christ. This means
clearing the ground, the locker room of our souls, of
every obstruction of loose thoughts, dark desires and
impulses by being willing to fit into the structure of
life shaped by Christ. Who can help us men with this
horrendous task?

Thanks be to God—through Jesus Christ our
Lord!
So then, I myself in my mind am a slave to
God's law, but in the sinful nature a slave to the
law of sin.
Therefore, there is now no condemnation for
those who are in Christ Jesus, because through
Christ Jesus the law of the Spirit of life set me
free from the law of sin and death. (7:25-8:2)

Praise God! We have a new life in Christ, Paul says;
a new structure to fit into, shaped by the Son of God
to replace the strongholds of dependence. The world
system has labeled these strongholds with terms such
as dysfunctional, codependent, compulsive or ad-

dicted. Once they diagnose these symptoms, victims are left with only world-tools to try to break their debilitating grip on the human body and soul. Devoid of God-tools, the human body and soul are still dependent upon a deeper bondage—justified selfishness.

The world system, our sinful nature of dark desires and the influence of Satan entice us as males to choose a variety of fruit from the tree of knowledge of what brings us pleasure and gets rid of our pain. We can become enslaved to any variety of "fruit" that looks good and is desirable for gaining wisdom, anything that makes life outside the garden work without God.

Understanding the Nature and Power of Enslavement

> See that no one is sexually immoral, or is godless like Esau, who for a single meal sold his inheritance rights as the oldest son. Afterward, as you know, when he wanted to inherit this blessing, he was rejected. He could bring about no change of mind, though he sought the blessing with tears. (Hebrews 12:16-17)

Every sinful fruit we become enslaved to, whether it is work-function, ministry-function, substance abuse (of food, drugs, alcohol), pleasure-function, sexual perversion, violence-function, power-function or religiosity, is an effort on our part to somehow escape the design and call of God on our lives. This design and call is to rule, subdue, multiply and fill the earth in a balanced way as His image-bearers.

Every enticing fruit we become dependent upon tends to demolish our male soul passion. We become drained of the energy needed to impact our world, to grow in our love for a personal heavenly Father and to enter into relationship with image-bearing people around us, especially our spouses and children.

Enslavement to the fruits of sin, in particular to function which is investing all of the male soul passion we have into ruling and subduing the earth, is our attempt to escape the rich beauty of loving God and being loved by Him. It is our way of hiding from knowing and being intimately known by others.

Our understanding of slavery to our strongholds has been superficial and incomplete. As men we have often treated our struggles of ongoing enslavement as attempts to escape the pain and groaning resulting from the curse, which was God's judgment on the earth and on us as males. The groaning inside our souls is something we despise. But what we hate even more is the dread of soul nakedness before a holy God and significant others. So we become enslaved by believing that we can silence this awful, inner combination of male groaning and dread.

Most of us, when relating out of a pattern of functional abandonment or domination, become terrified of the empty loneliness and pain that ensue. We, like Adam, believe that we must hide and fill this hole. This is partially true. But it is more true to say that any enslavement, such as alcohol, workaholism or obsessive sex, is an escape. Knowingly or not, we use them to avoid relationship with God. We are afraid of the passion of intimacy with the Father.

When we try to control or stop our enslavement to someone or something, we generally try legalistic self-discipline to diminish our desires and passions. This in fact energizes them and makes the form of enslavement even less controllable. Every attempt to keep away from pornography or food, for example, serves only to intensify the passions within us.

Passionate about the Wrong Fruit

As men who believe in Jesus, our core struggle is not that we are always too passionate about wrong fruit from the tree of the knowledge of good and evil, but that we are not passionate enough about fruit from the tree of life. We desire too little when we lust for sexual perversion, money or power. We gorge ourselves on scraps, when God is offering us a feast. The problem with enslaving strongholds is that they are not designed to satisfy us; they are a feeble attempt to destroy much deeper longings within us.

Passion is what energizes our souls to have eternal impact for God's glory and the good of others. A soul thirst is what fuels our deep desires for intimacy in knowing God and being known by Him. When we destroy our passion for relationship with God, we then lose our hunger for intimacy with people. So we settle for function as the substance of our souls suffocates on the stressful treadmill of business.

Passions are the essence of our maleness. In our humanity we have two deep longings—impact and intimacy. We long for a sense of meaning that gives purpose and direction to our lives. Being a good dentist, carpenter, tradesman or farmer is a legitimate earthly longing. Wanting to experience human love, touch, trust, the joy of someone knowing our name, to be blessed by our fathers with identity, affection and affirmation is a normal human passion or longing.

But these passionate longings go much deeper than that within us. God has designed us to experience an eternal impact that transcends our earthly mortality.

Our impact of ruling and subduing the earth was originally designed for us as image-bearing men to be done
for the glory, delight and pleasure of our Creator-God.
Secondary male fullness, for our own glory, delight
and pleasure, was never to topple and replace this transcendent God-directed passion and purpose. To do so
leads to the idolatrous worship of the male self and to
enslaving, sinful patterns of relating and seemingly un-
breakable habits of the body and soul.

God designed us as male image-bearers to thirst for
an intimate experience of transcendent, divine love. He
made us to know a Father-heart love that blesses our
identity with a sense of sonship, that embraces our
eternal souls with divine affection and eternally affirms
us as good, faithful men.

The world system, our own sinful desires and the
ongoing influence of Satan marginalize and eventually
obliterate these two transcendent human longings that
so passionately cry out for expression and fulfillment.
In the midst of this battle, we are so poorly trained by
example and teaching that we are unable to infuse intimacy into our lives with any kind of balanced priority.

Almost anything accessible to us that brings a feeling of closeness—whether genitals or gourmet good-
ies—will do for intimacy. And almost anything that
comes along that creates a sense of intrigue, mystery
or adventure—from the miraculous in religion to
skydiving, river rafting or bungee-jumping—will do
for a transcendent touch of satisfying our longings. It
is no wonder a pagan culture under the influence of
the god of this world taunts us with pseudo-intima-
cies that dehumanize, like pornography and the ob-
jectifying of the female body and sex. Or experiences
of pseudo-transcendence that trivialize, like a weekly

diet of sports heros to worship, or business gurus to follow, or some far-out religious ideals to embrace.

Our longings for impact that involve our maleness but transcend our humanity are designed as a gift from God and are meant to serve as a pointer to Him. Likewise, our deep, passionate yearning for intimacy with another human—to become one flesh with a woman in a monogamous lifelong marriage, to hold our children in our hearts, to have brothers who we would die for in friendship—is a gift from our God. But it is a gift to awaken a deeper desire, a more intense hunger and thirst for closeness with Him.

Rechanneling Our Passions

When we as men reduce these two passions with the makeshift solutions of the world, then every enslaving habit that we become dependent upon will only destroy these two passions and longings of our heart. Every enslaving habit that consumes us has a passion that can never be lost, destroyed or changed; but that can be rechanneled into a deeper experience of the eternal and transcendent. Our only hope to break our enslavement to controlling habits—power, money, work, ministry, sports, substance abuse, masturbation, sexual fantasizing and lust, sexual perversions of pornography, homosexuality, fornication or voyeurism, to name a few—is in choosing to deepen these passions, not to diminish them.

For example, James and Roxanne had been married for two years. They were on the verge of separation. Listen to the confession of James' heart.

"My obsession with pornography and compulsive masturbation was like an addiction. I could no longer control it. I didn't have the willpower or the willingness to control it. I remember lunch hours when I would walk through a mall and feel the desire like a force drawing me, a desire that demanded to be filled. I was trying to meet a need and didn't know what it was.

"The more I got involved, the more I wanted it. It didn't stop by getting a little. It led me to strip joints and X-rated movies because after a while porn magazines got boring and I needed something closer to reality. Now I'm into computer-porn where you can hook up and network with everything beyond your own creative imagination. What is powerful about this kind of pornography is you can create it out of your own imagination as well.

"I also struggled with some voyeurism, peeping-Tom experiences, exhibitionism, where I took off all my clothes in a secluded area of a park. I was never caught, yet it was a deep urge that was part of me and my whole addiction.

"I recognize more clearly now, with help, that part of my use of pornography and the other sexual struggles was my way of searching for closeness that I never found in my family. There was a lot of tension in my family especially between my father and me. He abused me both physically and verbally. In real life I was afraid to get too close to people. In pornography I found a kind of intimacy that wasn't threatening. I also believe Satan was involved and using this to destroy my life.

"Pornography and masturbation were not only a sensual-sexual matter with me as a married man. If it were, my struggle would have ended when I married Roxanne. But very soon after I married I realized it was still a problem and wasn't going away even though my sexual needs were being met. This surprised me, as I had thought sexual expression in marriage would solve it for me. In a sense it was the reverse. Instead of an active marital sex life eliminating my need for pornography and masturbation, those things ended up damaging our sexual and relational intimacy. I was leaving Roxanne out of it to find my own pleasure. I was treating her sexual gift to me as garbage. I felt guilty and hated myself for it. But not enough to stop.

"I used porn as an escape from my problems as well. I felt less drawn to a magazine rack, or computer networking when I was feeling better about myself and life. But when I felt down, lonely, like no one cared about me or that my work really didn't make much difference to anyone, I was more susceptible to masturbating and using pornography as a temporary escape. I just couldn't get close to my wife or anyone else. The locker room door of my soul was closed tightly to relationships and open wide to pornography."

Hank's Story

Listen to Hank's story of what went on in the locker room of his soul.

"Throughout my life I struggled with control over my sexual imagination. Erotic images from videos, movies and magazines since I was ten have left me addicted to the need to have my fantasies fulfilled. I came to the belief, albeit a wrong belief, that it was acceptable for me to have these fantasies and live them out within our marriage. But it ended up putting pressure on Jill to become like my fantasy lover. Now she tells me she never enjoys sex. In fact, she says she hates sex because I always pressure her to do things that she does not agree with and then she hates herself and me for it.

"This led me to further sexual frustration, less sex and more fantasy. So things only got worse between us. I began seeking self-gratification through masturbation. And so the vicious cycle of unfulfilling sex with Jill, leading to fantasy, leading to masturbation resulted in further personal and relational distancing and a build up of resentment and hurt between us.

"My retreating as a man into my own world of sexual lust and fantasy resulted in a loss of intimacy with God and with my wife. In my relational isolation, I began to work harder and longer and watch far more TV when I was at home."

For both James and Hank, sexual lust and fantasizing was a selfish, self-centered, perverted use of a God-created sexual eros desire for expression with one's own wife in a God-ordained sexual union. Uncontrolled and misdirected, this sexual desire ended up enslaving them to masturbation, pornography and prostituting their wives in their marriages as a way of meeting their deeper longings for intimacy with God and others.

Slavery Is Idolatry

Like James or Hank, we know that our sinful human nature is always inclined to move toward false worship. All forms of enslavement that keep us in bondage involve, first and foremost, idolatry. This kind of enslavement can be the worship of any person, object or idea that enables us to quiet, deaden or kill our inconsolable longings for heaven and intimacy with our God or people. It also serves to shift the blame for our not being able to have eternal impact for His glory and the good of others. When James and Hank bow down to their false gods of sexual fantasy, masturbation, pornography and using their wives as sexual objects, they engage in a form of self-worship that absorbs their male souls. Men, any false god will eventually consume our souls in perverted worship of fruit from the tree of knowledge of good and evil. When this happens, fruit from the tree of life becomes tasteless and unattractive.

What does your idol look like? Let me suggest a few that are common, not just to Hank or James. For some of you your idol is symbolized by your desk calendar. Some of you bow down to it many times a day. Others of you bow down to your four-wheel drive tractor which symbolizes your ever-increasing need to expand your farming acreage, not for survival but to prove your manhood through how much ruling and subduing of the earth you can actually do. You are not doing it for God's glory, but like the rich man Jesus addressed, you are satiating your soul needs by building bigger barns.

For some of you, your computer has become your idol. You worship the creative power it has given you. You find life in creating even good things like manuscripts, course material, music and drafting specs. You use it to fill your emptiness, to escape the reality of the tension between you and your son or deaden the ever-lurking sadness of little or no closeness between you and your father.

You know what? It works! False worship does work for a season, but remember, it always leads to death. You are not getting any closer to your son or to your father. In fact, you feel less guilt, sorrow and loneliness. Hours at your new idol marginalize your thirst for intimacy and deaden your passion and desire for worship of your God.

Our forms of idolatry are many. Our willingness to face them and call them what God calls them is difficult, humiliating, humbling. It is hard to open up the locker room of our souls and let our idols be seen for what they really are. When we as men continue to let our enslaving, sinful desires rule us; when we continue to leave our soul wounds and deep pain go unattended; when we continue to handle our threatened male sexuality by abandoning or dominating others in the way we relate, then the three enemies of our maleness overpower us and seduce us into false worship that becomes a stronghold, an idol.

The Bible and Idolatry

God had some strong words to say to his people about idolatry.

> All who make idols are nothing,
>   and the things they treasure are worthless. . . .
> The blacksmith takes a tool
>   and works with it in the coals;
> he shapes an idol with hammers,
>   he forges it with the might of his arm.
> He gets hungry and loses his strength;
>   he drinks no water and grows faint.
> The carpenter measures with a line
>   and makes an outline with a marker;
> he roughs it out with chisels
>   and marks it with compasses.

He shapes it in the form of man,
of man in all his glory,
that it may dwell in a shrine.
(Isaiah 44:9, 12-13)

This sounds like what we do with sports figures as we install them in our various halls of fame. It is also what we do with our shrines of pornography, temples of sports arenas and stadiums, and our city business towers of power as they reach ever upward to exalt man and not God.

He cut down cedars,
or perhaps took a cypress or oak.
He let it grow among the trees of the forest,
or planted a pine, and the rain made it grow.
It is man's fuel for burning;
some of it he takes and warms himself
he kindles a fire and bakes bread"
(44:14-15).

Here God through Isaiah is describing how men are taking dominion by ruling and subduing nature for good purposes. But they don't stop there.

But he also fashions a god and worships it;
he makes an idol and bows down to it.
Half of the wood he burns in the fire;
over it he prepares his meal,
he roasts his meat and eats his fill.
He also warms himself and says,
"Ah! I am warm; I see the fire."
From the rest he makes a god, his idol;
he bows down to it and worships.

He prays to it and says,
  "Save me; you are my god."
    (44:15-17)

Are we really any different, men, in the idols we
fashion? We use our pocket calendars to govern our
schedules, help us be efficient, good stewards of our
time and resources. And we say, "You are good, God; I
am fed, clothed, sheltered and have added blessings of
life. Thank you, Amen!" And then we too slip into becoming workaholics, ministry-aholics who sacrifice our
spiritual and relational birthright with our God, our
spouse, our children on the altar of the other half of
our desk calendar. We subtly move from being a rec-
reational golfer, done for enjoyment and legitimate exercise, to leaving our wives and children golf widows
and orphans.

They know nothing, they understand nothing;
  their eyes are plastered over so they
    cannot see,
  and their minds closed so they cannot
    understand.
No one stops to think,
  no one has the knowledge or understanding
    to say,
"Half of it I used for fuel;
  I even baked bread over its coals,
  I roasted meat and I ate.
Shall I make a detestable thing from what is left?
  Shall I bow down to a block of wood?"
He feeds on ashes, a deluded heart misleads
    him;
  he cannot save himself, or say,

"Is not this thing in my right hand a lie?"
(44:18-20)

Our hope, men, is not in our own idols, often crafted
to serve two purposes, one for which God intended,
the other for our own self-worship. When good things
like sex, money, work, food, even certain drugs, ma-
chinery, academic and professional training are used to
"save us," then is not that which is in our right hand
now a lie? We too become an idol worshiper from
making a detestable thing of what is left of the good
thing God has given us.

Men Who Light Their Own Fires

Isaiah offers us hope and warning, both for our
good.

"Let him who walks in the dark,
    who has no light,
trust in the name of the LORD
    and rely on his God.
But now, all you who light fires
    and provide yourselves with flaming torches,
go, walk in the light of your fires
    and of the torches you have set ablaze.
This is what you shall receive from my hand:
    You will lie down in torment." (50:10-11)

When Adam and the men we have talked about in
this chapter faced someone or some situation they had
no idea how to enter into as men, to rule and subdue in
a God-ordained way, they chose not to rely on their
God. Instead of fearing the Lord and obeying His
Word, they chose to light their own fires and provide

their own torches. God says this will set about a blaze that will torment. We have a choice, men. We are not just victimized males who are in need of some light thrown from the torch of some self-help group. We are moral, image-bearing males who are in desperate need of radical soul surgery. We are men who need to repent of our sinful patterns. We are drinking from broken, idolatrous cisterns that hold no living water.

If living water is ever going to entice us to drink in order to touch the deep thirsts of our souls, then we will need to stop lighting our own fires when we face darkness. This calls for a greater fear of our God than we have for the darkness and our nakedness of soul.

Fearing God begins with a necessary but painful pilgrimage—repentance. A.W. Tozer said, "God will take nine steps toward us, but He will not take the tenth. He will *incline* us to repent, but He cannot do our repenting for us."[1]

Going back will often involve pain. When God circumcises hearts, as Pascal's words express so vividly, pain is the "loving and legitimate violence" necessary to procure our freedom from our enslaving strongholds of idolatry.

Jason's Story Continued

Let's finish Jason's story about his pilgrimage out of his stronghold of dependency.

"I started attending Sexual Addicts Anonymous in a Bible-believing church. It was attended by men who had grown up naming Jesus as Lord. I found a group of Christian men there whom I could talk with, pray with and depend on. They too had struggles. It was a safe place to be. I was also surrounded by men who were gifted intercessors. They made me accountable. They gave me permission to call them day or night. And when I traveled, I could and did call them night after night.

"I faced my stronghold of sexual addiction that had so dominated me in the context of my three enemies— the world, my flesh and the devil! I prayed in Jesus' name against my motivational lie and vow. I took ownership of my abandonment-passive pattern of relating. Being with these men confronted my fear of relational closeness head on!

"All of this helped to make my problem of sexual addiction worse! I couldn't stand it! All the other men were getting it together with God and I was actually slipping further into myself and the gaping hole inside of me. God was not supposed to work this way. I thought He had promised to make it all better. What He really promised, of course, was that He would be with me. Big help that was! I wanted Him to fix me. The least He could do was fill up my horrible pit and right now! I had prayed, hadn't I? He was the Mighty One, wasn't He?

"I felt helpless, deserted and alone. Something was wrong here. I hadn't prayed right, long enough, hard enough. I must not have done my devotions correctly or early enough.

"The only thing that comforted me was the Psalms. David was a man in pain, and I was too. He cried as I did, 'God, where are You?' There was no hope. I tried everything I could think of. All the landscaping around my hole was uprooted and I stood staring down into a crater. 'God, where are You?' I cried. This time instead of a hollow echo over my hole, I thought I heard Him answer, 'Wait.'

"No! I couldn't do that. I had to get healing. I had books to read on healing the sex addict. I had spiritual people to pray over me and pray me out of this. But Jesus said, 'Wait. I will be your Good Shepherd, but you need to wait and let Me shepherd you out. I want you to learn to hear My voice while you wait. It will not be easy, but My rod and staff will be there to guide and discipline you.' Wait! Learn to listen to the Shepherd's voice! I had exhausted all the alternatives. I had to do what God asked.

"I'm gaining more confidence in hearing my Shepherd's voice. At times I feel His love wash over me as He leads me beside the still waters to restore my soul. I have started a journal about my pilgrimage with my Good Shepherd. I began to write what I think He is saying. Then I write my responses. I say, 'Thank you, Lord.' He answers, 'You are welcome My son; you are chosen and marked by My love; you are the pride of My life.' Other times I think I will never stop weeping from so deep within this hole. But now He is in there with me, weeping, too.

"Jesus never said He would just zap me and fill my hole, leaving the core of who I was as a man unmarked. He did promise He would never leave me nor forsake me and that nothing, not even this hole would separate me from His love. I'm getting to know Him in my pain and struggle. He really is my Good Shepherd! I'm learning to see Him on the cross. Sometimes when I ask Him for forgiveness for failing, I see Him taking my debt of sin upon Himself as I hold it up to Him. I sometimes sense Him severing my sinful connections of unhealthy relationships from the past. I see those bonds disappearing into the nail prints in His hands and feet.

" 'Lord Jesus, as my Shepherd, thank You for pursuing me as Your lost sheep. For using the pain in my life to teach me to stand before Your cross, to wait and listen for Your voice. Thank You for my tears and Yours which are just beginning to fill my crater. I'm still vulnerable and scared. Thank You for Your shed blood that keeps on forgiving me from all my unrighteousness. You are the Master Landscaper who can take my internal disaster of sin and pain and create a beautiful garden for Your use in Your time.' "

Jason's glory has been shattered. But God is committed to restoring His glory in Jason, in James, in Hank, in you and in me because "He has made everything beautiful in its time. He has also set eternity in the hearts of men; yet they cannot fathom what God has done from beginning to end" (Ecclesiastes 3:11).

A Call to Battle

We need to go to war with our pagan world system, with ourselves and with the enemy of our souls, Satan. We are in a battle! Playing with the world system, ignoring the locker room of our souls and dismissing the god of this world will not lead us into a passionate celebration of our redeemed manhood. We have reason to celebrate, men. God our Father is waiting to clothe us with new, clean garments of manhood. Remember, God's initiative toward Adam and his wife: "The LORD God made garments of skin for Adam and his wife and clothed them" (Genesis 3:21).

Remember also, our battle with Satan is real and he keeps trying to rot our garments with his accusations! This is one of his primary ways of paralyzing our celebration of manhood. Let's be alert, on our guard and stand against the accuser of our male souls. Understanding him and his way of working is our way out of the darkness of our struggles to be men after the heart of God, but first we have to deal with our sin, idolatry, pain and wrong patterns of relating.

Often the devil tempts us to commit sin, private or public, and then he tries to destroy us with accusations. Satan works with our guilty consciences to make us feel hopeless, coaxing us to light our own torches. Because every Christian man sins every day, our problem of sin and guilt may be a continual blockage to celebrating our restored glory. Satan condemns us by telling us we are not worthy to be restored, not worthy to even be a follower of Christ.

The Spirit of God who is holy also ministers to us by bringing us face to face with our guilt and shame, but He does it as conviction, not condemnation. Satan wants us to wallow in despair and the stench of death; the Spirit wants us to humble ourselves as men and confess our sin and experience repentance which leads to further celebration of our restored manhood.

Remember Satan's accusing work in Zechariah 3. This chapter is part of the "night visions" of Zechariah. In one of these visions, the prophet sees the current high priest, Joshua, standing before the Lord on behalf of the people. "Then he showed me Joshua the high priest standing before the angel of the LORD, and Satan standing at his right side to accuse him" (3:1).

What was Satan's accusation? We see it in verse 3: "Now Joshua was dressed in filthy clothes as he stood before the angel." The filth represented not only Joshua's own sins but also the sins of the whole nation, which he represented. Normally the high priest wore "garments of glory and beauty" (see Exodus 28:2, KJV), which symbolized his position as God's anointed and glorified leader. Now, however, Joshua was dressed in degrading garb. His filthy garments represented the defilement of his life and of his office. Satan was pointing these out to the Lord, and Joshua was standing ashamed. But, "The LORD said to Satan, 'The LORD rebuke you, Satan! The LORD, who has chosen Jerusalem, rebuke you!' " (3:2).

God refused to hear Satan's accusations, and instead stripped Joshua of his filthy garments and dressed him with beautiful clothes.

> The angel said to those who were standing before him, "Take off his filthy clothes."
> Then he said to Joshua, "See, I have taken away your sin, and I will put rich garments on you."
> Then I said, "Put a clean turban on his head." So they put a clean turban on his head and clothed him, while the angel of the LORD stood by. (3:4-5)

In this lies our hope to enter the battle, men! This is how God deals with all we are as men, as written about in these pages. God refuses to hear Satan's accusations because He deals with us only through His Son, the Lord Jesus Christ. Likewise, we must learn to rebuke Satan's accusations, knowing we are clothed in Christ's garments of righteousness. His breastplate of righteousness covers our hearts.

Move into battle! Do not allow Satan to burden you with your sin. Rather, keep on confessing your sins because we are confident that God keeps on forgiving and cleansing us from all our unrighteousness—our enslaving, sinful desires, our sinful patterns of relating, the fruit that we keep eating that fuels our idolatry. Do not wallow in guilt and shame that God the Son has taken and lifted from your male soul. His forgiveness is real and final. Remember, Satan condemns; the Holy Spirit convicts! His conviction awakens your thirst for intimacy with God the Father and with others.

That is why I have sought to sound the battle cry and like Gideon, to call out men who would believe in their God; men who would defeat their enemies not with conventional weapons, but with God-tools; men who will venture into the darkness of their souls without lighting their own fires. Men who will venture into the night of other men's souls and do battle, their vessels of a broken and contrite heart exposing the light of the fear of God. Those who would respond to this "call of Gideon" would have their identities as men affirmed, as though proclaiming with a sudden, certain shout, "The sword of the LORD and of [your name]! (Judges 7:18, 20).

It's time to stop minimizing the impact of Adam's sin on us. The legacy of his enslaving, sinful desires is ours. The curse of God upon the earth is a memorial to us males for our sin. Work will be filled with pain and sweat. Weeds, thorns and thistles will daily remind us that we are broken and sinful. Our woundedness and resulting pain are additional memorials to the consequences of sin on our soul as it contorts our sexual identity. Instead of fearing God we light our own fires in our darkness by abandoning or dominating in the way we sinfully relate and enter our world and the lives of others. Our own torches of fire torment us with enslaving strongholds of dependency leaving us as shattered men in desperate need of Someone to restore our glory. With the words of Paul, I invite you to move into celebrating your restored glory of redeemed manhood:

> For what the law was powerless to do in that it was weakened by the sinful nature, God did by sending his own Son in the likeness of sinful man to be a sin offering. And so he condemned sin in sinful man, in order that the righteous requirements of the law might be fully met in us, who do not live according to the sinful nature but according to the Spirit.
>
> Those who live according to the sinful nature have their minds set on what that nature desires; but those who live in accordance with the Spirit have their minds set on what the Spirit desires. The mind of sinful man is death, but the mind controlled by the Spirit is life and peace; the sinful mind is hostile to God. It does not submit to God's law, nor can it do so. Those controlled by the sinful nature cannot please God.
>
> You, however, are controlled not by the sinful nature but by the Spirit, if the Spirit of God lives in you. And if anyone does not have the Spirit of Christ, he does not belong to Christ. But if Christ is in you, your body is dead because of sin, yet your spirit is alive because of righteousness. And if the Spirit of him who raised Jesus from the dead is living in you, he who raised Christ from the dead will also give life to your mortal bodies through his Spirit, who lives in you.
>
> Therefore, brothers, we have an obligation— but it is not to the sinful nature, to live according to it. For if you live according to the sinful na-

ture, you will die; but if by the Spirit you put to death the misdeeds of the body, you will live, because those who are led by the Spirit of God are sons of God. For you did not receive a spirit that makes you a slave again to fear, but you received the Spirit of sonship. And by him we cry, "*Abba*, Father." The Spirit himself testifies with our spirit that we are God's children. Now if we are children, then we are heirs—heirs of God and co-heirs with Christ, if indeed we share in his sufferings in order that we may also share in his glory. (Romans 8:3-17)

Men, welcome! Enter into the celebration of your restored glory!

Endnote

[1] A.W. Tozer, *That Incredible Christian* (Camp Hill, PA: Christian Publications, 1964), 30.

PART II

RESTORED
GLORY

CHAPTER 15

Sonship that Cries Out

Bob poured his heart out to me in my office. "I tried to fill the emptiness in my soul from age eight to forty-five with sensual pleasures, especially sex and sports. I sinned much in many ways sexually, including immorality with many women. Eight years ago when I came in brokenness and repentance to God, another man put his arms around me and brought the Father-heart of God to me.

"As he held me in his arms and incarnated the Father God's love and forgiveness to me, I sobbed—his words became the words of my heavenly Father, his arms like the Father's arms. I felt deep in my inmost being the ministry of the Father to me as His son. I actually began to enter into a moment of the Father's rejoicing over me. I sensed His delight in the depth of my heart. In that moment of unspeakable ecstasy and pleasure, the Father said to me, 'No woman can ever do this for you!' My whole life was changed as a result of that encounter with God."

What Bob experienced was not unique. The Lord desires to have a deeply intimate relationship with all of us. He simply awaits our willingness to respond. In the Old Testament David is shown to be such a man. He was more than a great musician, warrior and king. He was a man after God's own heart. Samuel said, "[T]he LORD has sought out a man after his own heart" (1 Samuel 13:14).

David was also a passionate man who loved God deeply, who expressed his fears, doubts, anger, conflicts and sins. His love, trust, adoration and submission to his sovereign King is a model of intimacy between a man and his heavenly Father. Even though David had his bouts with sinful passions, he worshiped and adored God most of his life. The very purpose and direction of his heart was to get to know God the Father more intimately. David lived with an integrity and uprightness that flowed from the relationship he had with his God.

God's promises to David were based on His relationship with him as His son and extended to his children.

> [A]nd I will establish his kingdom. He is the one who will build a house for my Name, and I will establish the throne of his kingdom forever. I will be his father, and he will be my son. When he does wrong, I will punish him with the rod of men, with floggings inflicted by men. But my love will never be taken away from him. . . . (2 Samuel 7:12-15)

From deep within the inmost place of our male soul comes the cry of sonship with our beloved Abba Father. No deeper passion and soul thirst exists for us than the yearning to be intimately connected as sons with our Father God. Both Bob and David experienced this and so can we! The Holy Spirit testifies and confirms that our identity is rooted in our relationship as sons with God the Father.

Every New Testament occurrence of the term "Abba Father" is found in the context where Jesus is in great pain, crisis or struggle. This is not a cry outside of pain, but from within it. In Romans 8, where it is also used, it is in the context of our suffering as God's children. Furthermore, to say "Daddy" is not the mark of immaturity, as with a little boy, but rather a denotation of sonship. Saying "Abba" is a mark of maturity in love and relationship. We need to keep in mind that this is a cry of the Spirit. It is not self-induced or forced. It is not mere rhetoric or magic.

> [Jesus came] to redeem those under law, that we might receive the full rights of sons. Because you are sons, God sent the Spirit of his Son into our hearts, the Spirit who calls out, "*Abba*, Father." So you are no longer a slave, but a son; and since you are a son, God has made you also an heir. (Galatians 4:5-7)

Biblical metaphors such as panting after God (Psalm 42:1), thirsting for the living God (Psalm 63:1), our heart yearning within to see Him (Job 19:27), tasting God (Psalm 34:8), drinking living water (John 7:37), eating bread from heaven (John 6:32-35) make it clear what moving into the Father-heart of God as sons is all about. It is not merely an academic act of acquiring knowledge about God, but a sensual and personal experience that is relationally intimate to the core.

Entering into the Father's heart as sons involves using our personal struggles to find God, to know

Him intimately. This intimacy can only be developed in the context of the realities of life. Knowing God is not restricted to Sunday morning. He longs to reveal Himself to us as we confront our sinful desires, our ongoing battle with the curse, our pain from our woundedness and our never-ending war with idolatry and Satan.

The Supernatural Rhythms of Soul Repentance

The process of entering as sons into the Father-heart of God often takes place in the supernatural rhythms of both spontaneous and planned times of repentance in our lives. Soul repentance begins with an upward look into the face of our Father God. Entering into His Father-heart is knowing what is in His heart. Paul writes: "Or do you show contempt for the riches of his kindness, tolerance and patience, not realizing that God's kindness leads you toward repentance?" (Romans 2:4).

Regardless of the father-son relationship you had or have here on earth, there is a deeper thirst in your soul for restoration and oneness that cries out, "Abba! Papa! Father!" Our earthly fathers were imperfect at best. Regardless of their efforts, they were unable to give us a true taste of the kindness, tolerance and patience of the Father God's heart. This lack leaves us afraid and unwilling to take off our fig leaves, to come out from behind our forms of hiding and stand naked of soul before a holy God and the eyes of another.

Walter Wangerin Jr., in his short story "For, Behold, the Day Cometh," tells us of a young son who caught a glimpse of the Father-heart of God through his own earthly father.

In those days my father was the President of Concordia Junior College, Edmonton, Alberta, Canada. One must capitalize that title throughout. It's a very high office that my father held. It holds an oaken authority, grim and altogether absolute.

Now, Concordia Junior College had a hockey rink in which, during the winter, students played hockey, but which, during the spring and summer, they abandoned. In the spring we faculty children claimed it for ourselves. We played football in its oval interior. The walls of the rink were a perfect border for privacy and for a football game; and the red and blue powder-paint had melted into the grass, leaving midfield and endfield stripes for play. The only problem with the field was stones. Winter always drove stones to the surface; and since we considered ourselves fleetest in stocking feet, we bruised ourselves on the occasional stone in the grass. But that was a problem soon mended. Every time we stepped on a stone, we tossed it over the wall, till none were left, and the summer was kind to the soles of our feet.

Now, I had my own method for tossing stones. I winged them toward one of the floodlights aloft on their poles, high and high above me. Because they were so distant, and I so indifferent a shot, I always missed the light bulbs. Winging and missing were traditional with me.

But there came the auburn afternoon when I winged a stone (and missed, of course), and a thrilling stentorian man's voice called my name.

"Wally!"

My father, the President of the College, had happened to be walking by.

I stiffened, so to be seen, but I said with creditable innocence, "What?"—as though he had merely called, and I was merely answering.

"What are you doing?"

"Nothing."

"Wally!"

"What?"

"What are you doing?"

My father, willy-nilly, makes a juridical presentation of himself. He wore a black suit in those days, with a clerical collar white. His hair was nearly black, his glasses black-rimmed, and he twisted the ends of his eyebrows up, so they reached to his temples like raven's wings. His aspect was symmetrical, louvered and sterner than he knew. Down the slope of those twin eyebrows came the gaze that turned his words to juggernauts. "What are you doing?" he said. How could I not respond?

"Winging," I said, "stones."

"At," he said, "six-thousand-watt light bulbs of great expense."

"But," I said—and I had a righteous defense— "I never hit them."

My father was not persuaded by righteousness or any reason. "Don't!" he said. His raven eyebrows raised their wings. "Don't ever throw stones at light bulbs again." Thus the commandment. My father departed.

But I knew better. I knew the undependability of my arm. My father simply didn't understand the way of the world, or of his son. I *always* missed. And besides: it was a tradition with me.

Therefore, I continued to wing stones at the rink lights.

I suppose it was the last stone of the season. After that stone, there would be clear running on a clear field, all heels unbruised. I picked it up, drew back, and winged it, then stood watching with my jaw wide open.

The instant it left my hand, I knew I had launched, for the first time in my career, the perfect shot. It sailed upward on a precise and beautiful trajectory. I should have been elated. Just below the light bulb (which I saw with dreadful clarity) the stone slowed and bent its path into an easy turn. But it closed the distance. Its zenith was the light bulb, which it barely touched as it passed underneath. That touch was enough, and down with the stone came a rain of the finest glass, twinkling, joyful, and nasty in the sunlight—

Don't ever throw stones again!

My poor heart sank.

My brother and my friends all gaped at me.

Don't you ever—

I thought I saw the cloud of judgment touching down to earth, the wheel of the chariot, the prow of the ship—the black shoe of my juridical father! I thought I saw him striding toward the rink, his raven's wings sweeping the sky with threat. The President of the College, glorious authority, altogether absolute.

But I had my plan, and *bang!* I went straight into hiding. That is, I rounded on my brother and aimed a violent finger at him and thundered,

"Paul, don't you ever tell Dad." Then I pointed at Feller and Randy and Dick and Jimmy Demos:

"Don't none of you ever breathe a word of this. Not ever, hear me? Not ever. Swear!"

They swore.

And so it was that I slipped into my boiler room, never, never to emerge until my father was busied by the multitudes, the masses of problems that all College Presidents must turn to one day and another.

I shut from my father a piece of me—forever.

It worked.

Or, let me be accurate: it worked for a while. He didn't know. He couldn't punish me.

But in time it began to seem that I'd shut more from my father than merely a piece of me; maybe it was the best piece; maybe it was most of me. Maybe, if he didn't know this piece of me, he didn't know me at all. I began to suffer the solitude.

Well, we would sit at the table for supper, and all my brothers and sisters would chat right openly with my father—but I couldn't. Not openly, at any rate. He'd ask some lightsome question, and I would reflect before I answered: what to answer, what not to answer. I would squirm, trying to remember little lies and strategies. He would give me a curious look, and I would know that he wasn't seeing all of me. Something of me was missing. So it felt as though most of me hadn't come to the table at all. My brothers and sisters had it so easy. I had it so hard.

And he used to call me an affectionate nick-
name in those days: "Ah-vee" he'd say, and
chuck me on the shoulder, and maybe want to
hug me. But I knew that I wasn't "Ah-vee" any
more, that I didn't deserve the chuck—and that
he would cease the affection immediately if he
knew what sort of kid I really was. *Don't you
ever!* But I did. *Six thousand watts!* Yes, and I
broke it.

So when he said "Ah-vee," now, and smiled, it
burned in my ear, and it shamed me crimson. I
was growing so old so fast, so distant from my father, and he didn't know. He kept playing the old
games. But "Ah-vee" wasn't here any more. . . .

That evening, my father smiled at me where I
lay on my bed. He said, "Ah-vee," and I burst
into tears. His love scorched me, because it was
a lie.

No, *I* was the lie. I'd fled to my boiler room.
The room grew hotter than I could handle. I
was so lonely, so desolated. I wanted to be "Ah-
vee" again—but how could I be? My father was
involved with the multitudes, the millions and
trillions who presented themselves with honesty
and humility, above ground, openly. They deserved his attentions. His eldest son deserved
just nothing. Therefore, anything his father did
for him intensified the worthlessness of his
heart: *You liar! Look how you insult your father by
making him play the fool!*

My father's love for me made him seem piti-
ful. But oh, what a wrath he would rise to, if he
knew who I was truly! What a straking of the
wind his raven's wings would leap to then!

So therefore I was caught between loneliness and corporal punishment, between the father whose love was a shame, and the father whose authority was Judgment Day. My dad or the President of Concordia Junior College: I had neither one.

Did I say I'd hidden in my boiler room? Well, now it felt more like a torment. Now it was my Hell. And lo: the Jaws of Hell had not reached out to snatch me; rather, I'd simply walked into them. My plan had sent me in precisely the wrong direction, not from the weeping-and-gnashing-of-teeth, but to the solitary heart of it.

"Ah-vee."

"Dad, don't say that!"

"What? Why not?"

"Just—don't."

"Is my son growing up so fast? Is he a man now?"

"Just—don't."

And I burst into tears. I covered my head with my pillow and cried. . . .

So, then I couldn't stand my isolation any longer. So then, by main force and willpower, I determined to come out and to climb the mountain of God and to confront him with the truth. Then he could bundle me to Hell right properly. At least there would be honesty between us, and he would know whom he was sending to Hell. Then let the stars fall down. Let the high and distant Son of man sweep his hand across the sky to blacken the sun, to bloody the moon, to shake the earth, and to make the graves disgorge. At least I'd feel a deserving pain—a righteous pain, if you will—and in that sense would participate in one propriety. My stroke for justice. It seemed no little thing to me any more, even though I'd pay for it with my hide and the scorn of the Deity.

All of which is to say: I decided to go and tell my father what I'd done.

Strangely enough, his Judgment Day seemed easier to me than my own.

I came out of hiding.

Early morning on the next day, I crept from our house to the Administration Building of the College and entered its holiness.

I walked, with an echoing click of my heels, down long halls with high ceilings and dark oak woodwork. This building diminished me. *Authority*, it murmured all around me. *Sanctity, Probity. None of which are you.* My poor butt tingled and talked to me too: *You got us into this,* it said. *But I get the licking.* My butt felt big with anticipation, a heavy load behind me. I was apologetic, even to my butt.

And here was my father's office door. Huge. Oak. Dark. On a crosspiece of wood was affixed the legend: W.M. WANGERIN, PRESIDENT.

I tapped the door down low, little roach-kicks for a knock.

"Come in."

Ah, me! There was life in there.

I turned the knob and nudged the door a little open. And a little farther open. And peeped in.

"Wally! What do you want?"

My father sat behind his desk, facing this door.

A huge oak desk, it seemed to me. Dark wood. In the shape of a coffin.

My father's face was the focal center of the entire room. His black-rimmed glasses were circles of scrutiny, judging me, steady and unwinking, impartial and dire at once. He had brown eyes. He was twisting his left eyebrow between his thumb and forefinger, grooming the wing; for the raven of judgment was about to leap and fly before it stooped.

"Well?" he said, and I inched forward toward the desk.

"I," I said, laying a finger on the edge of oak wood, unable to look at him.

"You?"

"I . . . well—you know those six-thousand-watt light bulbs at the rink?"

"Yes?"

"Well, that's what I want to tell you." I waited, as if wanting *were* the telling.

"Yes?"

"Well. Yes. I broke one."

"Ah," said my father. "Did you climb a pole and bump it accidentally?"

"No."

"Ah. What then? What did you do?"

"I," I said, "threw a stone. . . ."

Slowly, my father arose behind his desk. I didn't look at him. Just as slowly, he rounded the far side and came toward me—black suit, black hair, black spectacles. Judgment cometh. The multitudes are gone. There are two of us after all. Only two.

I was prepared for the spanking. The order of

things would be righted in my punishment. I lowered my head.

But I was altogether unprepared for what my father did. . . . I think I would not have cried if my father had spanked me. But he knelt down at my side, and he took me in his arms, and he hugged me, and then I began to cry, and I couldn't stop crying.

Love killed me. I hadn't expected love. I hadn't expected the most undeserved thing, to be forgiven. That fire of my father's love—it melted me altogether, reduced me to a little mess, to a child again, for sure.

Oh, how pitifully I loved my father then! How God-like his love for me.

And he whispered, "Ah-vee, Ah-vee," and I didn't dispute his name for me; for I was, again, "Ah-vee."

Sonship with our Father God can only happen when we come out from our boiler rooms and face a holy God who longs to display the passion of His heart for us. Repentance is the biblical expression of this process, which we examine in detail in the next chapter.

Endnote

[1] Walter Wangerin, Jr., "For, Behold, the Day Cometh." *The Manager Is Empty Stories in Time* (New York: Harper-Collins, 1989), 164-171.

CHAPTER 16

What It Means to Repent

Jesus tells my favorite story—you can read it in Luke 15:11-24—which shows what the Father's love is truly like. The supernatural rhythms of the process of repentance are clearly lived out for us in this parable of the loving Father and the prodigal son.

The natural rhythms of being an illegitimate son of God are very evident in this story. The sinful enslaving desires of the younger son spill all over his life, impacting his father, older brother and others: " 'Father, give me my share of the estate.' . . . Not long after that, the younger son got together all he had, set off for a distant country and there squandered his wealth in wild living" (Luke 15:12-13).

These sinful desires flow naturally from our hearts before we are sons in God's family. They are also evident when we as sons don't have much expressed need for intimacy with our Father God!

What doesn't flow from our hearts are the beautiful rhythms of supernatural hunger for God. The Father's supernatural passion constantly reaches out to us, but we typically don't respond. Something blocks us from taking that which is offered. How can we feast and eat the Bread of Life and drink the Water of Life? By entering into this supernatural rhythm of repentance like the younger son in this story.

The process of repentance begins in the depths of our soul. It is pictured by the young man running out of money, experiencing famine (economic collapse) and beginning to hurt. He was in need. He was so hungry he would have eaten the pig slop but no one would give him any.

Physical starving hurts! It got his attention. When we try to nourish our own souls, or empower ourselves without God, the slop of our own self-nourishment and self-empowerment will end in soul famine. Soul starvation hurts, too! Soul emptiness comes as a result of relating as a man through abandonment or by domination. It will ultimately end in an intimacy vacuum, an impotency of impact that will create an awareness of deep personal need. Sonship that cries out for the Father's heart needs to begin with the cry of our own neediness and brokenness.

The supernatural rhythm of repentance continues with our coming to our senses. Having no money, experiencing the pain of famine and finding out that no one would give him any corncobs from the pig slop brought this young man to his senses. He began to look at reality and himself from God's point of view. Specifically, he realized that being a farmhand and working for his father at least meant three meals or more each day. It suddenly dawned on him that his physical need could be met by going home and working for his dad.

Sonship begins with a broken, contrite spirit where we realize our unworthiness to be a son of the Father. Un-

worthiness is a different heart posture than worthlessness. Unworthiness is based on the deeper awareness of
the sin of our hearts—our idolatry! Unworthiness recognizes the wounds our sin has inflicted on both others and
the Father-heart of God. When we are able to say, "We
are no longer worthy," our Father-God is able to say, "I
give you My worthiness."

We don't have to change clothes to go home. We
don't have to wash off the stench of pigs. Home is
where we are accepted even though we smell. We can
go home dirty, broken, diseased. The only thing necessary to go home is a heart that says, "I'm no longer
worthy."

Three Levels of Conviction

1. I have been caught.

There are three levels of conviction regarding the sin
of our hearts. The most superficial level is the awareness that I have been caught. I have been found out. I
have been seen as naked of soul. At this level, all I want
to do is hide behind my fig leaves. I am more concerned as a man about my reputation, or of finding
some excuse so I can blame my circumstances, someone else or even God.

This level of response results in our taking no responsibility for the fruit of our sin. At best we come to
God in false repentance, asking, pleading or demanding that God set us free from or forgive us for our sinful behavior. And we wonder why the same sinful
expression of our hearts returns the next day, next
week, next month. And so I get on the repentance
treadmill, making mockery of God's forgiveness.

Why is my repentance and therefore my sense of
sonship so shallow and passionless? Because conviction

and confession of sin go no deeper than being concerned with being found out, being embarrassed or changing the way I feel, without being willing to go to the next level of heart response. Repenting from the fruit of my sin will never lead to radical change.

2. *My sin has impacted others.*

The next level of conviction results in our willingness to observe and own how our sin has hurt and wounded someone else. Our sin brings the reality of relational death to others. When we withhold the substance of our souls from our spouses, they become lonely and feel distanced from us. Does her loneliness grieve your heart as a man? Does the lack of relational oneness with her trouble your soul? When we shut our spirit up and withhold our hearts from our children often their hearts and spirits close up in response and their affection for us suffers. Does the pain in their eyes touch and move you?

Seeing the impact of our sin on others and the death it brings to our sense of relational oneness reflects the deepening supernatural rhythm of repentance. It is not a natural response of our hearts to pay close attention to how our sin affects others.

3. *I have sinned against God.*

In this story, when the son recognized his neediness and came to his senses, he said, "Father, I have sinned . . . against you" (John 15:18). This awareness is a work of the Spirit of the living God.

Moving into sonship with our "Papa Father" means that we will let the Spirit of God, the Word of God and the people of God—our spouses, sons and daughters, other men friends—expose and convict us of how deeply our sin wounds others in our world. To express with a broken and contrite spirit that we are wrong is the critical expression and fruit of a repentant heart. To confess our guilt to our wives, children, fathers, mothers, brothers, sisters and others, that we have sinned against them and that we see the damage we have inflicted on them and our relationship, is further confirmation of true repentance.

Coming to our senses means that at the deepest level of our being we embrace the truth that our sin has grieved the Holy Spirit and brought pain to the heart of our heavenly Father. The son in this story said, "I will . . . go back to my father and say to him: Father, I have sinned against heaven" (Luke 15:18).

The supernatural rhythms of repentance go to the core of our souls where with David we say to God, "[Y]ou desire truth in the inner parts; you teach me wisdom in the inmost place" (Psalm 51:6).

Joseph is a man who lived with a deep sense of his heavenly sonship and this is reflected in his godly response to Potiphar's wife:

". . . My master has withheld nothing from me except you, because you are his wife. How then could I do such a wicked thing and sin against God?" And though she spoke to Joseph day after day, he refused to go to bed with her or even be with her. (Genesis 39:9-10)

When we live with a deepening sense of sonship we will be aware that our sin is ultimately against God. If you do not sense this in your spirit, then I invite you to follow the path of the younger son in Jesus' story. Recognize your need. Your soul is starved and hurting. Come to your senses! Get up and go home to your heavenly Father. He's waiting for you to come, to be His son. Come!

If you have entered into God's family but have very little awareness of the Lord as "Papa! Father!" then I invite you, too, to come back home to the Father by coming to your full senses. The Holy Spirit wants to make that intimate conversation with God a daily experience for you. He wants to move you from your shallow sense of relationship into your true inheritance as a son of the living God.

How do we get up, and keep getting up, and come home to our heavenly Father? By realizing that it is His kindness that invites us. The pivotal place in the process of entering into our sonship—either initially or as a wayward son—is to get up from the pig slop and go home to the Father. Repentance involves the redeemed rhythm of going home to where we belong.

Spontaneous and planned times of getting up and going home can and need to happen as a lifestyle for us as men. Our sin and idolatry of heart are often exposed by the Spirit of God, the Word of God and people in our lives at both unscheduled and scheduled times.

As you read this, if you are sensing the Spirit of God drawing you to the Father-heart of God to become His son, then come by praying this prayer: "Dear Father God, I am a sinner, an orphan. I am not Your son. I confess and agree with You that I am a sinner and I can't save myself. I humbly invite You, Lord Jesus, to enter into my life. I ask You to become my Savior and Lord, to make me Your son. I ask this in Jesus' name. Amen."

Ambushed by the Spirit

Sometimes the Spirit of God ambushes me by exposing my sin when I least expect it. I remember the

morning when I sinfully expressed my anger at my
son as he was leaving to catch the bus to school. I
yelled at him! My daily practice has been to walk my
children to their bus. It's one way I bless them with
my involvement as they go off into their world. I express my love and affection for them and my prayer
backing just as the bus comes to pick them up.

That morning, after I yelled at him, he turned and
walked out the door and left without me. I saw the
pain in his eyes. His countenance reflected a downcast
spirit. I quickly put on my coat and followed fifty feet
behind him. Then he stopped and turned around and
looked at me as if to say, "Are you going to catch up
and walk me to the bus?"

At that moment I felt convicted for the fruit of my
sin—my yelling at him in anger. Then I felt convicted
for the root of my sin, my idolatry, my trying to empower my impotent soul by using verbal and emotional abuse to control my son's behavior. As I saw the
impact of the sin of my heart on his spirit, I also became more aware of how my sin grieved and pained
the Spirit of God.

I quickly caught up and walked with him to the bus.
I was not ready to confess my sin against him then, but
I put my arm around him as I walked. During the day
I pondered what happened and grieved. When he came
home that afternoon, I confessed my sin to him before
the rest of the family at the supper table. (I had yelled
at him in front of the whole family.) I asked him to forgive me. He did! I had come home as a father to the
heart of my son. I had also come home to my heavenly
Father as His son.

Like the son in this story, repentance can be thought
through over a process of time and planned. We can set

a time to meet with a friend, a spouse, a son or daughter. We can knowingly go to a seminar, a church service, special renewal meetings and there experience the redemptive rhythms of repentance at work.

To get up and come home to our Father God reflects that a deep, inner reality in our soul has been stirred and brought to the surface. This happens often over time; it could be hours, days, weeks, months or years. Or it can ambush us in a moment. But our deep soul hunger and thirst for intimacy with God is the consequence that turns our hearts toward home. When we get up and go back to the Father, we experience the most unexpected, undeserving, merciful, grace-filled rhythms of the fruit of repentance. "But while he was still a long way off, his father saw him and was filled with compassion for him; he ran to his son, threw his arms around him and kissed him" (Luke 15:20). When our image of God is biblical and accurate, and not a distortion of our own creation, then we will get up and come home.

The picture Jesus gives us of His heavenly Father is the most important part of this story. None of us will want to come home unless we realize that we have an Abba-Papa-Father who is standing at the gate, watching and waiting for us to come back where we belong. And even when our repentance is just beginning to stir in our hearts over a broken or superficial relationship—or over some other stronghold of idolatry like sexual compulsions, overeating, work- and ministry-aholism, substance abuse—and we are still a long way from getting through our struggle, He will be there waiting, watching and running toward us.

What a powerful truth about the very heart and nature of our Father God. That means we can get up from the pig slop and in the stench of our garments of shame, guilt, soul dread and self-condemnation, we can come home. We have a Father in heaven, men, who will literally run to us. This is the only time in all of holy Scripture that it says that God runs. Here are a few lines from a beautiful song that moves this truth from our minds deep into our hearts:

> With forgiveness in His voice, I felt His love
>   for me again!
> He ran to me! Took me in His arms! Held
>   my head to His chest!
> Said, "My son's come home again!"
> Lifted my face, wiped the tears from my eyes,
> With forgiveness in His voice, He said, "Son!"
> He said, "Son!"
> "My Son, do you know that I still love you?"
> Oh, He ran to me! And God ran![1]

This is no impotent, passive, passionless Father in heaven! We have a Father who runs to us as His sons. He embraces us, kisses us. The emotion of our Father is a passionate, affectionate love that envelopes us, making our sense of sonship what we have always longed for it to be—personal, alive, heartfelt and full of loving compassion.

Closed-up Fathers, Closed-up Sons

Many of us sons have not experienced the affection of our earthly father's heart. Many fathers' muscles of affection have atrophied, died for lack of use. Often this has been passed on from generation to generation, where the sins of the fathers stifle the third and fourth generations' capacity to be like our heavenly Father.

Sonship cries out for the affectionate embrace and kiss of Father God. This is the kind of Father in heaven we have to come home to. Come, men! Enter into your sonship! Home is a far better place than the pigpen!

We don't need to prepare a speech for our heavenly Father. Our speech, our good works may be important to us, but God sees when we get up and turn around to come home. And it's as though He is not listening to our planned speech because He's too busy preparing to celebrate. Too many of us have never been celebrated over and certainly not for our repentance.

This father was filled with delight which led to a wonderful time. Our Father God will re-dress us for the celebration. He will replace our old, smelly clothes of sin, guilt, shame and self-hate with the best robe. The robe stands for honor. You are going to be welcomed back home with honor. Not only will you be re-dressed, you will also be adorned. Instead of being told, "As soon as you are properly dressed you are welcome home," the Father Himself says, "I will dress you from My wardrobe. You must wear My clothes because you are My son."

Next came the family ring which stands for ownership, belonging. When you wear the father's ring, you represent the father which signifies that sonship has been restored.

Sandals were worn by family members. The hired hands went barefoot. This declared that he was a son, not a hired man. As sons we are no longer slaves to sin, but have a son's full inheritance to enjoy.

After the son was clothed, the father had the banquet prepared with one of his choice calves. God the Father has a theology of celebration unlike most earthly fathers. His heart is so filled with delight that nothing less than a celebration will do! "Music and dancing" and the best of food were not too much to express the Father's joy.

When was the last time—or has there ever been a time?—that you have been celebrated over, that your sonship has been affirmed? We need to celebrate our sonship, to be blessed in a ceremony that confirms our deepest yearning to belong and be cherished, to cry out, "Papa! Father!"

God did not condone what the prodigal did. Jesus called his lifestyle foolish and morally deficient. But equally foolish and wicked was the heart attitude and lifestyle of the elder brother. Both sons were prodigal. One wasted his father's inheritance and was miserable; the other stayed home, kept all the family rules and was miserable. The father had to go out to them both. In this story Jesus is saying that simply keeping the rules does not give a man the deep enjoyment or status of sonship.

The elder brother had problems with his father rewarding irresponsibility. However, neither son fully understood mercy. One was trapped by riotous, selfish living; the other by religiosity. God is bigger than both and longs for both to enter into sonship with Him.

The father said to his elder son, "Son, you don't understand. You are with me all the time, and everything that is mine is yours. No, you never got a calf because the whole herd is yours!"

God is a Father who longs to give good gifts to His sons. Not only to the prodigal, but to the self-righteous brother. Keeping the rules and trying to be religious does not make us less sinful than the man who squanders all he has on selfish, riotous living. Both sons needed salvation and an invitation to enter into sonship. All God asks of us is a broken and contrite heart where we acknowledge our neediness, come to our senses, get up and show a willingness to come home. He takes care of the rest.

The Blessing of Sonship

The most passionate demonstration of sonship is modeled for us by God the Father with His Son, the Lord Jesus. At two of the most significant times in Jesus' life God the Father blessed Him.

The first occasion was when Jesus was baptized by John the Baptist. As He came up out of the water two important events took place: "At that moment heaven was opened, and he saw the Spirit of God descending like a dove and lighting on him. And a voice from heaven said, 'This is my Son, whom I love; with him I am well pleased' " (Matthew 3:16-17).

In preparation to face a strong spiritual battle with Satan—and here Jesus models for us how Adam should have resisted and rebuked the devil in his deception of Eve—Jesus fasted forty days and forty nights. And then He confronted Satan with the truth of Scripture: " 'Man does not live on bread alone, but on every word that comes from the mouth of God.' . . . 'Do not put the Lord your God to the test.' . . . 'Worship the Lord your God, and serve him only.' Then the devil left him, and angels came and attended him" (4:4, 7, 10-11).

This is how God designed us as sons to initiate entering into spiritual battle—resisting and rebuking the devil with courageous strength from above. Like Jesus, the second Adam, we too need to be filled with the Holy Spirit; we need to be blessed by God the Father.

The second time Jesus, the Son, was blessed by His heavenly Father was on the mountain of transfiguration. In preparation for His upcoming Gethsemane struggle—His sorrow over carrying the sins of the world, suffering on the cross and being separated from God—His Father in heaven spoke clearly these words of blessing: "This is my Son, whom I love; with him I am well pleased. Listen to him!" (Matthew 17:5).

If the Son of Man, the Lord Jesus, was blessed by His heavenly Father in preparation for spiritual battle, then we too as sons need to be blessed with this confirmation and affirmation of our sonship. Only God can strengthen us for ministry and for the deep pain and sorrow of life.

Across this continent many men have knelt and received the blessing of sonship. We make this a part of every men's course and weekend seminar. An invitation is given to those who want to become sons of the Most High God or who want to affirm their sonship. As each one kneels, an older man lays one hand on his head and raises the other to God the Father and speaks into his spirit the blessing.

Many of us as men have never been blessed by our earthly fathers in any kind of formal or informal way. Because of this lack, we often question ourselves in the deepest parts of our male soul. This doubt and questioning leaves us with serious struggles with our manhood, with our relationships with our fathers, sons, daughters, wives, or with the opposite sex, and with our heavenly Father. This ceremony of speaking the same truth into our spirits that the Father God did at two critical times with His Son deals directly with what we cry out for.

The blessing of sonship has three specific parts to it: the blessing of identity, the blessing of affection and the blessing of affirmation. These parts are indicated by the use of italics and are not meant to be read or spoken as part of the blessing. Here it is:

God the Father said to His Son and He says to you as a man, "(Your Name), You are My son." *(The blessing of identity)*

Whether your earthly father ever has, or ever will say from his heart that he is delighted to have you as his son, you have a heavenly Father who celebrates over you by confirming your identity. He says to you, "You are My son! Your identity is secure and certain!" *(The blessing of affection)*

Whether your earthly father has ever or will ever celebrate over you as his son by expressing the affection of his heart by telling you that he loves you, and by embracing and kissing you, you have a Papa-Father in heaven who longs to give you the blessing of His affection. Receive it as a man and as His son. *(The blessing of affirmation)*

Whether or not you ever felt held in the heart of your earthly father as his son, your heavenly Father is proud of you as His son. And He is saying to you now, "As My son, whom I have marked with My love, you are the focus of all My delight. I am proud of the direction of your heart. You want to come home. Come home, My son! Receive My blessing. It is part of your inheritance. Let's celebrate!"

What more does a son want from his father? We long for a sense of security that comes from our identity as his son. We hunger for his warmth and affection to seal his love for us. And we thirst for his affirmation. There is no one else that we as sons so deeply want to know is proud of us and delights in us. If this is true of our relationship with our earthly father, then our longing, hunger and thirst for the same realities to mark our inheritance and relationship with our Father God goes eternally deeper in our souls.

A sixty-year-old man, who has pastored for over thirty years, came up to me after praying this blessing of sonship into several of the men in the church and said, "Will you pray this blessing of sonship into me?" So he knelt in front of 115 men and I had the privilege of praying this blessing of sonship over him. When he got up, tears were running down his cheeks and his eyes were sparkling with the delight of his heavenly Father's blessing and his deepened experience of sonship. Then he hugged me and whispered in my ear, "Thank you. It's never too late in life to deepen your relationship with God!"

I have prayed this blessing into many men and the majority get up off their knees with tears flowing because all their lives they have wanted their earthly fathers' blessing and never received it. Now the floodgates open as their souls' deepest longings are being touched in this ceremony that ritualizes and celebrates their sonship. Truly, the Holy Spirit is bearing witness to their spirit that indeed they are sons of their heavenly Father. And their spirits are finally able to cry out, "Abba-Papa-Father."

Our heavenly Father is waiting, watching, running, embracing, kissing and celebrating. Why hesitate to enter into the joys of your sonship? Why miss out on the Father God's delight in us? Come home, men! Come home where you belong.

> The LORD your God is with you,
>   he is mighty to save.
> He will take great delight in you,
>   he will quiet you with his love,
>   he will rejoice over you with singing.
>   (Zephaniah 3:17)

Endnote

1 Benny Hester. "When God Ran," from the album *Personal Best*. Copyright 1985 by Word Music (A division of Word Entertainment, Inc.). All rights reserved. Used by permission.

CHAPTER 17

Redeemed Desires That Bring Life

As we go deeper into the Father-heart of God, we find that our sinful tendencies are being disrupted and replaced by our redeemed desires that have come alive through salvation and sonship in Jesus Christ. Our sinful desires run deep. They will enslave us until we develop a growing sense of confidence in the Father's passion to delight in and bless us as sons.

Our redeemed desires are waiting to be encouraged, called forth and released by the Spirit of God, the Word of God and the people of God.

> And do not grieve the Holy Spirit of God, with whom you were sealed for the day of redemption. . . .
>
> And I pray that you, being rooted and established in love, may have power, together with all the saints, to grasp how wide and long and high and deep is the love of Christ, and to know this love that surpasses knowledge—that you may be filled to the measure of all the fullness of God. (Ephesians 4:30; 3:17-19)

We all become aware as we grow older that our sinful desires are very fleeting, sensually arousing and superficially satisfying. But as our sonship deepens in intimacy with our heavenly Father we joyfully discover that our redeemed desires are more deeply stirring and eternally fulfilling. We focus more and more on seeking first His kingdom and righteousness, finding that His rewards are more satisfying. The redeemed desires within us are released as we enter into our sonship with our heavenly Father. They become the transmitters of our deepest passion to worship, serve and love God with all our hearts, mind, soul and strength.

Redeemed Desire One

Just as there were sinful desires, so there are redeemed counterparts. The first redeemed desire has to do with choices and moral integrity: I am free to choose to initiate entering with gentle strength into life and relationships with moral integrity. Note the contrast between this redeemed desire and Sinful Desire One: I must choose to hide who I really am behind whatever fig leaves I can create.

David as a man after the heart of God lived with integrity. He wrote: "May integrity and uprightness protect me, because my hope is in you" (Psalm 25:21); "In my integrity you uphold me and set me in your presence forever" (41:12).

He demonstrated this redeemed desire to live with moral integrity by refusing to kill King Saul, even though the king was attempting to kill him. David was very aware that he stood accountable to God: "But the LORD forbid that I should lay a hand on the LORD's anointed" (1 Samuel 26:11).

After Nathan confronted David with his sin of adultery and murder, David owned his transgression. He did not try to hide or blame shift like Adam. In this, David is once again living with moral integrity in a very self-exposing situation before both Nathan and God. "Then Nathan said to David, 'You are the man!' . . . Then David said to Nathan, 'I have sinned against the LORD' " (2 Samuel 12:7, 13).

Job was another man who was highly committed to expressing this redeemed desire to live with moral integrity before God, others and himself.

> His wife said to him, "Are you still holding on to your integrity? Curse God and die!"
>
> He replied, "You are talking like a foolish woman. [The Hebrew word rendered *foolish* denotes moral deficiency.] Shall we accept good from God and not trouble?"
>
> In all this, Job did not sin in what he said. (Job 2:9-10)

By contrast, Adam acted without integrity when Eve was being deceived by the serpent. And when she gave him some of the fruit from the tree of the knowledge of good and evil, he again acted in a morally deficient manner—he listened to his wife and ate from the tree. He should have followed Job's approach in dealing with the temptation given to him by his wife. When she told him to curse God and die, he confronted the very nature of her temptation by pointing out the immorality of choosing such thoughts and behavior. He didn't call her foolish. He simply said, "You are talking like a morally deficient woman."

In so doing, Job models how a man is to enter with gentle strength into a woman's life where the temptation to distrust God's goodness is the bottom-line issue and agenda. He then demonstrates how to spill the redeemed substance of his integrity into her and the situation. In this way, spiritual life and light can be created and/or maintained to counter Satan's efforts to bring about death.

They also said this about the second Adam, Jesus: "Teacher, we know you are a man of integrity. You aren't swayed by men, because you pay no attention to who they are; but you teach the way of God in accordance with the truth" (Mark 12:14).

Sonship with our Father God through Jesus Christ results in our hungering to live with moral integrity. Such living releases us from having to hide behind our fig leaves; it frees us to live like David, Job and Christ, completely committed to doing the will of the Father.

Non-authentic males hide behind fig leaves. Authentic males are free to celebrate their manhood by living with moral integrity with God, others and themselves regardless of the personal cost.

Jim's wife, Anne, came to him one night after he had been down-in-the-mouth with discouragement for about a week and a half. "Jim," she said. "I know you are not doing well. Would you like to tell me what's troubling you?"

At this point, he had to make a choice as to whether or not to open up to her, which was an issue of moral integrity. His other choice was to hide this struggle by either lying, only telling her part of the truth or by just becoming quiet. Jim chose to open up.

He said, "I'm not sure where to begin or if you'll understand my heart, but this is what's going on inside me in the best way I know how to say it. About two weeks ago my boss came to me and asked if we could talk. He began giving me feedback on how I was doing in my job. He said some real hard things and some encouraging things, too! But I just can't shake this feeling that at the bottom line I'm a failure. It feels like he found out about the real me and now I'm afraid he is going to lower the boom and get rid of me.

"I just don't know how to handle constructive criticism. No one ever gave me feedback as I grew up. Dad never said anything good and encouraging, or anything negative or bad. He just didn't talk. I really don't know what to do with all these unsettling, bad feelings I have toward myself. My self-confidence seems to have been really shaken! I have worked there twenty-one years!"

Jim's choice to live with moral integrity before Anne, himself and God left him with more hope and help to move in a redeemed direction.

Redeemed Desire Two

The second redeemed desire has to do with defending and protecting life: I am free to choose to initiate entering with gentle strength into my God-designed and assigned creatorial responsibility in order to defend and protect life at personal cost and self-sacrifice. Contrast this with Sinful Desire Two: I will choose to abandon my God-designed and assigned creatorial responsibility by blame shifting to ease the dread in my male soul.

Paul wrote, "Be on your guard; stand firm in the faith; be men of courage; be strong. Do everything in love" (1 Corinthians 16:13-14). Another time he said, "[T]his all-surpassing power is from God and not from us. We are hard pressed on every side, but not crushed; perplexed, but not in despair; persecuted, but not abandoned; struck down, but not destroyed" (2 Corinthians 4:7-9).

Sonship involves choices that lead to being surrounded and battered by troubles, but not demoralized; of being unsure of what to do all the time, but learning to know that God knows what to do; of being personally and spiritually terrified, but knowing God has not left our side; of being put down personally and physically, but never having our spirits broken. This is what it means to live as a redeemed son. Sonship means that what they did to Jesus, they might do to us—trial, torture, mockery, death. What Jesus did among those who treated him this way, He does in us as His sons—He lives!

As sons, who do not blame shift, but enter into ruling, subduing, multiplying and filling the earth to the glory and enjoyment of God and for the good of others, we will find our lives are at personal and physical risk for Him. This makes the life of Jesus all the more evident in us.

Jack, the Defender

Jack went alone. Every Saturday morning from 10 a.m. to 11 a.m. he left the comfort of his home and drove to one of the many adult, X-rated, pornographic stores in his neighborhood.

He remembers well the first time he drove into the parking lot in the part of the city zoned for this store. He was more than nervous; he was afraid and literally shaking physically.

Jack told me that he had never been inside an adults-only store before and only speculated on what he would see. However, he said, "My purpose was to go

in and boldly, in love, confront the owner. I had prepared my message."

Jack said that the Spirit of God had prompted him
to go to this one store which was closest to his neighborhood. He ran it by his elders in his church and they
said they would back him and maybe go with him. He
had hoped for support that first time, but ended up going alone.

Here was his plan. It was simple and straightforward. He walked into the store that Saturday at 10
a.m. and said, "Hello, my name is Jack. I have come to
tell you that every Saturday morning from 10 a.m. to
11 a.m., I will drive into your parking lot and park over
in that front corner and pray that God will bring circumstances to bear on your life and store so that your
business will be shut down."

Jack came faithfully. His intercessory prayer for the
salvation of the owner went forward every Saturday.
His spiritual warfare of resisting Satan and claiming
God's victory over this place of idolatry and sin went
forth from his lips and spirit. He wrestled and took his
stand not just against flesh and blood, but also against
the rulers, against the authorities, against the powers of
this dark world and against the spiritual forces of evil
in the heavenly realms. After an hour of praying in the
Spirit with all kinds of prayers and requests (Ephesians 6:18), he drove home.

No one ever came out and harassed or made fun of
him, but he felt the attacks of the powers of darkness.
He often doubted himself, questioned himself, felt all
alone and terribly stupid sitting there. He would ask
God if He really was listening and if He really could
use His power to close this place. Jack's faith was
tested like never before.

He had felt a burning passion inside of him to defend and protect in some way the dignity of sexuality and the purity of the children and younger and older men in the area. He never knew what the cost to him personally and spiritually would be.

Almost to the day, eight months from the first Saturday that he had walked in, the place closed down. He never knew why. But he did know that God defends and protects the righteous. And as a Christian man, this was his calling as well.

God's Word is clear on this, that the only reason evil flourishes and reigns in our lives, homes, cities and country is because righteousness is not defended and promoted.

Joseph was highly motivated to defend and protect the reputations of God, his master, himself and even Potiphar's wife (see Genesis 39:7-20). This cost him his job and led to a jail sentence. Even more so, it cost him the personal pain of being accused unjustly. Joseph's life is a refreshing example of what a redeemed man's heart is really like under severe temptation and testing.

Fred's Story

Marg had not wanted any children. But Tommy came along. Having a boy was even more frightening for her as a woman and mother because she had grown up as an only child. As Tommy grew, Fred noticed that often his own stomach would knot up in fear, mixed with a defensive, angry response, when Marg would ride her son. She was often all over the boy trying to tame him and get him under her control. Sometimes Fred agreed with Marg that Tommy needed a firm word or some discipline.

Fred wondered though, *If I feel fear and anger inside me when Marg is on Tommy's case, I wonder how Tommy feels as a young nine-year-old male?*

Tommy was becoming more and more distant from his mother. Fred noticed him pulling away. As Fred faced some of his own wrong and sinful, defensive responses to Marg, he slowly began to take more initiative to enter into Tommy's life and into more of the confrontations he had with his mother. He actually found himself defending Tommy and protecting him from some of her angry, controlling outbursts.

Fred found this involvement foreign to his way of handling relationships because the pattern he was used to while he grew up was watching his own dad back off and abandon him to his mother's fury. Fred said, "Dad was so afraid of Mom, he just got real quiet and went into the den and switched on the TV."

Fred knew that he was pretty angry at his own father for not defending his tender, sensitive male spirit while he grew into manhood. But one thing he determined was that this generational sin of relational cowardice and passivity was not going to be passed on to his son. The sins of the fathers to the third and fourth generation would be broken.

Fred repented before the Lord, confessing his selfish commitment to passivity and abandonment. He faced up to how this way of relating, when he felt threatened as a man, was his own way of protecting himself and playing it safe. In this way he never needed to depend on God's resources to be a man and a father.

Fred confessed to Marg the sin of his heart and how his own passiveness had hurt her and their sense of oneness in marriage. He renewed his love for her by committing himself to taking more initiative, to enter with gentle strength into parenting Tommy and in husbanding her.

Then he went to Tommy and confessed his sin of failing to be strong before him and for him. He owned his own sense of inadequacy and the cowardice that flowed out of that dread. He told Tommy he was sorry for not protecting him from the outbursts of anger and harshness from his mother. He asked for his son's forgiveness. He told him, "With God's help, I will be a godly father. I will hold you in my heart by protecting you from unwarranted harshness and anger."

The whole family embarked on a new and redemptive journey that day. It was another stage of Fred's pilgrimage in learning to be a man. And Tommy had a different role model.

Redeemed Desire Three

The third redeemed desire is this: I am free to choose to initiate entering with gentle strength into life and relationship by taking dominion in order to express my maleness so that I provide life and empower others through sacrificial love. Contrast this with Sinful Desire Three: I will choose to dominate in order to prove I am a male with enough of the right substance.

The Bible gives some clear direction for husbands and men.

> For the husband is the head of the wife as Christ is the head of the church, his body, of which he is the Savior. . . .
> Husbands, love your wives, just as Christ

loved the church and gave himself up for her to make her holy, cleansing her by the washing with water through the word, and to present her to himself as a radiant church, without stain or wrinkle or any other blemish, but holy and blameless. In this same way, husbands ought to love their wives as their own bodies. (Ephesians 5:23, 25-28)

Husbands, in the same way be considerate as you live with your wives, and treat them with respect as the weaker partner and as heirs with you of the gracious gift of life, so that nothing will hinder your prayers. (1 Peter 3:7)

And masters, treat your slaves in the same way. Do not threaten them, since you know that he who is both their Master and yours is in heaven, and there is no favoritism with him. (Ephesians 6:9)

Do not rebuke an older man harshly, but exhort him as if he were your father. Treat younger men as brothers, older women as mothers, and younger women as sisters, with absolute purity. (1 Timothy 5:1-2)

We loved you so much that we were delighted to share with you not only the gospel of God but our lives as well, because you had become so dear to us. (1 Thessalonians 2:8)

When we enter into our relationship of sonship, our redeemed manly desire to take dominion manifests it-

self in wanting to provide life from the substance of
our new life in Christ. Our aliveness as sons will move
us in the direction of enjoying the empowering of others. Each of the above passages speak directly to how
this redeemed desire takes on a male flavor and expression in the context of the various roles God has assigned us in taking relational dominion.

Being a provider of life is a deep passion in the core
of a man's soul. By God's design a redeemed man in
his role as a husband is now free to learn how to love
his wife "as Christ loved the church and gave himself
for her" (Ephesians 5:25). In his fidelity, he is now
wanting to serve her and help her flourish.

Ed came home sick in the middle of the afternoon.
He found Judy, his wife, on the bed crying. They
were both surprised to see each other in the middle of
the day. Ed wanted to just climb into bed and disap-
pear from sight. Judy had not wanted Ed to know she
was upset.

Ed knew he had a choice—climb into bed or take
some time and try to enter into her pain and distress.
Ed found himself justifying his not wanting to move
toward Judy. Yet it had startled him to see her crying
so hard. Something deeper than his excuses and his
nausea seemed to motivate him to ask her if she
wanted to talk.

At first Judy tried to use his flu as an excuse to just
let it go.

Ed, who by now had laid down on the bed, said he
was serious. "Judy, what's wrong?" he asked insis-
tently.

It was hard for her to tell Ed that she had just mis-
carried fifteen minutes before he had come through the
door.

When Ed heard what happened, he began to weep. He couldn't ever remember crying in front of Judy. He shared in her sorrow and grief in a depth of sadness he had never known. Then he just held Judy in his arms as they lay on the bed.

Weeks later Judy took Ed out for a special meal. She wanted to express her deep gratitude for his pursuit of her even when feeling so sick. She told him that the effort and energy that he used to find out what was troubling her gave her the strength to share their loss. His tears and grieving were a gift to her that he had never given before. It helped release her grief and contributed to her healing.

As Ed listened to his wife reflect back to him the impact his love and gentle involvement had had on her, he now was more aware of that deep manly desire that kicked in somewhere deep within him. He had helped move his wife from death into life, from suffering into restoration. Giving his life away for her sake tasted good.

Joseph was a man in power. He could have dominated his brothers when they came to Egypt. Instead he used his own personal presence to empower them. He provided them not just with food, but with love, forgiveness, hope and restoration of their family (see Genesis 45:1-15). That is what taking dominion is all about—using the resources and abilities God has provided for the good of others and the glory of God. What a powerful act of providing life to his brothers is demonstrated in this story!

Woven into the very fabric of our maleness is something deep within that echoes God's nature by providing and caring for the physical needs of food, clothing and shelter. My father is a living example of this in action.

My father's sense of calling and the resulting joy he exhibited in serving God is eternally set in my soul. Dad and Mom moved to Alberta's Peace River Country in the early 1940s. For sixteen years my father sacrificially served the Lord in teaching Bible and providing leadership at the Peace River Bible Institute. Six children (one daughter and five sons) came into the family while living in the rugged, early development of that great part of northern Canada. Dad was never paid a salary in his sixteen years. He and the rest of the staff lived by faith. Yet we never went without food, clothing and shelter. God the Father was faithful to provide. Dad made sure that we were cared for as he trusted God.

Then we moved to central Alberta to Prairie Bible Institute. There Dad taught for twenty-six more years until he retired. Again, he was never salaried as far as receiving a personal paycheck with a set amount of money to work with each month. Yet again, over all these years my father faithfully provided for our physical needs without complaint. He trusted God and took care of his family. He lived by faith in his heavenly Father who gave us our daily bread. In so doing, Dad became a picture of our heavenly Father—a faithful provider.

Thanks, Dad, for the gift of your manhood!

Men who are sons do not have to dominate to prove their manhood. They have been liberated to provide life and empower others. That's dominion, not domination!

Redeemed Desire Four

The fourth redeemed desire concerns creating life: I am free to choose to initiate entering with gentle strength into life and relationships in order to create life from out of my redeemed soul so that I can share in Christ's suffering and glory. This is the exact opposite of Sinful Desire Four: I will choose to find life outside the garden in order to find relief from the stench of evil, pain and death within and around me.

> But thanks be to God, who always leads us in triumphal procession in Christ and through us spreads everywhere the fragrance of the knowledge of him. For we are to God the aroma of Christ among those who are being saved and those who are perishing. To the one we are the smell of death; to the other, the fragrance of life. And who is equal to such a task? (2 Corinthians 2:14-16)

> Dear friends, do not be surprised at the painful trial you are suffering, as though something strange were happening to you. But rejoice that you participate in the sufferings of Christ, so that you may be overjoyed when his glory is revealed. (1 Peter 4:12-13)

Every single sperm is alive with only one purpose—to find and enter the egg so life can be conceived. Only one of thousands of sperm ever succeed. The journey up the birth canal to the waiting egg is one that the sperm makes in order to create life. The sperm enters and moves and initiates seeking out the egg. With great effort, it penetrates the surface and the greatest miracle of life takes place. This description of physical reproduction is a picture, a metaphor of how our sense of maleness longs to be expressed.

God has designed us to initiate with gentle strength into life, our world, into the lives of others and spill the substance of our male soul so that life can be created. This will be done at great personal cost. It is never a selfish act, but is initiated to glorify God with our maleness. It is an other-centered commitment that involves giving important parts of our manhood away so that the essence of life can be brought to the physical and soul needs of others. Often out of our own sacrifice of blood, sweat and tears the seeds of life are planted in our world, our work, our relationships.

Shadrach, Meshach and Abednego were three Jewish men who gave all of themselves in passionate, loyal worship of their God (see Daniel 3:16-29). Their act of obedient worship created a response in the heart of King Nebuchadnezzar that had never been there before. But the cost was the furnace, from which there was no guarantee of rescue.

Bringing about spiritual life and change cost the death sentence for these three men as they spilled the substance of their love and loyalty for their God all over this pagan nation. They literally poured their physical lives out for God and their captors. Life came at great personal cost.

Stephen's life provides us with another example of creating spiritual fruit at great personal cost (see Acts 7:54-60). As they stoned him for speaking out for Jesus, he prayed: " 'Lord Jesus, receive my spirit.' Then he fell on his knees and cried out, 'Lord, do not hold this sin against them.' When he had said this, he fell asleep" (7:59-60). The seed of Stephen's life, nourished by his own blood and death, brought spiritual life to Saul who became Paul the apostle.

Creating life at the cost of personal suffering is the mark of sonship and true manhood. Spilling our brawn, our intelligence, our hands (giftedness), our time and our hearts for the glory of God and the good of others is one of the deepest, most passionate expressions of maleness.

The man who has never entered into sonship, or the man who has very little sense of his sonship with the heavenly Father, is a man who will be driven to find life, find relief, find pleasure in temporal reality that will never satiate his thirst and hunger for the eternal. The man after God's own heart will pay the price, sacrificing personal pleasure, at the cost of his own time, energy, virtue and life.

God may not ask us to be a Shadrach, Meshach, Abednego or Stephen in like experience. But as His sons He has created us to live with the same spirit as these men:

To bring life to women by treating them with deep respect as equals who bear the image of God with dignity;

To enter into the mystery of my wife's soul and explore and get to know her; to cherish and give up my life for her in servant headship so she can be free to be a woman and my wife;

To spill my time, energy and heart into my sons and daughters; to let my sons know that I hold them in my heart; to let my daughters know that I prize them, that they are the apple of my eye;

To spill my life into spiritual battle so the kingdom of God will flourish and grow, and so that the evil tide will be stemmed and righteousness will prevail.

God has designed us to penetrate our world to spill

the substance of our maleness in order to create life out of death, healing out of pain, calm out of chaos.

Entering our world and relationships with gentle strength and courage calls for a radical sense of sonship with our Father God. There is no better place to discover how God would enter into a situation and spill His life than being in an intimate relationship with Him. This truth tested me as a man, husband and father.

Doing Battle in My Home

I will never forget the night. It was 12:20 a.m. and I was alone in the room of our house that I used for study and class preparation. One of our teenage daughters came up from her basement bedroom trembling and crying. "Dad," she said, "I can't sleep! There is something evil in my room and all around me!"

I called my wife Jackie and all three of us went into the living room. We took authority over the spiritual forces of evil in the heavenly realms (Ephesians 6:12) by resisting the devil and by claiming the pieces of the full armor of God. She settled down and was able to go back to her room, but her night was interrupted with recurring attacks.

I was up and in the same room at 6 a.m. Around 6:20 the door opened and in came my daughter, distraught and trembling to the point of collapsing at my feet. I sensed that the enemy was attacking me through harassing one of our children. I became righteously indignant and rebuked the enemy in the name of the Lord Jesus Christ. I laid hands on her and prayed the blood of Jesus over her and invited the Holy Spirit to manifest Himself in our presence. He led me to pray this prayer:

In the name of Jesus, we claim the truth of Your Word by tightening Your belt of truth around our waist as a family. Thank You for Your righteousness which is our breastplate shielding us from the enemy and from our unrighteousness. Take our feet and use Your shoes to ready us with the peace that comes from Your good news. We lift up the shield of our faith which is in You, Lord Jesus, to extinguish these flaming arrows of the evil one. And Lord, we humbly thank You for the helmet of Your salvation which protects our heads, our minds, the way we need to think right now. And we take and speak Your Word which is the sword of the Spirit and move offensively right now against these spiritual forces of evil. In the powerful name of our Lord and victorious Savior Jesus Christ! Amen! Yes! Amen!

She stopped shaking. Peace flooded us and the room. The attacks of harassment stopped.

Paul said, "Therefore put on the full armor of God, so that when the day of evil comes, you may be able to stand your ground, and after you have done everything, to stand" (Ephesians 6:13). My daughter and my family were standing! Praise God!

As the spiritual head of our family, God has designed me, in my role as a husband and father, to enter into spiritual combat. He has made me to spill my very self into the battle, to push back the darkness and evil and be instrumental in bringing the life and light of Jesus Christ into our home and into the lives of each family member. Was I afraid? Yes! Was I angry at the enemy? Yes! Was it my place as a father to take authority over the spiritual forces of evil? Yes! By so doing, I was modeling and teaching my family, right in the midst of life and the spiritual battle, how they could take the same authority in Christ's name over their enemy.

Sonship frees us to express our redeemed male passions and desires, to live with moral integrity. It frees us to defend and protect life and righteousness, to provide and empower others with life and to create life at a personal cost and sacrifice. In all this, sonship allows us to glorify our heavenly Father and share in the sufferings of His Son. That's being a redeemed man who is after the heart of God.

CHAPTER 18

Chivalry—Strength that Is Safe

As sons of God we have a glorious gift and promise from the Holy Spirit—to be empowered, not by brute force, but by a glorious inner strength. Jesus Christ, the very Son of God, manifests Himself in us as we keep opening ourselves and inviting Him into the deep places of our inmost being.

From what the Bible tells us about Adam, we can draw the following conclusions. He proved, by listening to Eve and eating the fruit she gave him, that he was not a man who could be depended on to listen, obey and radically trust in his God. Depending on the fruit from the tree of knowledge of good and evil left Adam an unsafe man and husband.

As Adam was consumed with his own inability to manage the curse, he became self-centered and selfish in his focus on survival. Eve realized that she no longer was the focus of his complete love and affection. Out of this grew her desire to seek to control the nature and direction of their relationship.

Adam hated being relationally controlled and manipulated by Eve. In fact, he was downright afraid, even personally threatened by her controlling attitude.

Scripture says that Adam's way of sinfully managing her controlling, manipulative spirit and behavior was to rule over her (Genesis 3:16). *Rule* here means for Adam to take his heal and grind the essence of her femaleness into the dirt. This consequence of their sin makes them unsafe to each other. Men, we need to deal with our responsibility in becoming safe males!

Women long to feel secure in the very depths of their souls. One of the best gifts we can give to women is a sense of "soul-safeness." Yes, physical safety is also very important, but if we are committed to making them feel safe in the deepest parts of their feminine soul, then they will also feel secure physically in our presence.

Jesus' View of Women

Jesus set the standard by which women are to be treated by men. Nowhere in the accounts of the gospels do we ever see women afraid to approach the Lord. He demonstrated purity of motive and integrity in speech and behavior in all of His relationships with older and younger women.

He honored His mother throughout life. Just before His death while hanging on the cross, His concern for her was paramount as He asked John to care for her (John 19:25-27). Jesus believed in women. Throughout His ministry He freely blessed them, healed them, confronted them about their sin without degrading or humiliating them. He thoroughly enjoyed their ministry to Him and their love, loyalty and worship of Him as the Son of God. He did everything He could to free them from personal and cultural restraints so they could be all that He had created them to be for His glory and their good.

In keeping with His high view of women, Jesus spoke forcefully about what is in our male souls that needs to be attended to—fornication, adultery and sexual lusting after women. He was also very straightforward in confronting men who used divorce to do away with an unwanted spouse. Women, in Jesus' eyes, were every bit as much image-bearers of God as were their male counterparts.

Paul's View of Women

Paul also held a very high view of the value and dignity of women. He instructed Timothy and Titus on how and what they were to teach men about relating to others, especially women. To Timothy, he wrote: "Don't let anyone look down on you because you are young, but set an example for the believers in speech, in life, in love, in faith and in purity. . . . [Treat] older women as mothers and younger women as sisters, with absolute purity" (1 Timothy 4:12; 5:2).

His exhortation to Titus was equally pointed: "Teach the older men to be temperate, worthy of respect, self-controlled, and sound in faith, in love and endurance. . . . Similarly, encourage the young men to be self-controlled" (Titus 2:2, 6).

Safe Men, Secure Women

Paul breaks down his instruction to Timothy and Titus into several important qualities. Their personal relationships are to be marked by love, self-control, respect, temperance, faith, endurance and purity. Self-control, purity and love are mentioned more than once indicating their level of importance. In application of these qualities, Paul focuses on older and younger women separately.

Women in the days of Paul, Timothy and Titus were treated as second-class citizens to be used and objectified for the selfish purposes of the male population. Not much has changed throughout history on this relational level. Men are still fulfilling the consequences of the curse, which is a memorial to our sin. They continue to rule and dominate women in every imaginable way.

Women are still abused physically, relationally and sexually. Some husbands sexually "use" their spouses in marriage. Many young men are date raping women they know and raping women they don't know. In the workplace there is much sexual harassment. They are being seduced by men in offices of trust—doctors, priests, pastors, rabbis, counselors, psychiatrists, lawyers, teachers—put down, devalued, threatened, intimidated and otherwise exploited simply because they are female.

In Paul's day and in ours, men have failed to make our homes, the workplace and our communities a place where women and children feel totally safe. The cry of their hearts is for change: "Give us men with whom our daughters and other younger and older women can relate, with a deep sense and experience of relational, sexual and physical safeness."

God's response to this plea is to call us to become safe males. While the rest of the nation depends on the courts and legal system to set the boundaries regarding sexual harassment and politically correct speech and behavior, we as redeemed men need to demonstrate that this issue is not resolved in the courts, but at a moral, personal, relational and spiritual level.

Fathers, it begins with us. We need to be teaching our sons and the young men of today that it's not a matter of women's rights but a matter of loving and treating women as equal image-bearers of God. If we are going to become safe males, we must demonstrate before our sons the godly way to treat and relate to women. This revolution must begin in each individual home by example and verbal instruction, in the context of a father-son relationship. Where no father exists, then a surrogate father, a spiritual mentor, must come alongside and give assistance.

Treating Older Women as Mothers

Modeling is most powerful when our sons see us treat their mothers, grandmothers and sisters with dignity, equality and respect. Our sons need to see us love and honor our mothers and mothers-in-law. How we treat and relate to other women in public, in the workplace, in church, is of utmost importance to our sons and other younger males. The power of imitation can be awesome; our sons take their cues from us on how to show respect to older women.

Why would Paul tell Timothy to treat older women as mothers? Possibly the answer is found in his reference to the quality of Timothy's faith. "I have been reminded of your sincere faith, which first lived in your grandmother Lois and in your mother Eunice and, I am persuaded, now lives in you also" (2 Timothy 1:5).

Perhaps Paul's instruction to Titus about the important ministry and impact older women are to have will help us see why they need to be treated with respect and honor.

> Likewise, teach the older women to be reverent in the way they live, not to be slanderers or

addicted to much wine, but to teach what is good. Then they can train the younger women to love their husbands and children, to be self-controlled and pure, to be busy at home, to be kind, and to be subject to their husbands, so that no one will malign the word of God. (Titus 2:3-5)

What eternal influence older Christian women have in God's economy of relationships and ministry! We need to make room in our homes, churches and communities for these women to be all God designed them to be. Our own mothers and grandmothers long to be treated and seen as having a quality of life, faith and capacity to love that is of utmost importance to both their generation and the next. Let's rise up and honor all of the older women by treating them the way our own mothers long for us to relate to them as their sons. Jesus, Paul, Timothy and Titus have shown by their example and instruction that this is how we are to treat older women.

Treating Younger Women as Sisters, with Absolute Purity

Fathers, our sons desperately need to be taught by word and example how to relate to and treat young women. This begins in our homes with how we as husbands relate to and treat our own spouses. Paul's instruction to husbands is the standard by which we should live: "Submit to one another out of reverence for Christ" (Ephesians 5:21).

A safe husband demonstrates courteous reverence to his wife in the following manner:

For the husband is the head of the wife as Christ is the head of the church, his body, of which he is the Savior. . . .

Husbands, love your wives, just as Christ loved the church and gave himself up for her to make her holy, cleansing her by the washing with water through the word, and to present her to himself as a radiant church, without stain or wrinkle or any other blemish, but holy and blameless. In this same way, husbands ought to love their wives as their own bodies. He who loves his wife loves himself. After all, no one ever hated his own body, but he feeds and cares for it, just as Christ does the church—for we are members of his body. "For this reason a man will leave his father and mother and be united to his wife, and the two will become one flesh." This is a profound mystery—but I am talking about Christ and the church. However, each one of you also must love his wife as he loves himself, and the wife must respect her husband. (Ephesians 5:23, 25-33)

Characteristics of a Husband Who Is a Safe Male

Let me suggest some characteristics of a husband who is cherishing his wife like Christ does His bride, the church. First of all, he will strive to place complete and absolute value on her because she is made in the image and likeness of God. God's love is complete and unconditional for her and so is the husband's. As a safe male and loving husband he will cherish her worth and dignity based on absolute values rather than on cultural and relative values—her body shape, physical attributes, gifts, talents and relational style. If our sons see us model this fundamental relational truth in marriage, then they will include this most important concept in the development of their own sense of male identity. This in turn will help our sons treat the young women in their lives with a relational purity that will result in the younger women feeling respected and not objectified for their physical appearance.

Another characteristic of a safe male is a man who humbly receives rebuke, exhortation, instruction, encouragement and the incarnational love of Jesus from his wife. A new husband soon recognizes that he is not a very good relational lover and that his wife can become his best teacher. He will need to let her into the closed-up places of his soul when it's appropriate. As husbands we need our wives to incarnate Jesus to our places of sin, shame and weakness, as well as to our places of dreams, hopes and joys. Our sons need to watch and catch our spirit of humility, vulnerability and teachability before our spouse. This will help keep their male spirit sensitive and moldable. Hopefully it will also provide a sense of direction in helping them relate to younger women so they will become less inclined to manipulate, control and use them for the quieting of their inadequacies and fears.

Peter instructed husbands to learn this as an important way of treating their wives: "Husbands, in the same way be considerate as you live with your wives, and treat them with respect as the weaker partner and as heirs with you of the gracious gift of life, so that nothing will hinder your prayers" (1 Peter 3:7).

Women speak in a different voice, a female voice. They long to be heard and understood by men. Husbands, when we don't learn to listen and understand the inner worldview of our spouse, we become unsafe and virtually end up having a dialogue of the deaf. Developing closeness is of greatest priority to women.

Emotional intimacy that comes from a deep spirit and soul oneness is foundational to their feeling secure in friendships and/or in the covenantal bond of marriage. Our culture has promoted the view that emotional intimacy and love for a member of the opposite gender has to be expressed sexually in order to be satisfied. The reality is when wives sense that neither our spiritual closeness to God nor our relational intimacy with her are priorities with us before sexual intimacy, she will feel used relationally and sexually prostituted.

This priority in the marriage relationship needs to be pursued and cherished with a passion by the husband who is a safe male. When a wife sees that her desire for spiritual and emotional intimacy is recognized as a legitimate longing and that efforts are being made to satisfy this need apart from sexual intimacy, she will feel safe. This kind of loving will bring a rich sense of goodness and beauty to the home that will spill over into our sons. They will learn from us how to differentiate between relational and sexual intimacy and will be equipped to conduct their relationships with young women with absolute sexual purity.

We want our sons to learn first and foremost that relational love with the opposite sex is best celebrated in deep friendship and loyalty without mandatory sexual expression. We also want to teach our sons that God links sexual expression only with a permanent, monogamous commitment to a woman in marriage.

Another important female message concerns what she as an individual brings into the marriage. A woman does not want to be stereotyped in terms of how she will actively respond in inviting you into her soul. She wants us to realize that she brings her own life and relational experiences into the marital union. Discover what is safe, enjoyable, desirable and best for her. Be alert to what is uncomfortable and threatening to her. Husband her by not requiring her to move beyond her level of relational and sexual comfort to keep your passion of love alive. Work with God's help and strength to communicate that your love for her does not depend on her physical beauty and/or sexual performance. She is a mystery to explore, to get to know, not to be used and taken for granted.

As our sons observe us loving their mothers in this sensitive manner, they will also learn to relate to young women with this same kind of purity. They will no longer pressure their dates to respond in any way that makes them feel uncomfortable in order to feel loved or appreciated. Our sons will no longer encourage deeper levels of spirit, soul or body intimacy by making false promises of commitment. Through our modeling, we will help free our sons from the sinful, cultural pressure to compare, disarm and address women in demeaning ways. They will learn that a woman's true worth and value are not found primarily in her outer physical attributes and beauty, nor in her sexual presence and availability.

Treating the younger women as sisters will encourage younger men to work at setting safe, appropriate relational and sexual boundaries. Women who have been abused relationally or sexually, and young women who have grown up in a culture which says that their supreme value is in being a sexual object, need safe, loyal, consistent friendship. They need strong affirmation that their value and dignity are intact, without any sexual innuendoes or implications.

Developing Sexual Identity

Another important area of training for our sons has to do with their sexual identity as males. What we model before our sons as older men and fathers—our attitude and behavior about our bodies and sex—will produce the greatest possible fruit in their development of male sexuality.

A proper view of sexual identity must begin with a solid biblical perspective on the primary function and purpose for our physical body and sex. Paul lays it on the line in a straightforward manner. We need to do the same with our sons.

> Do you not know that the wicked will not inherit the kingdom of God? Do not be deceived: Neither the sexually immoral nor idolaters nor adulterers nor male prostitutes nor homosexual offenders nor thieves nor the greedy nor drunkards nor slanderers nor swindlers will inherit the kingdom of God. And that is what some of you were. But you were washed, you were sanctified, you were justified in the name of the Lord Jesus Christ and by the Spirit of our God.
>
> "Everything is permissible for me"—but not everything is beneficial. "Everything is permissible for me"—but I will not be mastered by anything. "Food for the stomach and the stomach for food"—but God will destroy them both. The body is not meant for sexual immorality, but for the Lord, and the Lord for the body. By his power God raised the Lord from the dead, and

he will raise us also. Do you not know that your bodies are members of Christ himself? Shall I then take the members of Christ and unite them with a prostitute? Never! Do you not know that he who unites himself with a prostitute is one with her in body? For it is said, "The two will become one flesh." But he who unites himself with the Lord is one with him in spirit.

Flee from sexual immorality. All other sins a man commits are outside his body, but he who sins sexually sins against his own body. Do you not know that your body is a temple of the Holy Spirit, who is in you, whom you have received from God? You are not your own; you were bought at a price. Therefore honor God with your body.

Now for the matters you wrote about: It is good for a man not to marry. But since there is so much immorality, each man should have his own wife, and each woman her own husband. The husband should fulfill his marital duty to his wife, and likewise the wife to her husband. The wife's body does not belong to her alone but also to her husband. In the same way, the husband's body does not belong to him alone but also to his wife. (1 Corinthians 6:9-7:4)

We are responsible to teach our sons this balanced view of sex and the body. Most sons are not taught biblical truth about their sexual desires and how it is an important aspect of their male sexual identity. When we do not teach the younger men, then self-control regarding their sexual desires often becomes an ongoing struggle. This absence of solid teaching contributes to their confusion about their male sexuality, frequently resulting in their becoming unsafe males. I can't say it any more strongly than the admonition found in Psalm 78:

> O my people, hear my teaching;
>   listen to the words of my mouth.
> I will open my mouth in parables,
>   I will utter hidden things, things from
>   of old—
> what we have heard and known,
>   what our fathers have told us.
> We will not hide them from their children;
>   we will tell the next generation . . .
> so the next generation would know them,
>   even the children yet to be born,
>   and they in turn would tell their children.
> Then they would put their trust in God
>   and would not forget his deeds
>   but would keep his commands.
>   (78:1-4, 6-7)

Fathers Set the Example for Sons

In a culture twisted by the chaos of careless change in gender identity and role, and in a time marked by sexual confusion, perversion, "safe" sex and sexually transmitted diseases, it is critical to let our sons know that there are practical answers to their questions. Our sons want to know what it means to be a man with powerful sexual desires. We need to provide biblical, satisfying, enduring answers. For the sake of the next generation, let's equip our sons in this most critical matter. Under God, they can become a generation of men who will make young women feel sexually safe and relationally blessed.

Several important and specific points of application flow out of modeling a biblical view of sex to our sons. We need to instruct our sons about the importance of a biblical sexual ethic. A safe male has learned to love his wife in such a way that it would be unthinkable to consider or commit adultery (sex outside of your marriage). This strong conviction will spill over to our sons so that they too will practice self-control in regards to fornication (sex before marriage).

We need to be an example to our sons in taking responsibility for our sexual desires. Our culture is saturated with erotic sexual images and messages. The most powerful transmitters of these sexual stimulants are rock videos, movies, television and pornography as accessed through magazines, video, telephone, computer—virtual reality is now being created for computer creation of pornography—and prostitution. Jesus warned us that we are responsible, regardless of the external sexual stimulus, for control of our thoughts, imagination and behavior.

> You have heard that it was said, "Do not commit adultery." But I tell you that anyone who looks at a woman lustfully has already committed adultery with her in his heart. If your right eye causes you to sin, gouge it out and throw it away. It is better for you to lose one part of your body than for your whole body to be thrown into hell. And if your right hand causes you to sin, cut it off and throw it away. It is better for you to lose one part of your body than for your whole body to go into hell. (Matthew 5:27-30)

What we watch and let them watch on TV and videos,

what magazines we read, and how we "eye" other women will all have a strong influence on our sons and their sense of sexual identity. Expecting our sons to be responsible for their sexual desires begins with our self-control in imagination and deed. As fathers we need to walk with our sons through the critical years of their sexual maturation and development. This is an ongoing involvement, not a one-time "embarrassed talk."

The revolution of change begins in the privacy of our own hearts and then spills into the lives of our sons and young men in our homes, churches and communities. We must call our youth back to sexual control and moral responsibility. The test of strength and courage to do this lies with us as older men. Consider yourself called by God, by your sons and by our nation. Being a safe male will not just happen. Righteous men must take an active stand against sexual evil by actively becoming involved in moral uprightness, passionately standing for righteousness in our land.

Safe males will be motivated to be at the forefront of the battle against pornography, sexual harassment and physical and sexual violence against women. We will be fighting for homes of refuge, safety and help for unwed, pregnant and battered women. Our sons and young men need to see us fighting these kinds of battles. Words are empty, teaching and instruction impotent, without the backing of active involvement in these battles. All God needs is a few good men!

Our best defense in all of this is a good offense. Helping train our sons to be safe males involves loving God with all our hearts, souls, minds and strength and our spouses and sons as ourselves.

Fathers, love your sons. Call out their maleness by modeling it, by learning to love, by growing in self-control of your sexual drive and desire, by treating the women in your life with dignity and respect. Be a safe male and you will improve the possibility that your sons will also be safe males, who treat younger women as their own sisters, with absolute purity of motive and behavior.

John took his thirteen-year-old son Scott out for a weekend canoe trip. Sitting around the fire Saturday night, John took out a small package and handed it to his son. "Open it son," he said with growing emotion.

As Scott began to open the package he wondered what it was and why his dad was giving him a gift when it was not even his birthday. He saw the ring and knew in his heart that this must be for a special purpose because it looked very expensive to him. It was shiny gold! He tried it on after asking his dad which finger it should be worn on. Then he looked at his father with a mixture of bewilderment and gratitude.

Noticing his response, John said to Scott, "This ring is made of pure gold. It symbolizes your sexual purity as my son and as a developing young man. I want you to wear this as an expression of your commitment to God, to me and to all the young women you get to know until your marriage; of being a young man who is sexually chaste, pure and a virgin. If at any time before you marry, you ever choose to give your virginity away to a young woman and you take the virginity of a young woman from her, I want you to take off this ring and bring it to me. Only wear it for what it symbolizes!

"Tonight marks your pledge before God, before me and to yourself of maintaining sexual fidelity, chastity and purity. This time around this fire is our little ceremony to ritualize our commitment to this purpose of God. I, in giving you this ring, want you to know that I will do all I can as your father to be an example before you of sexual purity and control, to love your mother and be faithful to her, and to walk with you through these coming years of your sexual development, struggles and joys.

"Son, I want to pray and seal this pledge in Jesus' name:

> *"Heavenly Father, in Jesus' name, Scott and I come into Your holy presence to seal this pledge of our commitment to sexual purity, to walking together through these important upcoming years, to be men who honor You with our bodies and with our sexuality.*
>
> *"Father, I pledge before You to be an example to Scott of a man who lives in sexual wholeness and fidelity with his wife. I pledge to encourage and help him in whatever ways I can to go through this time of development in his sexual identity. I pledge to not abandon him to the cultural and peer pressure of sexual confusion, temptation and perversions.*
>
> *"Father, thank You for giving me Scott as my son, for making him as a male with a sexual drive and desires. Give to him the desires of Your heart, that he would remain chaste sexually, a virgin until he should so choose to marry the woman of Your leading and directing.*

"I bless this pledge of sexual purity into your inmost being, Scott, as my son and as a male, in the name of the Father, Son and Holy Spirit. Amen! Yes, amen!"

Chivalry—The Lost Virtue of Male Protection

Our sons rarely see us practice the lost virtue of chivalry with our wives, our daughters and with other women in everyday life. A prime example of what we have lost as a society is powerfully portrayed in an incident that took place during the sinking of the *Titanic*. According to an article in *Reader's Digest*, when the ship hit an iceberg and sank, only about one-third of the passengers survived, and most of these were women and children. Later, a surviving ship's officer was asked why. He replied that "women and children first" was the law of human nature. Apparently, many male passengers refused to enter lifeboats until they were sure all the women and children were safe.[1]

It's a strange paradox that we have put women on the Supreme Court and in corporate chairs of executive power, made them judges, politicians and policewomen, all the while stripping them of the freedom to walk our streets in both city and country in physical and relational safety. This erosion of civility is due in part to feminists who saw chivalry as another form of male domination dressed in white gloves.

But the bottom line has more to do with the breakdown of authority structures where restraint, sacrifice, duty, self-control and self-discipline have all gone the way of chivalry. As life is cheapened by rampant pornography that degrades and subjects women to being sex objects for male sensual gratification, and by abortion that destroys the baby's right to live, we realize an even more serious area of protection is gone.

When manners and etiquette were a part of life, a certain degree of self-restraint was evident in homes, schools and churches. These restraints came to shield women and provide them with a sense of se-

CHIVALRY—STRENGTH THAT IS SAFE

curity. Men, it's time for a revival of old-fashioned restraint. Chivalry as a virtue and safety net has been replaced with a form of cultural anarchy that encourages immediate gratification and maximum self-expression, whatever the price. My sense is that women would welcome a little old-fashioned chivalry and restraint.

In the past, chivalry formed an additional element of control, over and above the law, which enabled society to protect itself against offenses which the law could not touch. This virtue of chivalry, like a code of manners, was far more effective than today's politically correct movement with its speech police and hateful speech laws.

Fathers, when we relearn and model respect for women and the self-restraint it implies, violence against women will decline in everyday life. Our sons and young men will begin to see how honor is given to women in practical ways. Incivility is a form of sexual harassment against women that is today a symptom of a far deeper cheapening of life. Older men, teach the younger men self-restraint by practicing some good old-fashioned chivalry with your spouse, your daughters and with older and younger women in your world.

Dad, Daughter and Dating

I will never forget our oldest daughter's first date. As the young man came to pick her up at our house, I stood—with the other four family members—behind the dining room curtains and sneaked a look to see if he would see her to her side of the car and open the door for her. I had told my three daughters that if the young men who came to date them did not pass their

first test—opening the door of the car to seat them—
they were history. The whole family held its breath.
He did it. He passed! He is now her husband and our
son-in-law! We love him and so does our daughter.

You see, my three daughters and one son see me
open doors for their mother, help her on with her coat,
walk on the street side of the sidewalk, carry heavy
grocery bags for her, wash the kitchen floor, vacuum
the house. Our three daughters have grown up to expect men to treat them this way. Our son will hopefully repeat what he sees his father practice—chivalry,
respect and self-restraint, all of which protect a
woman's sense of honor and femininity. Come on,
men, let's do it, and make our homes, churches, communities and workplaces a safe haven for women!

One other area that desperately needs teaching and
modeling is spiritual chivalry. Spiritual chivalry is
when we as fathers personally and publicly model being keepers of the Scriptures, defenders of the faith,
protectors of the poor and pursuers of justice. Our sons
need to see us personally reading the Word, praying
and living by the commandments of God in our
homes. They need to experience us reading the Word
and praying together with them and with the whole
family. They need to experience us challenging them
when they are out of line with scriptural truth. We
need to be passionate defenders of the church, loyal
and involved.

Incarnating the Word of God and the Spirit of God
to our sons, our families and to the world around us is
an important form of spiritual chivalry that will set us
apart as men after the heart of God.

One winter morning several years ago around 6:30
a.m., our son Scott came into the living room dragging

his portable hand-controlled hockey game. I was in the midst of my personal devotions.

"Daddy, Daddy," he said, "can you play hockey with me?"

"Not right now, son," I said. "When I'm done spending this time worshiping God, then I will have a game with you before you go to school."

He went off to play in another room. Fifteen minutes later he came back and asked a very profound question for an eight-year-old boy. "Daddy, do you *have* to do that or do you *want* to?"

"Son," I said, "I enjoy doing this with the Lord."

What an opportunity to speak into my son's life, to bless him by living out before him what it means to be a defender of that which is most important in life—to worship and love the Lord my God with all my heart, soul, mind and strength.

Fathers, be spiritually chivalrous before your sons. As they too become defenders of the Word, the faith, the church, the poor, they will also be men who defend and protect life, women and children. Imagine the result—safe fathers, safe sons; safe homes, safe schools; safe churches and safe communities.

Christ has called us to follow in His steps regarding our attitudes and behavior toward women. I encourage all men whose hearts are after God's to hold this aspect of their maleness up to the light of Christ's love and allow God the Father to guide them. Only then can we as men express more of our male potential. Only then can our women live in a community that is truly safe.

Endnote

1 Linda Lichter, "A Little Chivalry Wouldn't Hurt," *Reader's Digest*, Canadian edition (December 1993), 71.

CHAPTER 19

Real Men Are Servants

God designed male and female image-bearers to be personally involved in relational dominion. Both genders are necessary in order to be fruitful in filling the earth as part of God's creation mandate. Within the roles they fill there is certainly much overlap. The fruit of the Holy Spirit is one example—being honest, caring, loving and moral are qualities that are expressed by both genders.

Manly relational involvement, however, has a distinctiveness that separates it from that of women. It is best expressed when a man decides what direction to go when the path is unclear and physically or morally dangerous. A man of God does not sit back and wait for a no-risk situation. Male distinctiveness is also expressed when a man chooses to initiate by taking hold of hard, painful situations with a confident dependence on God. This encourages others in those situations to wait and trust on the Lord as well as to rest in who they are.

Perhaps more than anything else, men are to reflect passionate enjoyment in God's desire to Father us. This intimacy releases within us the passion and courage to initiate entering into someone else's life having in mind both their good and the reflection of God's glory.

This man will refuse to retreat into abandonment. He will not dominate when he finds out his son is on drugs or his daughter has been diagnosed with cancer or his wife begins to show the early signs of MS. He is in tune with his developing sense of manhood; he understands that life is filled with a certain mystery that can often leave him afraid, paralyzed and at other times challenged and alive.

Frequently, as he enters into the challenge of relating, he feels a sense of dread that makes him question, "Do I really have the male substance to be a man after the heart of God?" Not knowing how, or not wanting to initiate strongly entering into someone's life, does not feel manly at all. We soon become very aware that we cannot initiate entering with gentle strength into the hearts of others by sheer use of willpower. Such strategies will always end up deficient at some level when faced with the mysteries of life.

Entering the Mystery of Relationships

As we grow into manhood, we quickly learn that entering into relationships and staying meaningfully engaged is a very painful and deeply threatening part of the creation mandate. Becoming a man does not involve some easy relational formula; it's a process of development and change over the span of life. This process can be better understood in the following relational map of a man's pilgrimage.

It begins with a commitment to stop worshiping the "religion of the strong." We need to enter into humble ownership of our sinfulness and weakness. Paul wrote

about this when he took ownership of his propensity to
be proud and independent:

> To keep me from becoming conceited because
> of these surpassingly great revelations, there was
> given me a thorn in my flesh, a messenger of Sa-
> tan, to torment me. Three times I pleaded with
> the Lord to take it away from me. But he said to
> me, "My grace is sufficient for you, for my
> power is made perfect in weakness." Therefore I
> will boast all the more gladly about my weak-
> nesses, so that Christ's power may rest on me.
> That is why, for Christ's sake, I delight in weak-
> nesses, in insults, in hardships, in persecutions,
> in difficulties. For when I am weak, then I am
> strong. (2 Corinthians 12:7-10)

What a paradox for growing into manhood—the
weaker we become, the stronger we get in Christ and
the more evident His power becomes. It takes real
courage for us to take ownership of our weakness in a
legitimate way. This process involves an ongoing
choice to be willing to let the mystery of what is happening in the lives of others and in our world paralyze
us. I call this "redemptive paralysis," which is when I
come to the place where my resources are not enough,
when only God's presence and involvement will empower me to go on. As He takes over, He enables me
to reflect His character and enter as He would enter.

Letting life provoke a "redemptive paralysis" in us
will result in our having permission to be afraid, confused, directionless and hardest of all, powerless. And
in the face of this to resist resorting to passive or aggressive forms of violence in order to feel manly and in

control. It takes courage to name and take ownership of that situation which threatens us. Acknowledging this threat allows us to let our dread of initiating come to the surface. Or it can also expose in some men a sense of soul impotency, for which they compensate with rage and anger in order to dominate and control. This is not an easy personal journey to take because our natural inclination is to be independent and self-centered.

Entering into the mystery of relationships also means being willing to face the impact of our sin and weakness on others. When a man chooses to abandon entering into someone's life, as a general patterned response when threatened, he will end up doing nothing about what matters most to God and this person. That leaves a man feeling less afraid, but empty and very unmanly. It leaves the other person involved with us both sinned against and wounded.

When a man's general pattern of relating is to dominate, then others will end up being intimidated and controlled by his abuse of male power. This may temporarily remove feelings of powerlessness, but in the end leaves all involved feeling relationally raped by arrogance, loneliness and rage.

Entering into a total brokenness before God will also mean that we need to embrace the reality of the relational death of those around us because of the impact of our sin. Then we need to pay attention to what is dying inside of us. The first passion to die will be our sense of sonship with our heavenly Father, causing our desire to love Him and others to subside. As this passion dissipates, our sense of maleness will shrivel up until we no longer think and feel like a godly man. As a sinful replacement to cover the stench of our dying redeemed passions there will be a new thirst for self-adoration. False gods leading to superficial and temporal sensual worship will surface to tempt us to preempt our deepest passion for worshiping and serving God.

When we face the reality of relational life spilling all over the floor of our male souls, we experience from our inner being the renewed stirring of our redeemed desires. Deep within the bowels of our soul we will sense a growing yearning to begin entering into the threatening situation that has paralyzed us. Though we still fear that we lack what it takes to make a difference or to enable us to move in a redemptive direction, we are in a place of legitimate brokenness and humility of heart before God. Now we are free to come boldly into the Father's presence in our time of need. We can submit to His authority in reverent obedience.

Therefore, since we have a great high priest who has gone through the heavens, Jesus the Son of God, let us hold firmly to the faith we profess. For we do not have a high priest who is unable to sympathize with our weaknesses, but we have one who has been tempted in every way, just as we are—yet was without sin. Let us then approach the throne of grace with confidence, so that we may receive mercy and find grace to help us in our time of need. . . .

During the days of Jesus' life on earth, he offered up prayers and petitions with loud cries and tears to the one who could save him from death, and he was heard because of his reverent submission. Although he was a son, he learned obedience from what he suffered and, once made perfect, he became the source of eternal salvation for all who obey him. . . . (Hebrews 4:14-16; 5:7-9)

Coming as desperate, dependent men before the face of God the Father often means that we will wrestle with Him in prayer. This wrestling involves seeking to know Him and how He would enter into this relationship. It means time studying and reflecting in His Word. It means times that we weep, plead, agonize and wait on Him. Why? So we can use Him to solve our present relational problem? No! Our primary purpose is to enter into His Father-heart as His sons in order to know Him more passionately and love Him more deeply. Then we will begin to sense and experience the power of the Holy Spirit enabling us to enter the situation with a gentle strength and energy that reflects the character and heart of God.

In summary, we need to get to know God our Father well enough so that our ability to initiate entry into relationships reflects and models His character and His gentle strength.

Redeemed Male Patterns of Relating

Our love for God is most clearly seen and experienced by others in our pattern of redemptively relating with others, especially with women. Though this is manifest in different ways, the standard for such interaction is clearly stated by John:

We love because he first loved us. If anyone says, "I love God," yet hates his brother, he is a liar. For anyone who does not love his brother, whom he has seen, cannot love God, whom he

has not seen. And he has given us this command: Whoever loves God must also love his
brother. (1 John 4:19-21)

The following diagram graphically portrays the redeemed male patterns of relating. On a continuum
stretching from independent to dependent initiator
falls four basic types of male response: uncertain, predictable, ministering and servant. As we examine each
in turn, we need to invite God's Spirit to show us both
where we fall on this chart and where we ought to be.

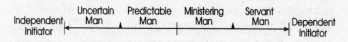

Redeemed Male Patterns of Relating

Independent Initiator

The beginning glow of the glory of God's presence
in our male soul is reflected in our redemptive relational style and strategy as an independent initiator.
Paul writes about this glory that is beginning to shine
through us in the way we relate:

But whenever anyone turns to the Lord, the
veil is taken away. Now the Lord is the Spirit,
and where the Spirit of the Lord is, there is freedom. And we, who with unveiled faces all reflect
the Lord's glory, are being transformed into his
likeness with ever-increasing glory, which comes
from the Lord, who is the Spirit. (2 Corinthians
3:16-18)

Men who begin to reflect the glory of God become
men who initiate, but do so with a lingering inde-

pendent spirit. Christ has set them free to begin to love others and give the substance of their maleness away; however, they are often reluctant to enter into their freedom to love and give to others. Here are some general characteristics of this type of man.

Eric, a married man, says, "I will die for my wife and children if I can, but I'm not sure I always know how or when or what it means to give up my life for them. This idea of dying to my own sinful desires is new to me. It all sounds kind of mysterious and too spiritual. Someone needs to tell me how to pull this kind of relationsip off. I need a formula, a relational road map."

Jim says, "With what I know about being a godly man, I will love my wife, my children and my friends as Christ loves the Church, but God better be around to pick up the pieces when I blow it!"

Ed, in talking to his single male friends, said, "I will love and give of myself in the best way I know, but don't any of you get too personal or ask me to open up!" Ed was also becoming more aware that he was still single by choice and by lack of courage rather than by calling and the gift of singleness. "I will develop ongoing friendships with the opposite sex, but if any of them want to get serious and expect some long-term commitment, then I'm out of that relationship!"

Jerry told his wife, Sara, "I will do my best to live with you in an understanding and considerate way even if I don't always like what you do. So when I fail, don't be too hard on me."

Mike told his small group of four male friends, "When I'm ready I will try to enter into a richer relationship with my father, but don't any of you push me."

Howard sat down with his two daughters and one son and let them know that with God's help he would not provoke them to wrath.

All of these men are demonstrating characteristics of an independent initiator. They are also reflecting the beginning glow of the glory of God in their relational style.

To summarize what is still in their independent male spirit would be putting it something like this: "If I do my part as a man, God will have to come through for me because He owes it to me for my obedience to Him about all of this stuff. Besides, this dying business is scary so I won't really look for more new ways and opportunities to do this in my relationships. I have learned enough about my weakness and sinfulness and I'm sure further exposure won't really result in much more change."

The motivational core conviction that has begun to take root in these men as "independent initiators" is "I am a son of my heavenly Father; I am chosen and marked by His love, and I know I am the pride of His life (see Mark 1:11). I now am more and more aware of the Holy Spirit's witness to my spirit so that I cry, 'Abba-Father' (see Galatians 4:6)."

These men—Eric, Jim, Ed, Jerry, Mike and Howard—are all beginning to be motivated by a new redemptive vow that flows out of their growing conviction of truth. This motivational vow reflects what was happening in Paul, another man of God: "In all these things [I am] more than [conqueror] through him who loved [me]" (Romans 8:37). These men are beginning to get a taste of being conquerors in the way they relate, but they are still guarded in how vulnerable and courageous they will become.

Male other-centeredness, as expressed in their redeemed relational patterns of independent initiation,
could also be described in two general categories, uncertainty and predictability.

Uncertain Eric, Jim and Ed

Eric, Jim and Ed are classic examples of men who
still feel uncertain about their manhood. They still initiate entering into relationships with a somewhat defensive style of involvement. They are not alert to their
lack of relational intimacy and its impact.

All three love the Lord, but they need to be taught
and mentored by an older man on how to give up their
life for the sake of others. They are relationally un-
learned, but not unwilling to be taught. Their heart attitude can be summed up this way: "We will try to
give of ourselves." It is based on lots of uncertainty
about who they are as men, who God the Father wants
them to be and what He wants from them in their
friendships with other men. This attitude of uncertainty also involves being sons with their fathers, fathers with their children, and husbands with their
spouses. They want to love, but often don't know how.
What others get from them is all they have to give;
they should not expect more.

Eric, Jim and Ed are your status quo Christian
males. They too easily accept the pattern of relating
from the present generation of men as well as the modeling that's come from men from the past generation.
They have good hearts, but they too easily slip into the
mood of acceptance of those around them. Their
hearts are not unteachable, but they have lost their
spirit of inquisitiveness and intrigue. They have settled
into a relational pattern that only faintly reflects the

glow of the glory of God. Their redeemed soul is turning numb toward heaven, others and themselves.

What begins to seep into their hearts is a demanding
spirit that in time comes out something like this:
"What I have to give as a man is supposed to result in
God's blessing my marriage, my family and my
friendships. He had better bless me, after all I'm trying
to be and act as a man!"

This trio's male other-centeredness is evident at
times, but is not very passionate and gripping to those
closest to them. Their relational pattern more reflects a
chosen uninvolvement than a strong movement into
relationships. There is little here that motivates them
to know their Father God more intimately.

Predictable Jerry, Mike and Howard

Jerry, Mike and Howard are predictable men who
still reflect a certain spirit of independence from their
heavenly Father and from others. This is evident in
their relational pattern. There is more self-awareness
of how they determine when they will initiate involving the deeper parts of themselves with others.

There is also growing awareness on their part that
there is very real personal cost to loving God and
others. The catch in these predictable men is their
bottom-line commitment to staying in control by
choosing when they will pay the personal price.

These men have developed a strong denial system
that yields very slowly to the work of God's Spirit, His
Word and other people. Part of what slows these men
down in their pilgrimage into godly manhood is their
justified self-centered reasons for picking and choosing
when to count the cost and enter into deeper relational
ways.

Jerry always seems to be too physically, mentally and emotionally weary to initiate entrance into his three sons' lives. Meeting other people's needs during the day is what has gripped his life.

Mike is always on the go. High intensity is the hallmark in all he does and who he is. He's busy all the time, seven days a week. What he has left personally to give, he portions out to a couple of other single friends every third or fourth week. Needless to say, they can predict when Mike will phone, stop over, and about how much they can expect from him relationally when he does come. Mike's friendships don't go very deep and tend to become stagnant over time. He rarely if ever lets them into what's going on beneath the surface of his life. The gap between his public image and private reality is growing and is really starting to create some inner stress and discontent. To cope, Mike just gets busier.

Howard justifies his relational predictability by hiding behind his I-don't-know-enough-yet attitude. "I mean, my wife doesn't need a failure as a husband. She deserves the best of what I can give of myself to her. I don't want to hurt her or disappoint her. I'm sure once I get to know more about how to husband her, our marriage will deepen and become more enjoyable. I'm open to learning. Just last week I asked her for some feedback on how she was doing. That took some real courage and sure felt like a risk. I don't do that too often. I'm hoping to try to be more sensitive and aware of how she is faring as I find out how to do it. It's tough figuring her out."

All three of these men protect whatever sense of manhood they have come to experience by being very predictable and controlling about when they choose to enter into relationships and when to let something go by. It's in this ability to choose that Jerry, Mike and Howard experience a real sense of male impact. Dying to even their legitimate desires as well as to their sinful ruling passions gives them the ability to measure their growth and progress as men of God. They like to be able to quantify the quality of how they are doing as men with their creation mandate of relational dominion. They believe that God will honor their predictable openness of how to handle life by picking up the relational pieces that fall between the cracks of their male soul.

These men are predictable in their sense of sonship with their Father God and in their human relationships. This predictable passion fuels their initiative to enter into relationships, but the fuel is not of the highest octane. There is more, much more available to the dependent initiator.

Dependent Initiator

The beginning glow of the glory of God's indwelling presence is now transforming the male soul from glory into glory. It is gradually becoming brighter and more beautiful as God continues to find entrance into the deeper places of his inmost being, conforming him into the likeness of Jesus Christ.

Paul expressed well what growing dependency on God involves:

> But we have this treasure in jars of clay to show that this all-surpassing power is from God and not from us. We are hard pressed on every side, but not crushed; perplexed, but not in despair; persecuted, but not abandoned; struck down, but not destroyed. . . .

Therefore we do not lose heart. Though outwardly we are wasting away, yet inwardly we
are being renewed day by day. For our light and
momentary troubles are achieving for us an eternal glory that far outweighs them all. So we fix
our eyes not on what is seen, but on what is unseen. For what is seen is temporary, but what is
unseen is eternal. (2 Corinthians 4:7-9, 16-18)

Men who choose to enter into a more radical lifestyle of dependence upon God develop a redemptive
relational style of initiating that becomes increasingly
evident to others the harder life gets. Unlike the independent initiator who struggles with his freedom to
love others and to give of himself in more controlled
patterns, the dependent initiator is released to not only
love and give to others, but also to be loved.

Here are some qualities and general characteristics
of this type of man:

Henry is committed to laying down his life for his
closest friend who has AIDS no matter what the cost
because it's what he as a redeemed man wants to do.

John's movement to initiate entering into relationships within his own family is growing in spontaneity.

Mark is ready to die so that his son can live. He is willing to be last in order to put his wife first. As a husband
and father, he is willing to lead by serving those he invites to follow. In order to find his life he is willing to
lose it for the sake of Christ and His kingdom.

Richard sat down with his small group of five men
and told them that he was finally willing to take the
risk and have both his sin and his virtues and their impact on them exposed on an ongoing basis.

Martin recognized in a far deeper way, as his and

Janet's growing relationship moved them toward marriage, that he wanted to protect the most sacred realities of their friendship.

Timothy recommitted his life to God and to missions. He knew that this would cost him all of his self-centeredness so that those without Christ could hear and receive the good news.

All of these men are demonstrating characteristics and qualities of a dependent initiator. They are reflecting the ongoing treasure of the glory and presence of Jesus Christ that is transforming them into men whose hearts are after His.

What motivates ordinary men like Henry, John, Mark, Richard, Martin and Timothy is this core truth that has gone down deeply into their inmost being: "I am a son of the heavenly Father, chosen and marked by His love, and the pride of His life" (see Mark 1:11). They are unashamed of the Holy Spirit's witness to their spirits of their sonship and they willingly and passionately cry out to him in worship and service, "Abba-Father" (see Galatians 4:6).

They are becoming freed up to choose to live more consistently by the gripping, redeemed, motivational vow of "Greater love has no one than this, that he lay down his life for his friends" (John 15:13). These men taste daily what it means to love by laying down their lives at home and in the workplace.

Male other-centeredness is expressed best when redeemed relational patterns of dependent initiation flow in both chosen and spontaneous acts of love.

Ministering Henry, John and Mark

Learning to trust and depend on the Lord, these three find that more and more they are able to initiate entrance into their most important relationships with a gentle strength that brings life and love. Their willingness to live with integrity, to create, provide and protect life reflects their deepening godliness as men. They also reflect a willingness to learn. They have teachable spirits which keep them on the outer edge of their relational comfort zone.

Henry was initially stunned when he heard that his closest friend, Ted, had contracted the HIV virus and now had full-blown AIDS. The two of them had been pals since elementary school. Ted was in his third year of engineering, but now had to withdraw as he fell victim to the ever-increasing symptoms of AIDS. Henry went straight to his doctor and learned all he could about the AIDS virus and the process of dying that Ted was going through. His heart opened up to new depths of compassion that he never knew existed.

As Henry began to enter into a new stage of their friendship, he discovered that so often he felt helpless when he was in Ted's presence. Ted was patient with him as he taught Henry all he could about how to love and care for him as he slowly entered into the valley of the shadow of death. Henry began to pay a relational price as his friendship with Ted took more and more of his time and energy. The more Henry gave to Ted the richer his compassion became.

John realized as his family grew in number and in age that he seemed to know less and less about what it meant to be a father. He had never had any sisters, so with two young daughters, fathering became a real challenge as he tried to learn how to relate. His inability to just "know how" to enter into their hearts exposed his weakness of character and where his manliness was inept. But he stuck with them even though he so often failed. Now as his eldest daughter reached her teenage years, John sensed a new challenge along with his low-grade fear of failing her. He felt alive as a man and a father. His focus remained on giving to them everything of himself, even out of his weakness.

Mark soon realized how selfish he was as a man when his wife and three sons asked for both his time and relational involvement. Life became more unpredictable as it spilled all over the floor of day-to-day living. He had always been a very predictable kind of person, ordering his life by a detailed schedule. He liked things planned and well thought through. He kept his life in control by worshiping his ability to be strong through self-discipline. Two of his three sons were totally opposite, free spirited and very out of control by his judgment. He tried to change both of them as their personalities emerged. The harder he tried to box them in, the worse their relationship became.

As they became eight and twelve years old, he began to reflect on the changes happening deep inside himself. He no longer worshiped the religion of the strong father. He was beginning to be more flexible, growing more spontaneous in how he handled the boys. Life still spilled all over and couldn't always be handled with some formula and relational script. Their lives were a mystery to enter, to explore, to get to know. He found this less threatening and increasingly more fulfilling.

He sensed his heart as a man was softening toward them and toward the Lord. He began to come to terms with his performance gap. He slowly, with God's help, began to accept that no matter what he offers his sons from his life, he will never be enough for what they need. They will always want and need someone stronger and something deeper than who he is as a father. That someone and something was the Father-heart of God. But he was learning how to reflect and give to his three sons a taste and shadow of what God had to offer. That to Mark felt manly and right. What better gift could he give to them than this?

Fathering was risky. But Mark realized now, in a much deeper way, how much God the Father had risked with Adam and the whole human race. There are no guarantees! Mark hated to live in that reality. But one thing he was discovering as a man and dad was that God the Father would never leave or forsake him. With that assurance, Mark continued to grow and learn how to father in ways that ministered to all three of his sons.

Servant Richard, Martin and Timothy

Richard, Martin and Timothy have walked with God for over twenty-five years. God the Father has passionately pursued them as His sons with gentle strength, often surprising them as to how and when He would enter into their lives. Their sense of dependence and trust in their heavenly Father seemed radical and overly simplistic to others. Yet their lives had a fragrance and aroma of Christ that was very enticing and appealing.

Richard had been meeting for about three years with a group of five other men. For the first eighteen months he had really kept himself closed up. But God continued inviting and discipling him through these men as they challenged and loved him. He recalls well the day he made a deliberate choice to risk letting the men into the deeper places of his soul. He remembers his first taste of their incarnational love of Jesus. They brought the love of God the Father into some deeply hurting and sinful places in his life. God the Father's love had previously been such a mental, rational experience. Now for the first time, after all his years of walking with God, he felt and experienced God's love in the deepest parts of his being.

These men were true brothers indeed. He knew in a fresh, new way what it meant to love others and to let others love him. This profound truth began to slowly transform Richard's way of relating as a man. He became far freer and more spontaneous in sacrificing his life for others. At work his colleagues often were surprised at receiving notes of written encouragement from him. At times when they were struggling in their work relationships, Richard would notice and help them work through the issues. He never seemed to be too preoccupied with his work to sense the spirit and atmosphere of the work place. His servant-heart began to make a real difference in both the quality of their relationships and in the quality and quantity of their productivity.

Richard is a man who has let God affirm his manhood through others, especially the five men in his small group and those people at work. God has also used the truth of His Word to enrich his life as he has applied it to the way he relates to others. God the Holy Spirit has been able to go into the deeper pockets of sin, the places of shame and inferiority in Richard's life. This vulnerability on his part has allowed the Spirit of God to empower him and not be quenched so often. As well, his sense of the Holy Spirit's presence has become more intimate instead of a previous pattern of grieving Him. This is all resulting in Richard becoming dependently spontaneous in serving others.

There is a gentle strength about his presence that allows the substance of his redeemed life and passions to flow freely into those around him.

Martin was being challenged in ways he had never known as a single man. He was now forty-five and his relationship with Janet was definite marriage material. His sexual desires were alive in ways he had never experienced. When he was with her he often struggled to stay in control of them. It was like his groin was on fire. He had remained chaste and sexually pure all his life and so had Janet. He was committed to protecting their virginity until marriage.

Martin had always been intrigued with his maleness. His sexuality had never been an ongoing burden to him, yet it had often been a mystery. Certainly, as a single man for these forty-five years, he had had sexual struggles. Sexual lust and masturbation had really controlled him for a seven-year stint in his late teens and early twenties. But Martin knew that if he was to ever see God bring his sexual desires under control he would have to become teachable, moldable and a willing imitator of other men older and wiser than he. So Martin sought out a man fifteen years his senior to mentor him.

Ken has stayed involved over these many years with Martin. He has poured himself into Martin in both good and hard times. No one has had more influence on Martin's sense of manliness than Ken. He has been unashamed in calling out Martin's maleness over the years. As a result, Martin has been redemptively intrigued by his maleness on an ongoing appropriate basis and holds his manhood in an open hand to God and to Janet. He embraces it as a gift from God to be treasured, exalted, admired, respected and accepted. What a gift to bring to his prospective bride! No wonder Mar-

tin was committed to protecting Janet's gift of femininity and sexuality that she was bringing to him. In this
way he humbly served Janet as a godly man.

Timothy realized that at the age of thirty-five to
leave his comfort zone of a stable job, a house one-half
paid and a family network of support was illogical according to a secular worldview. Missions had never
been his thing. Sure, he served on the church board for
one three-year term and had helped with fund-raising
for charities; but he had never even thought about going overseas with some mission board.

Timothy had started to sense his passion for God
and for others was waning. He was getting far too
comfortable in his current lifestyle. But his sense of
personal comfort seemed to be slowly destroying his
love for God and for others. One weekend he went to a
men's retreat and there was confronted with the perils
of personal comfort. The man who challenged him was
a retired missionary with forty years of overseas service.

When he broke the news to his wife Bev and their
three children about his sense of God's call to missions, it was rough. This shook their comfort zone to
the core and tested his own sense of manhood to the
limit. He doubted God, his own Christianity, his marriage and even his desire to be a father. But through it
all he began to move out of his personal comfort zone
and noticed his passion and love for God and others
were being rekindled. Two-and-one-half years later,
with the house rented, the car sold and their monthly
support at eighty-five percent, they left as a family for
central Africa.

Timothy was now experiencing both the fears of
facing the unknown and the passion of a radical de-

pendency on God that made him feel alive as a man in a way never before experienced. He sensed that he was beginning to tap into his redeemed male desires and now initiates in relationships and in new ways of loving and serving God and others. This is something he passionately wants to do out of a willing heart. He no longer fights being a man, but embraces his manhood as a rich gift from God. Fulfilling his God-assigned creation mandate is a privilege and calling to Timothy. It's no longer just drudgery and cold duty.

Three years into their second term, Timothy, Bev and the boys have now developed a growing freedom to spontaneously sacrifice their lives for others. They have truly found their lives and live abundantly.

In Timothy's heart there is little sense that his missions career and service has to compete with his love, affection and relationship with Bev and his three sons. Now at age forty-six, Timothy is enjoying loving God with all his heart, soul, mind and strength and his family and others as a man who passionately wants to. His gentle strength spontaneously spills into life and people. Timothy, as a servant man, is a true bond-slave and friend of God.

Each man I have written about is at a different place on the continuum of dependency. No redeemed man has characteristics of just one pattern. Depending on the depth of your trust in God when your male initiating is under personal threat, your relational pattern will come into increasingly sharp focus. When the threat level is more intense, the more your focus of relational response will fall into a single, identifiable, relational pattern that reflects varying depths of the glory of God. As men, like the twelve mentioned in this chapter, our pattern of how we initiate entering will always reflect the uniqueness of our own personality, gifts, abilities and character. Within this framework, God asks us to move into our world with gentle strength in order to pour out the redeemed passions and life of our soul into others and life itself.

As redeemed men, we have all been designed by God to express our manhood in a relational pattern that is servant-minded and Christlike. As sons, our love for God the Father is most clearly expressed and experienced in the way we redemptively relate to women, children, other men and our families.

Let's celebrate our manhood by entering into relationships that allow us to enjoy intimacy and love. Remember, the Holy Spirit moving and breathing in the most intimate part of your life is making you to be fit sons of your heavenly Father. Don't take your life and intimate relationship with Him and others for granted.

CHAPTER 20

Restoring Intimacy through Brothering

Our culture teaches us to separate intimacy and manhood. The Bible does not. Some of the greatest men of the Bible demonstrated personal strength, emotional transparency and long-term male friendships.

David was one of the great military leaders of his time. His masculine strength is not questioned, but how did he do with feelings, sensitivity and maintaining close friendships with men? We don't have to read long in the Psalms to understand his emotional transparency and sensitivity to feelings. He was able to speak and sing about his love for God, his fears, his guilt, his hurt. He and Jonathan established a deep friendship that endured at great price to both. Intimacy and manhood are comfortably joined in David, the warrior, the king.

Then there was Paul the apostle, a rugged traveler who covered much of the Near East on foot. His endurance of physical hardship and beatings is almost unbelievable, yet Paul's emotional transparency is akin to David's. In his speech to the Ephesian elders he mentions his tears on their behalf (Acts 20:19). When he departed with the expectation of not seeing them again, they wept, embraced and kissed (20:37-38). His deep friendships with Luke, Timothy and Apollos leap out of the text of Acts and his letters. Intimacy and manhood go together in Paul.

The Lord Jesus is, of course, our best example. He is a strong, sensitive, caring and available Man with a wide range of emotions. Purposeful but not reactionary, He confronted the power of the Roman and Jewish establishments without flinching. In the temple He turned over the money changers' tables. He confronted hypocrites and pronounced God's judgment on them. He walked knowingly to His own gruesome death. Personal strength marked His every step, yet He was also tender and caring with lepers, prostitutes, children and even Jerusalem, which rejected Him. In His ministry He developed a close group of friends, living and traveling with a dozen men for three years. John gives us a look at Jesus' willingness to have physical contact with men when he tells us that he (John) "leaned back on Jesus at the [last] supper" (John 21:20). Jesus' model of manhood includes personal strength, emotional sensitivity and the ability to make and enjoy enduring, intimate friendships.

Celebrating the Intimacy of Brothering

Manhood calls us to celebrate intimacy through loving involvement in some very important relationships, namely brothering, mentoring, fathering and husbanding. Join me as we explore the parameters of what it means to enter into manhood as God designed it to be, where intimacy can be richly celebrated. The first relationship we consider is brothering.

Friendship with other men is a very important relationship in which our redeemed manhood can be celebrated. Redeemed men hunger for and enjoy the fellowship and friendship of other males. In the company of men our developing sense of maleness is called out, a true sense of brotherhood developed. Manhood calls to manhood. Brothering involves a deep, meaningful relationship with one other man or a small group of other men.

There are a number of qualities and characteristics that define what brothering is.

1. Brothering is when a man or a small group of men is not ashamed to be your intimate friend and call you brother. "Both the one who makes men holy and those who are made holy are of the same family. So Jesus is not ashamed to call them brothers" (Hebrews 2:11).

If Jesus is not ashamed to identify with us as His brothers, then as men we have been freed to unashamedly have brothers with whom we can deeply identify. The biggest struggle for us in developing meaningful friendships with other men is not the problem of enough time, but is rather the issue of shame over being known personally and intimately, of being naked of soul before another.

To manage our dread of being seen and known by other men we do one of two things. We either retreat into relational passivity and then relationally abandon each other or we choose to dominate other men. By expressing a brand of macho independence that shouts out the message that we need no one, including male friendships, we insulate ourselves from intimacy. Lack of involvement, business and workaholism are only male fig leaves that we use to cover our shame and distract us from our dread of being seen and known.

We have every reason to call each other brothers and to develop a soul fellowship that celebrates our manhood! Jesus took our shame upon Himself on the cross. He has replaced our fear and dread with His love and eternal acceptance. He has covered all our unrighteousness with His righteousness. If we identify with Jesus, then we will want to identify relationally with other men as brothers.

After graduating from college, entering into a career, getting married and having four children, I was left very unaware of needing other men as close friends. I struggled with a deep and chronic fear of failing in my job so I worked harder and longer. Our marriage after eight years of this kind of pace almost ended in divorce. I was not good at cherishing my wife. I had very little relational substance left to give to her. God had to hit me over the head with His "two-by-ten"—a failing marriage and children who were closing up their hearts toward me as their father.

These relational crises began to cultivate the soil of the back forty acres of my soul, preparing to help me begin to humble myself and ask for help. Five years of slow growth began to take place, and in year thirteen of our marriage I became a member of a group of men. Two of the men were Australians, two were Americans and two of us were Canadians. We spent one year together learning how to move through our shame of being fully known and then we were able to enter into the relational joy of being brothers and soul friends. Our group disbanded when we all moved back to our respective countries, but for the last eleven years I have enjoyed the relational riches of being in another small men's group. These two small-group experiences have convinced me that brothering is a gift.

2. Brothering is when a man or a small group of men help you carry your burdens when they become too heavy for you to bear. Nothing cripples our sense and awareness of our manhood more than when we try to hide or carry our own burdens all alone. Paul exhorted: "Carry each other's burdens, and in this way you will fulfill the law of Christ" (Galatians 6:2).

Again Jesus is our best model and example of one who called on other men to come alongside in His time of dire need. He was very close to twelve men, but His most intimate male friends were Peter, James and John. They were so close in fact that He took them with Him into the deepest, darkest hour of His life. What trust! What failure on their part when they fell asleep when the Master was facing the imminence of death!

Peter, James and John are typical men and therefore represent most of us. Like them, we often betray each other by falling asleep and missing those special moments where we could keep vigil for each other as we enter into unknown danger zones. Jesus is saying to us as He said to Peter: "Watch and pray so that you will not fall into temptation. The spirit is willing, but the body is weak" (Mark 14:38).

Men, wake up from your relational sleep! "Brother" one another by helping to carry burdens that are too heavy to carry alone. In so doing, we keep Christ's law of love and relate to other men as He did.

3. Brothering is when a man or a small group of men will let you carry your own load when you are ready and capable of doing so. "Each one should test his own actions. Then he can take pride in himself, without comparing himself to somebody else, for each one should carry his own load" (Galatians 6:4-5).

When we incarnate Jesus to each other by relating and loving, we will then help empower our friends to better handle the burdens of life in a righteous way. Had I been faithfully meeting with a small group of men my first eight years of marriage, I believe I would have avoided the relational crisis that arose. Having a group of men pray with and for me and keep vigil with me about my fear of failure and the ensuing dangers it led to would have enabled me to become a more godly husband and father. Instead, my brothers and I were asleep when we should have been awake.

4. *Brothering is when a man or a small group of men know how and when to wound you.* "Wounds from a friend can be trusted. . . . As iron sharpens iron, so one man sharpens another" (Proverbs 27:6, 17); "Brothers, if someone is caught in a sin, you who are spiritual should restore him gently. But watch yourself, or you also may be tempted" (Galatians 6:1).

Loving brothers and friends will know how and when to do relational surgery on you in order for you to grow into godly, righteous manhood. Several months ago two of my closest male friends, Ted and Ian, confronted me about the same sin my wife had just exposed in me—my lack of true integrity in how I relate with her and them. They spoke the truth in love just as my wife had. The truth felt like a deep wound as it cut to the core of my sin nature. It hurt, but it was spoken in love according to Ephesians 4:15 and it did its work.

Faithful male friends will stand in your way relationally. They will call you on your sin and its impact on them, your spouse and children, on your employer or on your employees. Celebrating our manhood comes when we are faithfully wounded by our friends so growth can take place.

5. Brothering is when a man or a small group of men hold no secrets from you or you from them. "The purposes of a man's heart are deep waters, but a man of understanding draws them out" (Proverbs 20:5); "Therefore confess your sins to each other and pray for each other so that you may be healed. The prayer of a righteous man is powerful and effective" (James 5:16).

Don't go to your grave with any secrets. The amount of personal resources we must invest to keep our secrets hidden from others and even from our ourselves will rob us of celebrating our manhood. The power any secret has to squelch our manhood is in its secrecy. Satan works hard to get us to believe that telling our secret would destroy our life, that we are the only one who has this secret, this struggle. Remember, Satan loves the lone wolf, the man who carries his secrets all alone and thus isolates himself from being known by another. Our secret, deceitful motives and purposes of heart need to be drawn out and exposed so new redemptive directions can be entered into. Our sins need to be confessed so we can be whole and our prayers can be effective.

I will never forget when I told the five men that I meet with weekly about the patterns that sexual lust takes in my life in a yearly cycle. I told the men one of my secrets. I seem to struggle more with sexual temptation and sexual lustful thoughts when I have emptied myself out through teaching, counseling and ministry during the first three or four months in each teaching semester in the seminary. So around the first of December and the first of April I notice a greater struggle with sexual thoughts and temptations.

Having poured the substance of my soul into people, having enjoyed the deep eternal sense of impact from serving God and others, I am now legitimately emptied and in need of renewal. If I don't choose to refill and renew my soul and body as a man with appropriate nourishment—rest, exercise, worship, prayer, the study of the Word, a legitimate hobby, time for my children and wife to love me, time with my male friends—I will too easily be overcome by this wrong source of nourishment.

Letting these five close male friends know my weakness and my vulnerable times of the year gave them opportunity to intercede in prayer for me and with me. As well, they help me monitor my schedule and hold me accountable to ongoing sources of legitimate soul and body nourishment. These men entered into my secret and as a result incarnated the very presence of Jesus to my area of need.

6. *Brothering is when a man or a group of men will give their life for you and you for them.* "My command is this: Love each other as I have loved you. Greater love has no one than this, that he lay down his life for his friends" (John 15:12-13).

Are you this kind of friend? Do you have other men you would die for? Are there men who would die for you? David and Jonathan had this kind of friendship. When it was confirmed that David's life was in danger,

> . . . they kissed each other and wept together—
> but David wept the most.
>
> Jonathan said to David, "Go in peace, for we have sworn friendship with each other in the name of the LORD, saying, 'The LORD is witness between you and me, and between your descendants and my descendants forever.'" (1 Samuel 20:41-42)

Typically when we say "die for you" we think of physical death. Certainly that is the most significant form of dying one can give to his friend. But there are other forms of death that this kind of friendship needs. There is a death to our selfishness that must be entered into; death to our relational and personal comfort zone which we often prefer to live within to stay safe, unexposed and uninvolved; death to our personal reputation. David and Jonathan's friendship modeled many of these forms of dying.

Friendship and friendlessness have consequences in critical areas of life as Solomon expressed so well.

> Two are better than one,
>   because they have a good return for
>   their work:
> If one falls down,
>   his friend can help him up.
> But pity the man who falls
>   and has no one to help him up!
> Also, if two lie down together, they
>   will keep warm.
>   But how can one keep warm alone?
> Though one may be overpowered,
>   two can defend themselves.
> A cord of three strands is not quickly broken.
>   (Ecclesiastes 4:9-12)

Brothering in Real Life

Soon after Jack Benny died, George Burns, the quintessential song and dance man, was interviewed on a TV talk show. When asked about his relationship to Jack, George flicked his unlit cigar and answered with that distinctive voice so experienced in delivering

punchy lines. "Well," he said, "Jack and I had a wonderful friendship for nearly fifty-five years; Jack never
walked out on me when I sang a song, and I never
walked out on him when he played the violin."
Though couched in jest, Burns expressed the fact of
commitment. He and Benny were genuinely close
friends, committed friends. While they were not given
to a formal covenant, hardly a day went by when they
didn't talk, at least by telephone. Each would have
done anything for the other.

The story is told of a military patrol reconnoitering
enemy territory. Taut as piano strings, the little group
of men probed the shadowy images of uncharted terrain. Suddenly, the night was rent by a blinding flash,
and the point soldier was mortally wounded.

While the sergeant screamed for the unit to take
cover, a young recruit plunged insanely ahead to the
dying man. There he, too, was wounded. In extreme
pain, mustering his ebbing strength, he dragged his
now-dead friend back to the unit and collapsed. Above
the roar of the battle the sergeant yelled, "You fool!
Why'd you go get yourself shot for a dead man?"

The recruit replied, "Sarg, I had to hear him say, 'I
knew you'd come.' "

Such epic tales of friendship to the death have been
sung and celebrated throughout the ages. There is a
kernel of truth to them. In every genuine friendship,
some kind of death is involved. The best example and
perfect model is our Lord. He, our friend who sticks
closer than a brother, gave everything for us. He is
waiting for us to reciprocate—with Him and with one
another.

We must never forget that we need each other.
Many men in our culture are in deep bondage in two

ways. One is the bondage of loneliness that is the result of not being close to any other males. The second is the bondage of not ever experiencing either the receiving or the giving of healthy male affection.

In times of neediness we should gather around one another and embrace each other as Jesus is incarnated to the one in need; not as wimps, but as men who will literally hold their friend in their arms while he is weeping out the confession of his sin and pain.

I remember one morning when one of the men in our group poured out the agony of his soul over his wife's divorcing him. While he wept from the depth of his heart, all five of us men got up from the breakfast table and went and surrounded our dear friend and brother. We literally all embraced him in one, big bear hug as he wept. We were able to incarnate the physical affection of the strong arms of our heavenly Father to him in his time of suffering, grief and loss.

Legitimate Male-to-Male Affection

Cultural pressure had turned off legitimate male-to-male affection in many of us for fear of looking gay or feeling less manly. Sinful misuse should not rob us of what is rightfully ours. We have been created to touch in healthy and legitimate ways. We have been called to bond together in a deep experience of male bravado and relational joy. The closest we ever get to seeing this happen in our culture is when a hockey player scores a goal. The players slap each other on the helmets, butt helmets, wrap their arms around each other, slap each other's backs.

I believe God created us to show physical affection. In the four gospels, Jesus is constantly touching others. Touch communicates acceptance and love. But the cultural system and beneath this system, Satan himself, has denied us these experiences. It has locked many of us in our male fortresses so much that we are afraid to let each other know that today we are going through hell and we need help and encouragement.

Developing friendships in a small group of three to four men means giving each other permission to ask hard questions:

"How is your marriage really doing?"

"How do you spend your leisure time?"

"What's your thought life like?"

"Are you into the Word and spending time in prayer?"

"What are you doing to encourage your children to get to know the Lord?"

As one man said, "When your spouse asks those questions, it often feels as though she is on your case and you are a big failure. But when your male friends sit down across from you and ask the same questions, it shows that they care for you."

Many women share a common concern. Although they know that their husbands attend church and make all the right spiritual noises, they have no idea where they are with God. Many express regret that their husbands are not in a small men's group. They so love what they are experiencing with their friends that they hope their husbands will share the same and thus be encouraged to grow spiritually and relationally.

I can testify that my wife Jackie has been the number one supporter of my regular commitment to a group of men. She tells me that it has made me a better man, husband, friend and father. Many times crises have been avoided or defused through my involvement with my group of male friends. I personally don't know how I could survive being alone and relationally independent from other men.

Our heavenly Father longs for us to grow in our obedience and our knowledge and experience of Him. He wants us, by His grace, to mature as men into Christlikeness, but that takes time. We all want "five easy lessons to be an effective Christian" or "eight quick steps" or some code to get spiritual victory. "Formula Christianity" can never bring us to male maturity in the image of Christ. As men made in the likeness of God Himself, we are far too complex for such simplistic and mechanical programs.

For fruit to mature—and ultimately it is we ourselves who are the fruit of the Spirit—there has to be nurture! There is no substitute for the biblical path to maturity. Growth is a pilgrimage, a gradual journey through life. It must be nurtured in the context of active participation in the sacraments, community worship, fellowship and discipline of the church. Study of the Word in private as well as corporately is absolutely essential. Faithful, intimate, private and corporate prayer with God the Father, obedience, worship and service are necessary forms of nurture.

Each aspect of the fruit of the Spirit—that is, each aspect of you as you are transformed—is nurtured through personal relationships. Because our Christian character does not develop in a void, take the initiative to regularly participate in a small group of men if you are not already. Make one of your top priorities this year the making of one to three close personal male friends. I stand as a witness to this truth. I have been in a small men's group for the past eleven years. It has been a true celebration of our manhood!

CHAPTER 21

Restoring Intimacy through Mentoring and Fathering

Brothering is not the only means of restoring intimacy in male relationships. In this chapter, we will consider two others, namely mentoring and fathering.

A Celebration of Redeemed Manhood—Mentoring

I just passed the fifty mark. I have an older man, John, who mentors me. John is giving me much more than information. He has poured his life into me, transferring something of his own spirit. He is my spiritual father. Mentoring by John is a relationship of the older to the younger, the experienced to the inexperienced.

Paul expressed his mentor's heart when he said:

> [B]ut we were gentle among you, like a mother caring for her little children. We loved you so much that we were delighted to share with you not only the gospel of God but our lives as well, because you had become so dear to us. . . .

For you know that we dealt with each of you
as a father deals with his own children, encouraging, comforting and urging you to live lives
worthy of God, who calls you into his kingdom
and glory. (1 Thessalonians 2:7-8, 11-12; see also
2 Timothy 3:10-12, 14)

The primary purpose of mentors is to establish a relationship with a younger man that will cultivate his
growth into manhood, helping him experience the full
purpose of his sonship with God the Father. In so doing, the older man commits to a younger faithful man
the task of stewarding the mysteries of the kingdom of
God. This mentoring process may encompass some or
all of the following principles.

*1. Mentoring is an older man helping a younger man man-
age his grief over the loss of closeness with his natural father.*
The mentoring relationship is most obvious to us in
the father-son relationship. Every male has been designed by God to be fathered by Him and by an
earthly father. And to the extent that we have not been
fathered by our earthly father, we will often struggle
with our sense of sonship with our heavenly Father. As
we move into our older years we will pay a personal
and relational price for that.

When our fathering process has been seriously neglected, we carry the relational scars for a lifetime. That
is gloomy news. But it is good news if we face up to it! If
we name it for what it is—a "father wound" or a "father
hole in our heart"—and begin to develop a righteous response, we will avoid major problems. Ignored, the sense
of grief over the loss of intimacy with our earthly father
can erupt, often trapping us in sexual perversions, power
domination, eating-, chemical- or work-compulsions.

When our father intimacy deficit manifests itself, we can choose to move toward an older man as mentor. This spiritual father can then help us manage our grief over the loss of closeness with our own fathers. Rather than letting this loss of intimacy with Dad end up being a generalized and undermining sense of anxiety, fear or rage, we can localize it and begin to work it through with an older man. As men and sons we all long to be held in the heart of an older man. To the extent that we are not is the corresponding depth of our intimacy deficit and soul pain.

2. Mentoring is an older man holding a younger man in his heart. Older men, you have been designed by God to continually hold a younger man in your heart. To give you a sense of eternity and the experience of eternal impact you need a relationship with a younger man into whom you can feed the cumulative wisdom and experience of life and your walk with God. There is an echo of godliness in a man who never stops being a father to his own children and grandchildren and then beyond these relationships to other men who are younger.

3. Mentoring is an older man holding a younger man accountable in his Christian walk. John has implanted his life into mine. He has provided guidance, affirmation, physical and verbal affection where he gives me fatherly hugs and tells me he loves me. He has exhorted me, rebuked and helped me see some of my sinful motives and behavior. As I reflect on the spiritual father that God has placed in my life to mentor me, I find that John's main purpose has been to root out seeds of rebellion, arrogance, self-contempt and other defects that lay dormant in the unplowed soil of my heart. God has used him to zero in on underlying character flaws so that the Holy Spirit could bring me into His full purpose. In so doing he has chosen to invest a portion of his life in me.

This kind of spiritual fathering demonstrates what it means to be held in the heart of an older man. To give and take with an older, wiser man of God is a very personal and intimate experience for me. He is not afraid to look into my eyes, hear my words and say, "I like what I see and hear" or "I don't like what I see and hear you saying." John is a man who will test me as to what my walk with God is like. He is a man who affirms my good choices, but will also call me to account when he sees me drifting and making wrong ones. John and I continually celebrate our manhood together every time we meet.

4. Mentoring is an older man sharing his wisdom and advice with a younger man. Not too long ago I needed some input from John. At the time, I was struggling with letting go of our oldest daughter Lisa to her fiancé, Kelvin. I had prized her for twenty-one years. We were very close and now another man was wooing her heart. There was a real shift as she gave her heart to him; I was no longer the main man in her life. I had all kinds of ambivalent feelings that I couldn't find words or proper ways to express.

I liked Kelvin but was not always communicating that I did. Several times Jackie confronted me about how rude I was being to our future son-in-law. I claimed that I was not, but denial distorted my perspective. It was only after Jackie and I double-dated with Lisa and Kelvin by taking them out to dinner and then to watch Steve Martin in *Father of the Bride* that I finally could begin to see and understand my behavior and feelings.

I still needed some wise advice and godly direction so I met with John. John has four married daughters, the last of whom had just married. Now here was a man and father who had gone through this letting go process four times and did he ever lay on the wisdom! He shared how each time it was like his heart was being torn out; how he had to learn to accept each of these four sons-in-law for just who they were. He shared from his heart what it was like to learn to trust God for his daughters and their marriages.

Then he prayed for me. He knew exactly how to bring Jesus to my place of struggle and pain. I will never forget our time together. Without John as an older man speaking life and wisdom into my struggling heart, I would not have been able to grow a little more in my manhood and as a father. Thank you, John!

A mentoring relationship can provide a younger man with an extra shot of manly passion. Without a mentor, he often feels underpowered, that he is not living up to his true potential as a man.

The root of some of the problems in the church today can be traced to the older generation of men who are too preoccupied, too busy or too afraid to exercise their mentoring responsibilities to the younger men. Each of us as older men need to be investing ourselves into at least one younger person. And if we are younger, we need to be having a relationship with an older man who will hold us in his heart. That's a rich and intimate experience no man should miss.

5. Mentoring is an older man helping a younger man learn what it is to be a servant, to be under authority. Through my relationship with John, I have discovered an important spiritual truth. The only way to be adequately mentored is to submit to him in servanthood as unto the Lord until he releases me from this relationship. As a man who longs to continue to grow up into godly manhood, I must be under authority. Jesus said the way to greatness is through humble servanthood (see Matthew 23:11-12).

In fact, having a heart after God needs to take place in the crucible of servanthood and in being under authority. Being in submission to an older man like John helps bring to the surface my self-centeredness and the many forms it takes. This process of pruning that God is doing in my life through John is helping me to bear fruit that abides.

6. *Mentoring is an older man helping a younger man move more intimately into the Father-heart of God.* Being mentored is one way the Father moves us more intimately into His Father-heart and His fullness. Developing a godly and intimate relationship with a mentor can cause us to receive his mantle of manhood, his spirit of godliness.

If I were to try to seek a physical symbol, I would say the mentoring relationship is mostly characterized by the baby sucking at the mother's breast. Therein lies the activity of nourishment, the giving from older to younger. And that's what mentoring is all about—nourishment!

I suggest that older men have the primary responsibility in initiating a mentoring relationship with younger men. Older men, we rise up and bless you! We honor you by asking you for your life, wisdom and heart. You have much to give us because you have walked life's pilgrimage ahead of us. Show us the heart of your Father God. Pray for direction, then reach out and embrace a younger man. Ask him if you can pour your life into his. Invite him into yours.

There are at least three ways to handle your mentoring relationship. You can formalize it by meeting regularly. You can keep it informal and meet at each other's request. Or you can use a combination of regularly scheduled times like once a month and then leave the rest of the month open for informal times to meet. The agenda can be formalized by going through a prescribed study or it can be informal with life being your ongoing agenda. And don't forget prayer. Let an older man pray for you and teach you to pray.

Those who are younger, let an older man speak into the areas of your life where you need wisdom, encouragement, rebuke and blessing. Celebrate your manhood in the presence of an older man.

On a personal note, I would like to honor my mentor of ten years, John Unger. He died suddenly just a few months ago from a stroke. Thank you, John, for your love, for holding me in your heart, for bringing the Father-heart of God to me.

A Celebration of Redeemed Manhood—Fathering

Fathering is a wonderful celebration of manhood and is demonstrated in several ways.

1. *Fathering is when a man's heart and affections are toward his children and are set on them.* Luke wrote that John the Baptist would call fathers' hearts back to their children: "And he will go on before the Lord, in the spirit and power of Elijah, to turn the hearts of the fathers to their children and the disobedient to the wisdom of the righteous—to make ready a people prepared for the Lord" (Luke 1:17).

He also wrote about the loving father in the story of the lost son (Luke 15:11-24). Here was a man whose heart affection had never waned or hardened but remained steadfast. When he saw his wayward son returning, he ran to him, embraced him and kissed him. Then he ordered a celebration feast to be prepared in honor of his son's return.

John possibly illustrates best what it means for a father to hold his son in his heart when he wrote about the Son of God and His relationship to His Father: "As the Father has loved me, so have I loved you. Now remain in my love. If you obey my commands, you will remain in my love, just as I have obeyed my Father's commands and remain in his love" (John 15:9-10).

God the Father clearly set the affection of His heart upon His Son, the Lord Jesus. Jesus had no doubt about the love and affection of His heavenly Father. Why? Because God the Father clearly verbalized His affection for His Son at critical times, enabling Him to be at home in His love. The voice from heaven at both His baptism and transfiguration are two examples of this affirmation.

Jim stood up at a men's meeting and described how he had never heard his father tell him that he loved him. He added that his father had never heard those three simple words from his father. Then Jim called his eighteen-year-old son to stand beside him. "Son," he said, "I'm going to break a generational, sinful tradition in our family. I'm here to tell you that I love you as my son." With that, he gave his son an affectionate bear hug. The curse of silence was broken. Love and affection began to flow from Jim to his son and from his son to his children in the next generation.

Fathers, our sons and daughters long to know that the affection of our hearts is set on them. Malachi describes its importance:

> See, I will send you the prophet Elijah before
> that great and dreadful day of the LORD comes.
> He will turn the hearts of the fathers to their
> children, and the hearts of the children to their
> fathers; or else I will come and strike the land
> with a curse (Malachi 4:5-6).

When we as fathers do not love the Lord our God
with all our hearts, souls and strength then we will not
be able to love our sons and daughters as ourselves.
God spoke these words through Moses to His people
and to us warning us of the consequence of not loving
Him, telling us of His blessing when we do: "[F]or I,
the LORD your God, am a jealous God, punishing the
children for the sin of the fathers to the third and
fourth generation of those who hate me, but showing
love to a thousand generations of those who love me
and keep my commandments" (Exodus 20:5-6). Later
Moses wrote: "[H]e is the faithful God, keeping his
covenant of love to a thousand generations of those
who love him and keep his commands" (Deuteronomy
7:9).

Loving God and our children breaks the generational sin and curse bringing love to thousands. Let us
celebrate manhood by setting our affection on our sons
and daughters!

2. Fathering is when a man delights in his children. This
is closely related to setting our affections on our children, but brings an added dimension of relating that is
a reflection of our heavenly Father's heart.

David sang to the Lord the words of this song when
the Lord delivered him from the hand of all his enemies and from the hand of Saul: "He brought me out
into a spacious place; he rescued me because he de-

lighted in me" (Psalm 18:19). The Lord declared: "Is not Ephraim my dear son, the child in whom I delight? . . . Therefore my heart yearns for him; I have great compassion for him" (Jeremiah 31:20).

Isaiah wrote powerfully about the Lord's heart response of delight toward His people:

> No longer will they call you Deserted,
>   or name your land Desolate.
> But you will be called Hephzibah,
>   [means my delight is in her],
>   and your land Beulah
>   [means married];
> for the LORD will take delight in you,
>   and your land will be married.
> As a young man marries a maiden,
>   so will your sons marry you;
> as a bridegroom rejoices over his bride,
>   so will your God rejoice over you.
>   (Isaiah 62:4-5)

Zephaniah also spoke about this quality of delight in the Lord's heart toward His people: "The LORD your God is with you, he is mighty to save. He will take great delight in you, he will quiet you with his love, he will rejoice over you with singing" (Zephaniah 3:17).

On the mountain of transfiguration, God the Father's expression of His heart toward His Son best models this quality of relationship: "This is my Son, whom I love; with him I am well pleased . . ." (Matthew 17:5).

The following anecdote is based on a story told to me by a friend who has since passed away.

It was a cold, snowy Christmas Eve in Manitoba. There we were, tucked into the cozy living room—my sister, brother-in-law, the couple renting their basement suite and me. Five fully grown, functional, supposedly mature adults. Why, then, were we carrying on like half-crazed football fans, yelling, clapping, and cheering at a small object in the center of the room? The answer is simple. First steps.

The "object" who had captured our enthusiastic attention was Timothy, a barely year-old charmer who had chosen that Christmas Eve to take his first steps. His parents, understandably, were leading the frenzied cheering, but the rest of us had no hesitation about joining in.

The same script played itself out over and over again: Timothy, smiling wildly, would gaze around the room. Then, after securing our attention, he would take a few faltering steps—only to fall on the well-diapered section of his anatomy. He carried on undaunted, however, mainly because of his daddy's reaction. Immediately after each of his landings, he would rush over to him, set him up on his feet again, dust him off, and then back away a few steps. "That's okay! Come on Timothy! Come to Daddy!" he would call, arms wide open, his entire body inclined in his direction. Freshly encouraged, he would start out again with confident, albeit wobbly steps.

It didn't seem to matter to either of them that they had to repeat this procedure over and over again. He just continued to move toward his father's outstretched arms; he continued to invite him to move toward him. With love and encouragement embracing him, he found courage to walk.

Amidst the cheering for Timothy, I began to focus my attention more on his father. The gentle delight on his face was a study in itself. Not once did he yell at him for falling. Not once did he roughly yank him to his feet. Not once did he chide him for not learning faster. He was simply thrilled that he was trying, delighted that he was moving in his direction, thrilled that he was responding to his voice and presence.

Slowly the thought formed itself in my mind: "This earthly father's delight is just a reflection of the heavenly Father's. If Timothy's father could delight in him like this, how much more . . . "

My cheering abated somewhat. It became increasingly difficult to cheer over the lump that was forming in my throat. The thought persisted: "If an earthly father could delight like that—thank you, little Timothy, and little Timothy's daddy for showing me a picture of my Abba Father's delight in me. Dear Father, indeed!"[1]

Hosea describes this delight in graphic terms. God's love and delight for Israel tells the same story.

> When Israel was a child, I loved him,
>   and out of Egypt I called my son. . . .
> It was I who taught Ephraim to walk,
>   taking them by the arms;
> but they did not realize
>   it was I who healed them.

I led them with cords of human kindness,
   with ties of love;
I lifted the yoke from their neck
   and bent down to feed them.
      (11:1, 3-4)

If it is true that the Lord delights in us and wants to talk to us, why should not we enjoy and delight in Him? As one father put it, "My five-year-old son called me today in the middle of an important meeting, but I loved hearing from him just as I know the Lord wants to hear from us."

As fathers I believe we need to express delight in our children. In celebrating our manhood, we need to take the relational risk of verbalizing our enjoyment rather than just assuming our children will see and experience it.

If our fathers never delighted in us, then we need to enter more richly into the intimacy of our sonship relationship with our heavenly Father. Realizing that our Father in heaven delights in us as He always has in His people can then free us as fathers to delight in our sons and daughters. Knowing our heavenly Father well is the beginning of our entry into the delight of His heart. We need a theology of delight. Let's celebrate this theology with our own children and grandchildren.

3. *Fathering is when a man wants to say to his children, "Imitate me as I imitate the Father."* That is celebration! Paul expresses this truth well. He said, "You became imitators of us and of the Lord" (1 Thessalonians 1:6). In the next chapter, he carried on with this thought: "For you know that we dealt with each of you as a father deals with his own children, encouraging, com-

forting and urging you to live lives worthy of God, who calls you into his kingdom and glory" (2:11-12). In Ephesians, he wrote: "Be imitators of God, therefore, as dearly loved children" (5:1).

My son Scott and I were walking on a narrow road out in the woods on a late winter afternoon. After walking together for a while, I suddenly noticed he was no longer beside me. I turned around to see where he had gone. There he was trying to put each small foot into my footprints in the snow, stretching his shorter legs as far as he could. I realized that whether I liked it or not, my son was imitating me and would for many years to come.

What I want my son and three daughters to imitate and learn from me is that our heavenly Father is very personal, loving and holy; that His heart is set on us. I want them to know that their heavenly Father delights in them because I know and experience His delight in me. I want them to see that He is worthy of our total love, worship and praise. We can only expect our children to imitate what we model.

Children—what a glorious opportunity to imitate the Father-heart of God!

4. *Fathering is when a man celebrates his manhood by lovingly disciplining his children so they will get a clearer picture of One who is stronger, holier, more dependable and trustworthy.* As fathers we want our children to know and experience that God's glory is more central to life than our human promotion of their well-being. One of our highest callings as dads is promoting in our homes that God has designed us to glorify and enjoy Him forever. The writer of Proverbs says this well: "My son, do not despise the LORD's discipline and do not resent his rebuke, because the LORD disciplines those he loves, as a

father the son he delights in" (Proverbs 3:11-12; see also Hebrews 12:4-14).

5. *Fathering is when a man celebrates his manhood by not provoking his children to wrath by abandoning or dominating them, but rather by bringing them up in the training and instruction of the Lord.* "Fathers, do not exasperate your children; instead, bring them up in the training and instruction of the Lord" (Ephesians 6:4).

To be fathers who train and instruct our sons and daughters, we too must be men who are under the authority and Lordship of Christ where we are being trained and instructed in the ways of the Master. Learn from God's Word, from your times of intimacy through prayer and reflection with your heavenly Father. Men, we need to learn from each other as fathers, learn from our own fathers. A teachable and humble spirit will equip us well to continually celebrate our manhood by taking our children by the hand and leading them in the way of the Master.

Godly fathering is a wonderful way to celebrate manhood!

Endnote

[1] Connie Kondos, "Your Heavenly Father's Delight," unpublished story, Otterburne, MB, 1991. Used by permission of author.

CHAPTER 22

Restoring Intimacy through Husbanding

God has designed and equipped us as image-bearing males to imitate and reflect His husbanding heart for His bride, the Church. What a privileged way to celebrate our manhood! Let's look at some important ways for us as men to both understand our wives and follow Christ's example in husbanding them.

Paul instructs us as husbands in a very direct, clear way:

> For the husband is the head of the wife as Christ is the head of the church, his body, of which he is the Savior. Now as the church submits to Christ, so also wives should submit to their husbands in everything.
>
> Husbands, love your wives, just as Christ loved the church and gave himself up for her to make her holy, cleansing her by the washing with water through the word, and to present her to himself as a radiant church, without stain or wrinkle or any other blemish, but holy and

331

blameless. In this same way, husbands ought to love their wives as their own bodies. He who loves his wife loves himself. (Ephesians 5:23-28)

Understanding Our Wives

To husband our wives as Christ husbands the Church, we must first understand them, the struggles they face and the desires of their hearts. Women, like men, were impacted significantly by the fall. We need to recognize the impact that God's pronounced judgment on Eve has had on all women. We need to grow in our understanding of the enslaving, sinful desires that are released in the feminine soul because of their sinfulness, emotional wounding and soul pain. Here are several facts we should remember as we seek to husband our wives.

1. Our wives are deeply wounded. A woman's source of wounding is vast and varied. Wounds can be caused by a father who did not prize her with his love and affection, who did not make her sense from him that it was good to be feminine and a woman. He may also have abused her through relational neglect, abandonment or through emotional, mental cruelty or incest. There may have been sexual abuse by other males—brothers, cousins, uncles, grandfathers or other male acquaintances or strangers.

Or perhaps she grew up with a mother who was either critical and overbearing or helpless, dependent, and controlling, resulting in your wife not knowing how to be truly feminine. Remember, it was your wife's mother who God designed to teach her how to be womanly. It was her father who God entrusted with the privilege of affirming in her that it is good to be feminine and a woman.

Another common source of wounding is the lack of any real close girlfriends in whom she could confide and who made her feel special and loved.

Be sensitive to the pain of your wife's heart. Enter into her woundedness, not with the primary purpose of giving her answers, but of exploring it with her, understanding it and walking with her through it. This is something of what it means to husband her. Too many of us feel uncomfortable and therefore out of control with our wife's pain and so we either ignore her or we enter into her woundedness with the main agenda of trying to fix it. Often our motive is not for her good, but to remove the discomfort and dread that comes into our soul from being out of control. Most of us simply do not know what to do with her pain.

2. Our wives' sinful, enslaving desires are influencing her strategies for managing her pain and the uncontrollable things in the fallen, sinful world around her. In husbanding a wife we must recognize that she uses fig leaves too. As she struggles with the sinful, enslaving desire to hide her inadequacies, she chooses something of her own making to cover whatever she believes is shameful and unattractive on the inside and outside of her.

Explore with her who has shamed her and how. What has she done to shame herself and others? What is it about her being feminine that she is ashamed of—her body, her personality, her sexuality, her abilities, her intelligence, her gifts, her being a wife or a mother? Seek to find out with her how and when she hides and covers these feelings and areas of shame and ugliness about her. And by all means, cherish her with the gentleness of Jesus!

Genesis 3:7-8 tells us that Eve was involved with Adam in the use of fig leaves to cover her nakedness of body and soul. She too hid from the Lord God among the trees of the garden. Understand that your wife will want to hide when she feels shame, feels ugly, feels used, feels guilt as she experiences her sin or the sin of someone else, especially yours. Don't ignore her fig leaves, her ways of going into hiding. Also don't chide or make light of her sinful strategies. Let her know how they hurt and wound you and destroy any sense of spirit, soul and body oneness between you. Incarnate the mercy, grace and forgiveness of Jesus to her. That is husbanding. That is celebrating what a real man of God will do to minister to his wife.

3. Our wives struggle with the sinful, enslaving desire to take control of life and relationships. This is especially true with you and it comes into operation when she feels either the threat or reality of physical or soul pain that leaves her in an unsafe situation.

Genesis 3:16 reminds us that our wives will experience physical pain in childbirth and relational pain in marriage and family life. Her sinful, enslaving desire at those times will be to get back into control by manipulating you as her husband to be to her what you are not being, or what God is not being to her. She will demand that you or God had better make her world and relationships safe and pain free. Her natural, sinful tendency will be to avoid putting her trust and dependency in God.

As husbands, our natural reaction will be sinful. When we feel our wives' sinful passion to control and manipulate us, Scripture tells us that we will rule over her (Genesis 3:16). That form of ruling will not minister to her, but will result in our exercise of power to get back in control. Our manipulation through the use of relational, verbal or physical power will destroy any immediate hope of intimacy of spirit, soul and body.

As husbands, the only way to manage our reaction to our wives' sinful manipulation for control will be to radically depend on God to show us and teach us how to enter into her fear, pain and sin in the same loving way He would. Celebrating your sonship with your heavenly Father will free you to love and husband your wife as a man of God.

4. A woman will choose to close up and harden her feminine spirit when she feels exposed, vulnerable and afraid of being used or taken advantage of by you or someone else more powerful than she. In Genesis 3:13 the Lord tries to enter into Eve's life and involve Himself by asking her what she has done. Eve's response is to harden her heart, to close up her spirit toward the Lord and to her responsibility for betraying her husband and the command of God. Unwilling to admit her own responsibility, she blames the serpent for deceiving her.

Our wives have inherited this same sinful, enslaving desire from Eve. Recognize her battle with keeping her feminine soul open, soft and inviting to you as her husband. It is hard for her to feel safe in inviting you to enter into her soul and enjoy who she is and what she has to offer you. This is especially true if she believes her soul is ugly, shamed, abused or used.

When she feels out of control and unsafe, it will be hard for her to let you enter into her soul. Remember, if she believes, feels or perceives in any way that you treat her as ugly or unattractive, she will close her soul up and harden it toward you to protect herself from more pain and hurt.

If she has been mistreated and sinned against by others in her past, and she has not worked through it, she will have a heart that is impenetrable by you or by anyone else, including the Holy Spirit. If she is harboring an unforgiving spirit toward her perpetrator or toward you and a bitter spirit has grown up inside her, she will find it impossible to open up her feminine spirit to you or to invite you to enter in to enjoy the substance of who she is as a woman and wife.

Husband her by incarnating the presence of Jesus to her to create a haven of safety in your presence. Do not be critical! Be open to her feedback about ways that you mistreat her or take advantage of her. Ask her how you exercise power over her in ways that result in her feeling unsafe and therefore choosing to close up and harden her heart toward you as her husband. This is your way of husbanding her as a man of God in relation to this sinful, enslaving desire of hers.

5. A woman's sinful desire is to use whatever is at her disposal to manipulate her husband. She does this to get what she wants and believes she needs, in order to be more inviting to you, others and even to God.

Genesis 3:6 states that when she saw that the fruit of the tree was good for food and pleasing to the eye, and also desirable for gaining wisdom (which gives power), she took some and ate it.

Like Eve, our wives' sinful, enslaving desire will be to misuse food, or misuse whatever can make her pleasing to her own eyes or to yours—fashion and an overemphasis on external beauty or her sexuality. Or she will misuse wisdom and knowledge (education) to give her greater opportunities and power, so she will then be more successful and appealing. If people, or you as her husband, will be more enticed because of her external beauty, her sexuality, her power, position, personality and all of what she can offer, then she will become enslaved to that. Remember, the tree of knowledge of good and evil and all its alluring fruit to bring pleasure (good) and do away with pain (evil) is just as big a temptation to your wife as it is to you.

Be humble before your wife, owning your vulnerability to the temptations of the fruit from the tree. Model eating and nourishing your soul from the tree of life. Then in love lead her to the fruit of life that will nourish her soul and give to her an inner beauty that is of precious value in the eyes of God and to the eyes of your heart, as her husband.

Husbanding Our Wives

As sons of the Father and men after the heart of God, here are some important ways for us to husband our wives with gentle strength. Our motive and purpose is to provide leadership for our wives in the way Christ does to His Church, leadership that serves her in order to make her whole, to evoke her beauty and to bring the best out of her, leadership that allows the Holy Spirit through you as her husband to dress her in dazzling white silk, radiant with holiness.

1. Respect the uniqueness of your wife. Don't force her to fit into these sinful, enslaving desire categories like some tightly closed box. Let her take you to where she is and be humble enough to let her teach you how to enter into the mystery of her inner self, and when needed, to help her overcome her sin and pain.

2. Enter with gentle strength into the mystery of the redeemed desires that free her to be the woman God designed her to be. What an opportunity to minister to her the incarnational love of her Father God! As husbands we can enter into her heart and empower her with the mercy, grace and love of Jesus.

Husbands, in the same way be considerate as you live with your wives, and treat them with respect as the weaker partner and as heirs with you of the gracious gift of life, so that nothing will hinder your prayers. (1 Peter 3:7)

Husbands, love your wives and do not be harsh with them. (Colossians 3:19)

Husbands, we have a God-ordained opportunity to celebrate our manhood by blessing and empowering our wives through cooperating with the Holy Spirit's release of her redeemed desires. Because Jesus promised to be the Shepherd and Overseer of her soul, understand then what redeemed desires are released in your wife. Understand what motivates her to actively respond with a softness of spirit and tender strength to invite you to enter in and enjoy the richness of her inner feminine beauty. "For you were like sheep going astray, but now you have returned to the Shepherd and Overseer of your souls" (1 Peter 2:25).

3. *Willingly understand that she is free to actively respond in order to cultivate and express her inner beauty.* Remember that she as a holy woman is beautiful before God just like the women of old (1 Peter 3:4-6). She is a true daughter of Sarah, unanxious and unintimidated, because she is kept by the Shepherd of her soul. This is what God says is true about her.

As husbands we need to see our wives as God sees them. We need to cooperate with God's agenda and purpose for our wives which is to cultivate her inner beauty and free her to invite others to enjoy her expression of it. She longs to be enjoyed. She deeply desires to bring delight to the heart of her heavenly Father as His daughter. She has been designed by God to captivate you, her children and others with her holy beauty.

As husbands, celebrate your manhood by continually cherishing her on a daily basis. Prize and delight in her, keep finding ways to bless the deepest parts of her femininity. Keep her as the apple of your eye! Be creative by being teachable before God the Father, His Word and your wife. Spend some valuable personal energy and time learning how to invest in your wife's development of inner beauty. Discover what touches her soul. Find out from her what her language of love is, by what specific ways she longs to feel special and be cherished by you alone.

In your men's group seek the Lord together to discover how He wants you to let her know that it is good for her to be a woman. There is lots of room for us to grow in our husbanding skills. Water the seeds of inner beauty in her with your prayers. Bless her unique qualities of femininity with your continued personal ways of choosing her over and over as your wife.

4. *Let your wife go "off duty" in regards to the uncertainties that surround her.* Husbanding will call on you to pay attention, to grow in your awareness that your wife is free to rest more fully and respond more spontaneously, by going "off duty" in regards to the uncontrollable realities of life. In order for your wife to let go of what are not her God-designed creatorial responsibilities she will need to place her dependency, not in you, but in the truth that God wonderfully prizes her as His daughter.

5. *Be willing to lay down your life for your wife.* As husbands we have the creatorial responsibility to

sacrificially love our wives by giving our lives for them. Our initiative to lead them is to be marked by a servant leadership that fits who each of us is as a unique image-bearer. Jesus said that we are to lead as husbands by serving our wives! Giving this kind of leadership will free them to let go of our areas of irresponsibility as we assume our God-given role.

Take the risk to ask her what areas of your responsibility she has had to take on because of your sinful abdication of your husbanding or fathering role. We need to free our wives to rest more fully so they can spontaneously love more richly. This is how they will feel prized by both God and us. Husbanding our wives means we will treat them the same way we want our daughters to be treated by their future husbands, the same way we want our sons to treat someone else's daughter when they marry.

6. *Identify and discard that which is in you that blocks your wife from fully expressing her femininity.* Never underestimate the wisdom of God's design for women and wives. He planned for them to freely rest in who He designed them to be so they could spontaneously respond in giving their inner beauty away to others. We need to be sensitive to what it is in us that blocks our wives from being free to nourish us with their inner beauty. We need to make them feel safe in our presence. We can create a relational atmosphere of safety by defending and protecting the deepest realities of their feminine soul. Ask her what she values about herself, what it is that she would want you to defend and protect at the cost of your selfishness and even your life. She longs to take the uniqueness of her personality, her spiritual gifts, her personal and physical resources and use them to nurture relational life in you as her husband.

Does she know that you would protect and stand up for those qualities of inner beauty that she longs to use for God's glory and your enrichment? Ask her if she senses that you value and treasure her inner beauty to the point of defending who she is. This could be done in any number of ways. The important thing is that you ask.

7. Recognize and welcome her longing to invite you to enjoy her femininity. Husbanding involves being aware of the deep redeemed longings of our wives to invite us to enter into the deepest parts of who they are as women. Enhance your wife's sense of being an inviting woman by asking her to bless you, to minister to the deep places of your soul. Ask her to bring all of who she is and thereby incarnate Jesus to your places of need— your sinfulness, your pain, your anger, your weaknesses, your limitations and soul dread. Let her support and affirm your strengths, gifts, personal and physical resources, your joys, hopes and dreams.

We need to let our wives pray for us, to incarnate the love, grace, mercy and forgiveness of Jesus. Give her ongoing permission to speak the truth in love to you as her husband. Let her rebuke you, exhort you, encourage and edify you with the richness of who she is in Jesus Christ. If we treasure what she is able to bring to us so that we can grow and mature, she will then grow in her redeemed desire to invite others into the depths of her being. What a way to treasure our wives and celebrate our manhood. Husbanding is a God-ordained calling. He has designed us to husband our wives like Christ, the Bridegroom, husbands His bride, the Church.

God longs for us as men to celebrate our manhood by brothering and mentoring one another, by fathering our sons and daughters and by husbanding our wives. Why? Because He celebrated our freedom to be re-deemed, image-bearing sons of His by raising His Son up from the curse of sin, hell, Satan and death. We can do nothing less than celebrate our sonship, our re-deemed manhood, in these intimate and personal rela-tionships. What hope! What opportunities! What a privilege to be men after the heart of God!

CHAPTER 23

Humility that Entices

Ask most men what *humility* or *meekness* means and they will probably say, "Weakness." And to most of us that's a scary word. We would much rather hear talk of power, control, dominance—these are terms we can sink our emotional teeth into. Yet Jesus Himself said, "Take my yoke upon you and learn from me, for I am gentle and humble ["meek and lowly," in the KJV] in heart" (Matthew 11:29). On another occasion He said, "Blessed are the meek, for they will inherit the earth" (5:5). It is obvious that the Lord is calling us to something that is close to His heart, though unnatural to man.

One distinguishing characteristic of this meekness is its strength. Paul spoke of this meekness of character having an all-surpassing power: "But we have this treasure in jars of clay to show that this all-surpassing power is from God and not from us. We are hard pressed on every side, but not crushed; perplexed, but not in despair; persecuted, but not abandoned; struck down, but not destroyed" (2 Corinthians 4:7-9).

What is it about humility, this meekness, that it is so powerful? One alternate translation for meekness is "gentleness." It requires strength to be men who are gentle. Gentleness is the opposite of abrasiveness, and it flows from that kind of confident strength that is the opposite of arrogance. As men who grow from the security of our sense of sonship with God the Father, we do not need to intimidate, but can be kind and humble in our ways of entering into relationships and life. When we become meek or humble before God, we will exercise that inner strength that enables us to be gentle men rather than violent.

The mysterious wonder of New Testament revelation is that we see this humility lived out before our eyes in One who comes to us clothed in our own humanity yet saying, "Anyone who has seen me has seen the Father" (John 14:9).

In Jesus the ideal and the actual are one. He is the norm of truest humanity, that is, humanity as originally intended and created. As Professor Henry Drummond said, "Jesus is the perfect Gentleman—the exquisite blend of gentle and man, of tenderness and virile heroism; meek and lowly in heart, but with an awesome flash of ire in His eyes before which the temple money-traffickers cowered and slunk away."[1]

He was often in prayer, but He was no head-in-the-clouds dreamer. He enjoyed periodic solitude but He was no isolationist. There was moral separation, yet no social aloofness. There was a sanctity about Him but no sense of spiritual elitism. He despised hypocrisy, but was compassionate to those who were needy, broken and contrite. He did not play off or ignore the rich nor did He despise the poor. He neither coveted wealth nor condoned poverty. Jesus never compromised principle, yet He was a congenial mixer with an aliveness toward people, things and life. He had boundless love, friendship, understanding for children, for the elderly, for the sick, for the suffering, for the demonized, for the bad who wanted to be different and the good who wanted to become better. He saw God everywhere and in everything. His passion was to do the will of His heavenly Father. He was the greatest embodiment of gracious otherism ever known; and most significant of all, in revealing the one true Godhead, He revealed also the one ideal manhood.

Years ago in Manchester, England, a minister prayed this prayer: "O God, make us intensely spiritual, but keep us perfectly natural, and always thoroughly practical—even as Jesus was."[2] This prayer captured the dominant themes of the Lord's holy manhood—intensely spiritual, perfectly natural, thoroughly practical; the living expression of God who is spirit, light and love. God calls us to be like Christ in heart and life, men whose number one passion is to have a heart after God's.

Humble Men Are Intensely Spiritual

The only way to enter into life and the world in a way that entices others to Christ is to let our hearts be molded and shaped after God's own heart. Two men from the Old Testament can help us better understand what it means to be so shaped.

Saul, Israel's first king, was a man of the people's own choosing. True, he was anointed by Samuel at the Lord's bidding, but he was given to the people as one who fit their image of a king, not the Lord's. They wanted a king who could lead them into battle and defeat their enemies. Saul was tall, giving the appearance of strength and courage. He seemed to be everything they needed. Even Samuel was deceived by it all. When later it was revealed what kind of man Saul really was—that he loved sacrifice rather than obedience and the fat of rams rather than heeding the Lord (see 1 Samuel 15:22-26)—Samuel was deeply grieved.

Yet in the choice of Saul's successor, Samuel would once again look at what was outward. When he laid his eyes on Eliab, the eldest son of Jesse, he was convinced that the Lord's anointed stood before him, for he too was tall and strong. The Lord rebuked Samuel for such a hasty superficial judgment, warning him not to look at appearance or the height of stature. It is the heart that counts, and the Lord looks at our hearts (see 1 Samuel 16:7).

David, the youngest and most insignificant of the family, had not even been called to the anointing at first. He was left to tend the sheep. He was insignificant in the eyes of others, yet he was the man of God's own choosing. Why? Because he was a man after God's own heart.

This is the indispensable characteristic that is needed in order for humility to abide in us as men, humility that will entice others to Christ. David was reminded of this most forcefully when, having fallen into the sin of adultery and murder, he was brought under conviction through the word of God spoken by the prophet Nathan. His heart was convicted as he confessed to God: "Surely you desire truth in the inner parts; you teach me wisdom in the inmost place" (Psalm 51:6). Then David prayed that God would create in him a pure heart and renew a steadfast spirit within him, and grant him a willing spirit to sustain him (51:10, 12).

Our hearts are to be conformed—molded and shaped—after God's own heart. Why? So that we may love what He loves and abhor what He abhors; so that we are fit to follow and lead, to serve and be served, to love and be loved. To follow without this kind of heart is hypocrisy and deceit; to lead without such a heart is tyranny and an abdication of our role and function. To serve without such a heart is phoniness; to be served without is manipulation. To love without such a heart is sounding brass and tinkling symbol; to be loved without is to become hardened, needing no one.

What is in our hearts today? Is there truth in our innermost being? That is God's desire for us. Is there a willing spirit within us? God requires it of us. As we enter into our world, do our lives give evidence that we are on this kind of pilgrimage with hearts after God? This is God's challenge to us.

Jeremiah warned that our hearts are deceitful above all things and beyond cure and that we cannot understand this reality about ourselves (see Jeremiah 17:9). That is why David demonstrated humility by praying and asking God to search him and know his heart (see Psalm 139:23). We need God's searching in order that we might know what is in us, that we would know the deceitfulness and wickedness of our hearts.

All too often, we are unconcerned about what is deep inside. Like Samuel, we are more concerned with appearance than we are about substance. It is out of the heart that come the real issues of life. Thus we are exhorted above everything else to guard our heart because it is the wellspring of life (see Proverbs 4:23). On many occasions instead of guarding our hearts, we are careless and indifferent. Many of us will spend more time grooming our bodies than caring for and guarding our hearts. Can we possibly hope to be men "after God's own heart" by choosing to invest our time in living this way?

God is calling us to repent of our preoccupation with externals, appearance and reputation, and to begin focusing on substance and directing ours hearts after His. We must do this not only in how we deal with ourselves, but also in our relationships with others. Function is never to usurp substance in our relationships and the way we live life.

Let us be certain that we are not Sauls. To be sure, he was acclaimed to be among the prophets (1 Samuel 10:11). He also sought the favor of the Lord through sacrifice (13:12). He even erected an altar to the Lord (14:35). Yet his heart was not after the heart of God and God was displeased!

Let us purpose deep in our souls to be found pleasing in God's sight, even when He looks upon our hearts. Let us agree with David to have the kind of heart that was molded and shaped after God's, a heart that knows this about God:

> You do not delight in sacrifice, or I would
> bring it;
> you do not take pleasure in burnt offerings.
> The sacrifices of God are a broken spirit;
> a broken and contrite heart,
> O God, you will not despise. . . .
> Then there will be righteous sacrifices,
> whole burnt offerings to delight you;
> then bulls will be offered on your altar.
> (Psalm 51:16-17, 19)

Jesus described the kind of life that will delight God the Father. It is found in Matthew 5:3-12 in a portion of Scripture commonly known at The Beatitudes. In these verses He speaks of a righteous sacrifice of a broken spirit, a broken and a contrite heart.

What Jesus cries out for is radical discipleship, passionate spirituality and a dependency on God that is like no other. Too many men remain on the fringe of this kind of intense spirituality. One can see them standing apart, at the back of the church—if indeed they come at all—or bored, passive and detached among the congregation. Many men in Western cultures simply cannot relate satisfactorily to the Christian spirituality presented to them. One way to gauge this phenomenon is to take a head count at your local church next Sunday; the female-to-male ratio will often range between 2:1 and 5:1.

Sad to say, many Christian men and women have unconsciously come to believe that the church is a woman's natural domain and that a man can relate to God only through women or through becoming womanlike. This growing attitude in some areas of Christendom reinforces the sexist stereotypes that women are spiritual and men worldly, women moral and men pragmatic, women nurturing and men violent.

In some theological circles words like "Father", "Lord" and "Son" are terms that smack of patriarchal bias and are to be shunned. As the feminist movement exorcises the "demons" of male oppression from Christianity, it also threatens to cast out the spirit of manhood and masculinity as well. Radical feminism has tended to sterilize Christianity's life-giving manliness by leaving God a victim of a sex change—a God who loves no longer as a father, but as an abstract, neutered "warm fuzzy." Jesus becomes to many men so meek and mild that He no longer calls them to radical discipleship and the cross, only to nurturing and gentleness. In some denominations where liturgy was once a powerhouse of transformational symbols, it has now become a butterfly-banner-and-balloon affair with much fussing and fluttering about.

What happens to us men when we are divorced from a deep spiritual experience of our own manhood? When Christianity does not address issues that men face and fight every day, they often are left feeling that the church is irrelevant. When the church provides no safe place for men to address and deal with specific manly issues, men either drop out, shut down or become passive observers, mere spiritual spectators. This in turn carries over into their significant relationships where spirituality is never discussed or encouraged.

Men who suffer from spiritual emasculation are lacking in spiritual passion. They are life-preserving men, but not exactly life-giving. Newly neutered Christianity in some denominations is beginning to produce a generation of men with no spiritual intensity or passion, with no fight left in them. St. Ignatius' famous prayer has lost all meaningful impact for many spiritually passionless males: "To give and not count the cost, to fight and not heed the wounds, to toil and not seek for rest, to labor and not seek for reward, save that of knowing we are doing Your most holy will."

For many other men, the lack of an attractive male spirituality leads to more tragic results. Confronted with a religious system that seems to require abandonment of their male qualities and that provides more moral reprobation than spiritual guidance, large numbers unhesitatingly choose to exercise their male passion in pursuit of money, sports, careers and power. And major corporations, the military, coaches and sports institutions are all too ready to exploit their deepest male desires. The result is often a vicious, uncontrolled competitiveness, an unrestrained passion of "agony" that lets loose the worst "demons" inside men and wounds anyone unfortunate enough to stand in their way.

But the cost to our own lives is even higher as we are devastated by unspiritual masculine stress. This unbalanced masculinity has resulted in men having a substantially higher suicide rate, a life expectancy almost ten percent lower than women's, and over fifteen times as many males in prison as females. Men are not only overwhelmingly victimized by crime, but are also four times as likely to be arrested as are women.[3]

As Christian men, we urgently need to rediscover and enter into a life-giving spirituality that is like that which is seen in Jesus. I believe that around the world at this moment men are seeking after God. They are praying and fasting for revival and renewal, dealing with their sin, worshiping and singing praises, enduring hardships for their faith and for justice. We are deeply spiritual and we passionately thirst and hunger for an intimacy with our heavenly Father that is genuinely expressed in how we live life. May God grant that we recover all that we have given up or has been stolen from us!

Humble Men Are Perfectly Natural

When spiritual passion grows and begins to flow out of who we are as men, we need to be aware of spiritual arrogance. There is a danger of becoming so heavenly minded that we are no longer of any earthly good.

Humble men are not afraid to live according to God's design as male image-bearers, to express their humanity through their spiritual passion. The more spiritually passionate we become, the more human we are.

Jesus modeled His full humanity by getting adequate rest, eating properly, enjoying His Father's creation. He worked hard, but never became a workaholic; invested in relationships, but did not idolize them; gave totally of Himself, but never refused to receive or be ministered to. Jesus was fully human in that He felt comfortable with His maleness. His sexuality was not distorted or twisted by sin. He was personally respectful. He honored His earthly father, expressed love toward His mother and siblings and was very alive and intimately involved with His twelve disciples. When associating with women, Jesus was very comfortable with His sexuality. He made women feel loved, honored, valued, equal in dignity and free to be image-bearers who were fully feminine. He let them enjoy Him, serve and minister to Him.

Jesus was willing to suffer hardships in order to see the will of His heavenly Father accomplished. He was passionately forthright in dealing with sin, evil, religiosity, hypocrisy, disease, demonization, riches and the improper use of power amongst fallen humanity.

Getting closer to God the Father as His sons does not mean giving up our humanity and therefore our maleness; rather it means fully embracing all that He made us to be and expressing it for the glory of God and the good of others. This is what it means to be perfectly natural like Jesus.

Jesus made it clear that we as men will find and enjoy our maleness by following His example in these ways:

> Anyone who loves his father or mother more than me is not worthy of me; anyone who loves his son or daughter more than me is not worthy of me; and anyone who does not take his cross and follow me is not worthy of me. Whoever finds his life will lose it, and whoever loses his life for my sake will find it. (Matthew 10:37-39)

> Instead, whoever wants to become great among you must be your servant, and whoever wants to be first must be slave of all. For even the Son of Man did not come to be served, but to serve, and to give his life as a ransom for many. (Mark 10:43-45)

As sons of our heavenly Father, it is perfectly natural for our redeemed hearts to want to be like Jesus, who left His equal status with God to be clothed in humanity; who left sovereign rule to become a servant and die. Imitating this powerful example becomes a growing passion that infects our souls.

The apostle Paul's advice for living a perfectly and redemptively natural life is this:

> So I say, live by the Spirit, and you will not gratify the desires of the sinful nature. For the sinful nature desires what is contrary to the Spirit, and the Spirit what is contrary to the sinful nature. They are in conflict with each other, so that you do not do what you want. But if you are led by the Spirit, you are not under law.
>
> . . . Those who belong to Christ Jesus have crucified the sinful nature with its passions and desires. Since we live by the Spirit, let us keep

in step with the Spirit. Let us not become conceited, provoking and envying each other. (Galatians 5:16-18, 24-26)

Humble Men Are Thoroughly Practical

Like Jesus, we are to walk our theology, not just talk it. Truth must be lived out in how we relate, in how we enter into our world. Being thoroughly practical means being down-to-earth about spiritual realities. The only way we can develop this kind of Christlike practicality is to be men of prayer. The symbol of sonship with our heavenly Father is a man on his knees.

James addresses our need to be down-to-earth and on our knees about what matters most to our heavenly Father (see James 4:1-10). He warns us about selfishness and lust, worldliness and pride. And then he makes this plea:

> Submit yourselves, then, to God. Resist the devil, and he will flee from you. Come near to God and he will come near to you. Wash your hands, you sinners, and purify your hearts, you double-minded. Grieve, mourn and wail. Change your laughter to mourning and your joy to gloom. Humble yourselves before the Lord, and he will lift you up. (James 4:7-10)

In order to get on our feet and humbly enter into life, prayer must be the most basic, practical reality of our worship. While God certainly knows our needs and wants, He invites us to become intimate with Him by verbalizing these concerns. This is not to nudge Him out of slumber into action; it's because prayer deepens our reliance on Him. In prayer we acknowledge our dependence on the Lord and give Him glory. Until we are first men on our knees, we will never be able to enjoy Him in this life or the next.

Often in the Psalms, David recounts God's great works to Him. The Lord obviously knows what He has accomplished, but by telling Him of His glorious deeds, David strengthens His relationship with the Lord and worships Him in Spirit and in truth. Paul instructed us to do this very thing: "[P]ray in the Spirit on all occasions with all kinds of prayers and requests. With this in mind, be alert and always keep on praying for all the saints" (Ephesians 6:18).

Prayer is effective in keeping us thoroughly humble and practical because God has chosen it as a means to bring about His purposes. Therefore, it is important to know how to pray. Prayer should include adoration and praise, confession of our sins, passionate gratitude, as well as supplication or intercession. Prayer changes our lives, the lives of our families, neighbors and the events of life. The story of Elijah both stopping and starting rain through praying is a good example of prayer in action (see James 5:17-18).

Prayer never changes God's mind, but it does play an important part in His providential plan for our lives. That's why we are told to pray according to God's will in all things. This is also why it is important to know and cherish His Word and be directed by His Spirit when we come before Him in humility and dependence.

Praying according to God's will in all things presumes on the practical reality that we are living our lives like Jesus, being guided by every word that proceeds from the mouth of God. Jesus taught, "Man does

not live on bread alone, but on every word that comes
from the mouth of God" (Matthew 4:4).

David experienced the Word of God in many practical ways:

> The law of the LORD is perfect,
>   reviving the soul.
> The statutes of the LORD are trustworthy,
>   making wise the simple.
> The precepts of the LORD are right,
>   giving joy to the heart.
> The commands of the LORD are radiant,
>   giving light to the eyes.
> The fear of the LORD is pure,
>   enduring forever.
> The ordinances of the LORD are sure
>   and altogether righteous.
> They are more precious than gold,
>   than much pure gold;
> they are sweeter than honey,
>   than honey from the comb.
> By them is your servant warned;
>   in keeping them there is great reward.
>
> Who can discern his errors?
>   Forgive my hidden faults.
> Keep your servant also from willful sins;
>   may they not rule over me.
> Then will I be blameless,
>   innocent of great transgression.
>
> May the words of my mouth and
>   the meditation of my heart
>   be pleasing in your sight,

O LORD, my Rock and my Redeemer.
(Psalm 19:7-14)

When we humble ourselves before our Father in heaven, we will discover that He is most glorified in us when we are most satisfied in Him. And we will be most satisfied in Him when our lives are a living sacrifice, an offering of worship to Him, as Paul so strongly advocates in Romans 12:1-2. This is our reasonable service.

When we yearn to be intensely spiritual, perfectly natural and thoroughly practical in entering our world, our redeemed hearts want to offer our bodies as an alive sacrifice of worship. God has designed us to love and worship Him. At our deepest level, our hunger for eternal impact and relational intimacy cries out in worship back to Him: "As the deer pants for streams of water, so my soul pants for you, O God. My soul thirsts for God, for the living God. When can I go and meet with God?" (Psalm 42:1-2).

When David was out in the Judean wilderness he found God to be the great Satisfier of his life. Psalm 63 is a record of his passion and delight at that discovery. Feel the emotion of his heart: "I will praise you as long as I live, and in your name I will lift up my hands. My soul will be satisfied as with the richest of foods; with singing lips my mouth will praise you" (63:4-5).

David found that often God had to put him in a hard place before his worship would shift and focus on the Lord. That's happened to me, too. Worshiping and loving God do not come naturally for me. My passion has gone awry and become misdirected. Sin has caused my affections to stray, propelling me to worship relationships, achievement, work, ministry, forms of pleasure, sources of approval and countless other ways to maintain physical and soul comfort. As a redeemed man I'm becoming more and more aware that there is a war within me. There is constant conflict between the old and the new me, between vice and virtue, sin and obedience, my flesh and the Spirit.

In this ongoing war, we so easily have obsessions about these things. We comfort ourselves with them and fantasize about them. Why? Because we are all passionate worshipers at heart.

From God's perspective He is jealous of me. He says, "I will not share My glory with your idols—your worship of relationships, work, ministry, forms of pleasure, sources of approval and physical-soul comfort."

True worship and love for God the Father consist of tearing our affections off our idols and focusing them on Him. Our affections are the core part of our male being that orients our mind, will and emotions toward any form of worship. True worship is seeing what God is worth and then as men, giving Him what He's worth. Job said, "I have treasured the words of his mouth more than my daily bread" (Job 23:12). Worship is treasuring God, pondering His worth and then doing something about it. We give Him what He's worth—our lives, our love, our worship and our enjoyment of Him! This is what brings holy pleasure to our heavenly Father's heart.

Because God has literally set eternity in our hearts (see Ecclesiastes 3:11), He is asking us to stop measuring ourselves by how successful we are and to begin asking whether or not our lives have eternal impact and value. Oswald Chambers, in *Disciples Indeed*, said,

"Beware of worshiping Jesus as the Son of God, and professing your faith in Him as the Savior of the world, while you blaspheme Him by the complete evidence in your daily life that He is powerless to do anything in and through you."[4]

God the Father has equipped and filled us with the Spirit of His Son. He has designed us to reflect His likeness. In Him we have all we need to enter into life as redeemed men who can make an eternal impact in our homes, our world and our churches. Paul put it this way: "But the fruit of the Spirit is love, joy, peace, patience, kindness, goodness, faithfulness, gentleness and self-control. Against such things there is no law" (Galatians 5:22-23).

God is calling us to be men like this. All He wants is a few good men, not great men, but men after His own heart, some quiet heroes.

Mark R. Littleton tells a gripping fictional story, "Only the Beginning." It is about Jim Colter, a humble, quiet hero who, like Jesus, was intensely spiritual, perfectly natural and thoroughly practical. As you read this story, pay attention to the deep affections of your heart as they are turned toward home.

The story begins with Jesus' return and all the believers, who were saved by faith alone, following Him home to heaven. Then as countless millions stand before the judgment seat of God, each one is called to account for his life (see 1 Corinthians 3:11-15; 2 Corinthians 5:10). John Colter watches in great agony of soul, sure that his ordinary life holds no commendations for him. He wishes the Lord would just pass over him and go on to the next one in line. We pick up the story as the year of John's birth is reached and he hears his name being called.

Then He came to my year, 1950. Soon it would be my turn. What would He say? What could He say? I was practically jumping in place. I felt like a school kid waiting for his report card and not being sure whether he'd get an F or an A or something in between.

He finally spoke my name.

I wove my way through the crowd to the Bema seat. He motioned to me to stand before Him. He was so august, so resplendent. Like light. There was a warmth in Him. It filled me and made me feel confident. Love—that was it. He loved me! I could feel His love holding me and strengthening me.

He asked the crowd if anyone wanted to speak. My son stepped forward first. "There are many things, Lord."

"Tell them all," He said.

I was astonished. We'd had some bitter times on earth.

My son began. "I remember his playing with me, Lord. Piggyback rides. Singing songs in the car. Fun. He made life fun." He recounted all sorts of deeds. I was amazed and grateful. These were the things he remembered?

My wife said she had always loved the way I held her, even when I was tired and wanted to go to sleep. She spoke of how I gave her money to buy groceries and clothing with a smile and no resentment. She seemed to go on and on. A lump formed in my throat, and I fought to control my tears.

Others told of my teaching them in church a Bible story that had stuck in their mind and influenced them. "He told a story one time in Sunday school about Zacchaeus' giving his money back to the poor," one said. "Later in life it motivated me to help some homeless people."

My mouth dropped open. He remembered that? I didn't even remember that!

Johnny Martin—I'd taught him to throw a ball. Bill Briggs, a fellow salesman—I'd been patient training him, and he'd come to Christ years after he left our company. Doris Liston—my strong singing in church one Sunday had encouraged her. It went on and on. I couldn't believe it. Most of the time I was in tears.

A lady named Gracie Schwartz had been stopped by the road with a flat tire, and I had fixed it. I hadn't even known she was a Christian. I had witnessed to her, sort of, but at the time she was bitter about problems in her marriage and didn't tell me. She said my words had reminded her of the need to walk with Jesus again.

There was a boy, now a man, from my Little League team—Casey Szabo—who said I had encouraged him and given him a Bible verse. Even though he wasn't a believer at the time, it had come into his mind years later when he did believe.

The time I'd prayed for a friend during a funeral.

The time I'd turned off a leaky faucet in the company bathroom because I thought the Lord would be pleased.

The time I talked in church about the need to give sacrificially.

I'd forgotten them all. They seemed so insignificant. But He had said that anything done in His name would last. And it did.

It seemed that it would never stop. Every impression, every word—there were thousands of them—stitched itself into my heart.

Then the Lord Himself put the book in the fire. And suddenly there were gold, silver, and jewels. So many pieces I couldn't count them. Each one a remembrance of a deed, a word, a thought, a prayer. They were all remembered. Every one.

And He spoke. He reminded me that I had practiced biblical principles in my work. He recounted that nearly every day I had refused to lie or cheat or steal. That I had been honest, worked hard, and given a good day to my employer. I hadn't even known if it mattered.

He spoke of how I had worked to be a good husband, listening to my wife, changing, learning, responding to her needs. He pointed out that I had stuck by her even when there were problems that could have ended in divorce.

He remembered that I had tried to teach my family the Bible and to apply its principles. Even though He had not given me gifts in teaching or speaking, He said I had tried and had done well.

He reminded me of how I labored to be a good father. He brought out deeds of gentleness and patience that even my children didn't remember. For every time I had prayed in the car for someone, He pointed out the answer, and sometimes people stood and thanked me for my deed.

He showed me the accounting books of my giving to organizations and to the church. Missionaries, pastors, people all over the world—places I knew little about and had never visited—praised me for my deeds to them, although neither they nor I had known anything about them.

It went on and on. He moved on through my life, picking out each episode of good, showing who had benefited. There were people who had become Christians through the smallest particles of my influence—a kind word, a tract, a prayer in passing.

He spoke of others who were simply touched by my presence. He showed how many people in the gathering had been influenced by my family's saying grace in restaurants. Often at the time, I had been vaguely uneasy. But He showed that some of those people were moved toward faith by those small acts.

Then He asked how many people had been in some way influenced by something I had done—whether it was a prayer for a missionary in Europe or a small gift to an organization in Los Angeles. All of it was connected. I could not count the number of people who cheered and thanked me.

I couldn't stop feeling choked up. The things I had done—the little things I considered so unimportant—had achieved these far-reaching effects?

Finally, after it was all done, He stood to speak. He said, "John, look at Me."

I looked into His eyes. It was hallowed,

cleansing, thrilling. As I looked at Him, in that blinding moment, I saw His heart. I saw that my God had loved me from all eternity and that I had been in His heart before I was even conceived. I knew He had been with me through every experience. I knew He had ordered every detail of my life to bring me to this moment of triumph.

And I saw that long ago He had planned every opportunity for a good deed so that when I came to this moment He might reward me much.

I knew it all in that instant. And in that instant I loved Him as I had never loved Him.

He spoke, His eyes shining and true. "John, you have done all that I planned. You have done many good works in My name. You have touched the lives of millions. Well done. I welcome you into the joy of your Father."

He embraced me, and my fear and doubt fell away forever. Then He presented me to the gathering. "Welcome John Colter into the eternal bliss and reward of His Lord."

The cheering never seemed to stop. And it was only the beginning.[5]

Endnotes

[1] Henry Drummond as quoted in J. Sidlow Baxter, *A New Call to Holiness* (Marshall, Morgan and Scott, 1967), 113.

[2] Unidentified minister, as quoted in J. Sidlow Baxter, *A New Call to Holiness* (Marshall, Morgan and Scott, 1967), 113.

[3] Unless otherwise cited, the figures given were gleaned from the following sorces: *Sourcebook of Criminal Justice Statistics 1995* (Albany, NY: The Hingleang Criminal Justice Research Center, 1996); *The World Almanac and Book of Facts 1997* (Mahwah, NJ:

World Almanac Books, 1997); and U.S. Department of Commerce, Bureau of Census, *Statistical Abstract of the United States, 1996*.

[4] Oswald Chambers, *Disciples Indeed* (London, England: Oswald Chambers Publication Association Ltd., 1955), 5. Used by permission of Discovery House Publishers, Grand Rapids, MI.

[5] Mark R. Littleton, "Only the Beginning," *Tales of the Neverending* (Chicago: Moody Press, 1990), 223-232. Used by permission.

PART III

CELEBRATED GLORY

CHAPTER 24

The Blessing of Manhood

My ministry to men has taken me across the country many times. It has given me the privilege of meeting all kinds of people. Many tell me that they have never had their maleness blessed by either their father or another older male. Because many describe their fathers as either relationally uninvolved, alcoholic or absent, they have never been able to enjoy his formal or informal affirmation of their manhood. This lack of a father's blessing has left a path strewn with full grown "little boys" still looking for someone to affirm them as men.

In the past, older men, specifically fathers, helped their sons define their maleness as it matured into manhood. In today's world that role has often been deferred to women, first mothers, then elementary and Sunday school teachers. When a man is only blessed by a woman's attempt to affirm his manhood, he will only get part of the picture of what he ought to be like. As a result he becomes dependent and personally attached to her. For example, professional football players, when focused in on by a national television camera most often holler out, "Hi, Mom!" rarely, "Hi, Dad!"

When a man's primary source of blessing and affirmation comes from a woman, he will live with a deep dread of failure, inadequacy and rejection. He will be a driven man, not a called, responsible, blessed man.

A man learns best about maleness and manhood from the company of other men. With other males, he may experience some of the obvious realities of raw maleness: bravado, uncontrolled aggressiveness, abusive competition, earthy humor, braggadocio, drivenness and the instinct to ruthlessly conquer and dominate. These are not all bad or sinful male qualities, but left untamed and unredeemed, these male traits can leave a man obnoxious and hard to be around.

Hopefully he will be blessed and influenced by more righteous modeling of maleness and maturing manhood: quiet strength, integrity and the keeping of one's word, respect for law and order, pursuit of justice, thinking for himself, sticking to his convictions, standing up for truth and principle, treating the opposite sex with dignity, equality and honor, the ability to laugh at himself, initiative that creates life, loving that gives until it hurts, defending life at personal cost and providing life with sacrifice and denial of self-centeredness.

To bless means to bring life, to affirm life, to call life out of death, to shatter the curse, to bring God's presence near. One of the more helpful ways for fathers to call out their sons' maleness is to bless and affirm their maturing manhood, to bring God's presence near. The same holds true for adult men with each other. Since many men have never had their maleness affirmed and their manhood richly blessed, reciprocal times of blessing can soothe the woundedness and help fill their deep hole of uncertainty.

The following ritual of the blessing of manhood is one model that has been used by hundreds of men. I have stood and witnessed these men at the close of men's conferences confer on each other what they have always wanted—to be told by another male that he is a man!

Entering into the Blessing of Sonship and Manhood

A father can bless his son in the following ritual. The father and son face each other in a standing position. The father places his hands at arms length on his son's shoulders. The father and son engage in and maintain eye contact.

Now the most important stage of the ritual of blessing is ready. The father, looking into his son's eyes, speaks the following truth into his spirit and soul:

(Son's name), you are my son, marked and kept by my love and affection, the focus of my delight and pride.

(Son's name), you are now a man, made in the image of God. You have the right stuff as a man to initiate humbly entering into life, people and the heart of your heavenly Father.

(Son's name), I as your father bless you with this truth, in the name of the Father, Son and Holy Spirit, Amen. Yes, Amen!

I remember well a sixty-three-year-old father who was one of the independent, hard-working prairie farmers at a men's conference. He stood up at the end of a men's course and called his two sons to come and be blessed. Tears coursed down his sun-wrinkled, weathered face as he stood with his arms outstretched. The eldest son went first. You could tell that he had waited forty-two years for this moment. He sensed his father's heart as he felt the older man's hands on his shoulders and looked through his father's tear-filled eyes deep into his soul. His father's eyes were like freshly washed windows that now revealed the truest and deepest heart feelings for his son.

I watched this sacred moment of blessing wash away forty-two years of wondering, waiting, wanting. The father's presence and words of blessing brought life. They were powerful transmitters of a father's affirmation of sonship and manhood.

I watched the younger son, who was thirty-eight, standing just a few feet away. He was a witness to one of the most important gifts a father can give to his sons. It was like he was in another world as he awaited his turn.

The father embraced his eldest son and then released him and turned to his youngest son. What a joy to see the same transference of blessing of sonship and manhood flow from the father into the deepest places of this son's male soul.

When he had completed speaking this truth into the second son, the eldest son moved right back into the circle of blessing. I will never forget all three of these grown men in one huge embrace, weeping with joy and gladness. Indeed they were now celebrating their sonship and manhood like never before.

Another man at this same course stood and testified that he had five grown sons that were scattered all over North America. He had called each one and set a date to come and bless them as their father. He was like an excited boy with a new bike as he anticipated blessing

his five sons. When he sat down the 100 men in attendance applauded and many wept with mutual joy from
aroused longings.

Recently, a 102-year-old father came with his sev-
enty-five-year-old son to a men's conference. When
the time came for fathers to bless their sons, he stood,
motioned to his son to follow and with his cane, he led
the way to the front. Every man sat listening, not just
with his mind, but with his heart and spirit. What a
powerful moment of transformation as this aged father, with one hand on his cane, the other on his elderly son's head, spoke words of love, life and blessing.
There was not a dry eye! Something rich was passed
from father to son in those sacred moments.

Fathers, I urge you, make time to ritually bless your
sons and daughters. Speak the truth of manhood and
womanhood into their souls. There is a wonderful
source of God-ordained power that you have to speak
this kind of life into their manhood.

Entering into the Blessing of Manhood

Men can also have the wonderful privilege and joy
of being involved in transferring the blessing of manhood to one another.

I have stood in reverence, watching hundreds of
men at the close of men's conferences mutually bless
one another's manhood in a simple ritual.

The men pair up and place their hands on each
other's shoulders. As they look into one another's eyes,
they in turn speak this specific message of affirmation
to each other:

(Man's first name), you are a man made in the
image of God. You have the right stuff to initiate

entering as a man into life, people and the heart of your heavenly Father.

(Man's first name), I bless you with this truth in the name of the Father, Son and Holy Spirit. Amen and Amen!

Ron's Testimony

"The blessing of manhood was a very moving experience for me. From the first day of the course I was looking forward to this time of affirmation. When the actual time came, however, I felt a big wall go up and I could not respond. Finally I decided to just go ahead and trust God to use this time for His glory and my good.

"During the actual time of blessing, the wall went up again. My spirits sank and I thought to myself, *rejection again*, but finally something broke lose. When the man blessing me uttered the words, 'You are a man made in the image of God,' it seemed like a big dam broke lose in the bottom of my stomach. Slowly big sobs came out that eventually blended together until I was weeping and even unable to stand for a few minutes.

"It was a powerful moment in my life and a very healing experience for me to know and feel my manhood blessed and affirmed. I know it isn't magic, but I have never really believed I was much of a man and no one has ever told me I was till this moment. In that moment, something deep inside me stood up!

"Now when my own thoughts accuse me of not being much of a man or Satan sends his fiery darts of accusation, destruction and deceit with the same message, I can hold up this moment and this ritual of blessing of my manhood as a symbol and witness of my remembrance of the truth."

Men, I urge you to ritualize a blessing of one another's manhood. Get together, have a banquet and celebrate your manhood. Call for a time of blessing by coming together as men to honor the Lord God by blessing what He has said is true about you. Enjoy a theology of celebration as redeemed men of God. Walk in the truth of your manhood and let your spouse, your children, your employer, employees and other men and women in your world celebrate with you all the blessings that will flow to them from deep within you.

Manhood means moving to one other final level of experience in order to know the deepest realities of being male and a man. At the deepest level, the discovery of manhood must include actual experience, for maleness is not something observed or even blessed, not something imagined in your own mind, not something read or studied, but something *done*. It is not just a virtue given by God the Creator, but a capacity and capability achieved through risk.

After having our manhood blessed and affirmed, we need to become men of faith and *risk*! It means actually choosing to undertake the hero journey. It means repenting of and leaving the safe comforts of cowardly manhood; it means giving up our passive abandonment or aggressive domination of others and life; it means turning our backs on all our sinful, safe relating styles.

It means becoming quiet heroes who choose to gently initiate entering into relationships and the world with a strength that brings the blessings of life—providing, protecting and modeling servant leadership. It means leaving the comforts of your personal world for an adventurous exploration of God's kingdom work. It demands an ordeal—a struggle with your self-centeredness and selfishness, with the demons of spiritual warfare and the dragons of evil and injustice. And it requires, finally, a return to a life of service and responsibility on behalf of others. Maleness and maturing, blessed manhood is about heroic suffering, not for its own sake, but to provide good and righteous things for our families, our churches and our country.

Only when we as men choose to actually follow our creatorial design and respond to our own unique call of God can we understand the depths of our redeemed maleness and affirmed manhood. Our Father God has charged us to live by faith, to join the cloud of witnesses and heroes of faith who have gone on before us. Let us be obedient to that call.

Such a journey of quiet heroism will be unique to who God has designed us to be as men. It may lead to an intimidating medical school and a healing career; bring you to fight society's callousness on behalf of the poor and homeless; draw you into a foxhole or warship to defend your country against outside foreign attack. You might also find the warrior-self inside you by fighting forest fires in Manitoba or Montana, or the AIDS epidemic in a medical laboratory or on the streets of your community.

Perhaps you will simply choose as a husband and father to wisely and lovingly live out the role of servant headship of your home by shepherding your family to grow in wisdom, stature and knowledge of God. Or maybe the quiet hero within you will respond to work behind the scenes in your organization and vocation to provide faithful, quality work and encouragement to those over you and around you.

Quiet heroes will work in far-off places of the globe, in well-known public offices in government, in churches, in communities—provincial, state and federal representatives, trustees, school board members, mayors, town or city counselors.

In all of these experiences and many more, a man can find his maleness expressed in his maturing manhood etched deeply into every cell of his body and every niche of his masculine spirit. God has created us to celebrate our manhood by expressing our unique, individual gifts and abilities, granted through the miracle of our male sexuality, for His glory and for the good of others and the world we live in.

What is our true worth, men? It's a whole lot more than just being used for ideological target practice and rhetorical put-downs. God has redeemed our desires and manly passions. He has designed us to lay our lives down for His sake and the good of others. Manhood means undertaking the quiet hero's pilgrimage— leaving the safe comforts of self-centeredness and selfish pursuits for an adventurous life of faith, hope, love and sacrifice, taking up our cross and loyally following Him, even to death. That is living! That is manhood celebrated God's way!

The writer of Hebrews says it so well. Let us celebrate our manhood according to biblical directives:

> Therefore, since we are surrounded by such a great cloud of witnesses, let us throw off everything that hinders and the sin that so easily entangles, and let us run with perseverance the race marked out for us. Let us fix our eyes on Jesus, the author and perfecter of our faith, who

for the joy set before him endured the cross, scorning its shame, and sat down at the right hand of the throne of God. Consider him who endured such opposition from sinful men, so that you will not grow weary and lose heart. . . .

Therefore, strengthen your feeble arms and weak knees. . . .

See that no one is sexually immoral, or is godless like Esau, who for a single meal sold his inheritance rights as the oldest son. Afterward, as you know, when he wanted to inherit this blessing, he was rejected. He could bring about no change of mind, though he sought the blessing with tears. (Hebrews 12:1-3, 12, 16-17)

Marriage should be honored by all, and the marriage bed kept pure, for God will judge the adulterer and all the sexually immoral. Keep your lives free from the love of money and be content with what you have, because God has said,

"Never will I leave you;
    never will I forsake you."

So we say with confidence,

"The Lord is my helper; I will not be afraid.
    What can man do to me?" (13:4-6)

Men, join with me as we make this great closing prayer from the book of Hebrews the lifelong passion of our hearts:

Dear Heavenly Father,
  May you as God, who puts all things together,
    makes all things whole,
  Who made a lasting mark through the sacrifice of Jesus, the sacrifice of blood that sealed the eternal covenant,
  Who led Jesus, our Great Shepherd,
    up and alive from the dead,
  Now put us as men together and provide us with everything we need to please you,
  Make us into what gives you most pleasure, by means of the sacrifice of Jesus, the Messiah.
  All glory to Jesus forever and always!
    Oh, yes, yes, yes. (Hebrews 13:20-21)[1]

Endnote

[1] Eugene H. Peterson, *The Message: New Testament* (Colorado Springs, CO: Navpress, 1993), 377; wording adapted.

APPENDIX

Explanation of Terms and Definitions Used in This Book

Creation Mandate or *Creatorial Mandate.* When God created Adam and Eve, He designed and equipped them to represent Him as His image-bearers. They were to take dominion by doing two specific assignments: 1) To take functional dominion, which is to rule (to care for, as a caretaker) over His creation and subdue (work) it (see Genesis 1:26, 28; Psalm 8:6-8); and 2) To take relational dominion, which is to be fruitful, increase in number and fill the earth, which requires relationship between the male and female.

Creation Order. 1) When God who is a God of order created human life, He first made Adam, the male, out of the dust of the earth and breathed into him. He became a living being (Genesis 2:7). 2) God put Adam in the Garden of Eden to work it and take care of it (2:8, 15). 3) God then commanded Adam to eat from any tree in the garden but not from the tree of the knowledge of good and evil or he would die (2:16-17). 4) God said that it was not good for Adam to be alone—"I will make a helper suitable for him" (2:18). 5) So God took from Adam one of his ribs and made a woman (Eve) from his rib (2:21-22). 6) God brought her to the man (2:22). 7) Then Adam called her woman (Genesis 2:23). 8) They were naked, not ashamed and became one flesh (2:24-25).

This created order implies that: 1) As image-bearers of God, the male and female are to take functional and relational dominion together; 2) There is a function and role that they each have in fulfilling this creation mandate—the male is to be the primary initiator in ruling, subduing and filling the earth and the female is to be the suitable helper, the primary active responder in ruling, subduing and filling the earth; and 3) The male has a God-designed inner constitutional desire to be the primary initiator while still having a secondary desire to respond; the female has a God-designed inner constitutional desire to be the primary responder, while still having a secondary desire to initiate; and 4) This function and role assigned to both by God was given with equality of dignity, value, essence and authority.

The Right Stuff. What every male and female human being is born with. These are gender specific as the following metaphors portray.

Male "right stuff." These are the metaphors of male substance that make up his physical (body and biology) and personal (soul) essence: 1) Testosterone—a metaphor symbolizing that substance of maleness that gives a man the drive to initiate entering into his world, life and people to fulfill the creation mandate for the glory of God; 2) Testicles—a metaphor symbolizing that substance of maleness which gives a man the God-created desire to create life out of his redeemed heart; 3) Sperm—a metaphor symbolizing that substance of maleness which gives a man the capacity and desire to spill and provide life from the God-created essence of his redeemed heart; 4) Muscular Brawn—a metaphor symbolizing that substance of maleness which gives a man the capacity and ability to boldly and willingly defend and protect life at the sacrifice of his own life.

Female "right stuff." These are the metaphors of female substance that make up her physical (body and biology) and personal (soul) essence: 1) Estrogen—a metaphor symbolizing that substance of femaleness which gives a woman the God-designed desire to actively respond by warmly inviting others to enjoy the mystery and richness of who she is as a redeemed woman of God; 2) Ovaries—a metaphor symbolizing that substance of femaleness which gives a woman her God-designed capacity and ability to reproduce her life in her world and in others for the glory of God; 3) Egg—a metaphor symbolizing that substance of femaleness which gives a woman her God-designed capacity and ability to conceive and bring forth life from the depths of who she is for the good of others and her world, for the glory of God and for her enjoyment; 4) Womb and Breasts—two metaphors which symbolize that substance of femaleness which gives a woman the God created capacity and desire to be fruitful by bearing, carrying and nourishing life. She does this by offering her redeemed inner beauty in order for life and others to find rest, grow, develop and be fruitful.

Sexual Identity. The gender of a male or female person made in God's image.

Male Sexuality. The sexual drive and desires of a male.

Female Sexuality. The sexual drive and desires of a female.

Masculinity. How maleness is nurtured by one's background, nationality and culture and then is expressed through the grid of one's uniqueness of personality, abilities, resources, role and function.

Femininity. How femaleness is nurtured by one's background, nationality and culture and then is expressed through the grid of one's uniqueness of personality, abilities, resources, role and function.

Soul Dread. A deep terror of being naked before a holy God and being seen for who one really is, a sinner and an enemy of God, spiritually dead and bankrupt.

Male Soul Dread. A personal terror of 1) being incapable, inadequate or incompetent physically and/or personally to rule, subdue and fill the earth as a man; 2) not being needed by anyone; and 3) being exposed in relationships. Males fear relational closeness and intimacy where all of who they are is seen by another and rejected or not taken seriously.

Female Soul Dread. A personal terror of 1) being incapable or too flawed physically and/or personally to be a suitable helper in ruling, subduing and filling the earth as a woman; 2) not being wanted by anyone; and 3) being seen as ugly inside and outside. To be used. Not wanted relationally. Females fear relational distance and so hide the ugly, shameful

parts of who they are to maintain relational closeness and intimacy or connecting.

Redeemed. Being born again by the shed blood and sub-
stitutionary death of Jesus Christ on the cross;
made new. Also means: 1) To become spiritually
alive whereby one is able to personally relate to
God the Father in a new and eternal relationship;
2) Being filled with the Holy Spirit, the third person of the Trinity; 3) Being given a new nature
with new desires that motivate one to move away
from selfishness and self-centeredness to take on a
selfless, sacrificial ability to worship and love God
and others with all one's heart affections, sense of
self, strength of passion and personal might; 4)
One now wants to obey God and keep His commandments, serve and enjoy Him now and into
eternity; and 5) Entering into sonship with the
heavenly Father; being able as a man to cry from
the depths of your soul, "Abba, Papa, Father," because of the witness and work of the Holy Spirit.

Sinful, Enslaving Desires. 1) Because a man is conceived
and born with a sinful nature which is a perverse
state of personhood, made up of self-centered, selfish motives and desires that enslave a man's entire
being and which are then expressed in all that he
thinks, says and does; 2) Sinful enslaving desires
are the selfish affections of a man's heart, made up
of the idolatrous core part of one's being that orients a man's mind, will and emotions toward an
object, idea or relationship; and 3) A man's sinful
enslaving desires are an offense against God. They
are the result of his human capacity to choose and
are incurable by his own efforts.

Redeemed Desires. 1) When a man is born again and enters into a relationship of sonship with his heavenly Father and when he is filled with the Holy Spirit at his time of conversion, then his new nature, which is a redeemed state of personhood made up of other-centered motives and desires, will enslave his being and will be expressed in all he thinks, says and does; 2) Redeemed desires are the other-centered affections of a man's new heart—other-centered affections are God-created desires that are made up of the core part of a man's being that orients his mind, will and emotions to worship, love, serve and obey God; and 3) A man's redeemed desires are a delight to God and are the result of the work of God the Holy Spirit along with a chosen obedience from the core of one's heart.